The Study of
International Affairs

The Study of International Affairs

ESSAYS IN HONOUR OF
KENNETH YOUNGER

Edited by Roger Morgan

Published for
THE ROYAL INSTITUTE OF
INTERNATIONAL AFFAIRS
by OXFORD UNIVERSITY PRESS
LONDON NEW YORK TORONTO
1972

Oxford University Press, Ely House, London W. 1

GLASGOW NEW YORK TORONTO MELBOURNE WELLINGTON
CAPE TOWN IBADAN NAIROBI DAR ES SALAAM LUSAKA ADDIS ABABA
DELHI BOMBAY CALCUTTA MADRAS KARACHI LAHORE DACCA
KUALA LUMPUR SINGAPORE HONG KONG TOKYO

ISBN 0 19 214989 X

PRINTED IN GREAT BRITAIN
AT THE UNIVERSITY PRESS, OXFORD
BY VIVIAN RIDLER
PRINTER TO THE UNIVERSITY

Contents

Abbreviations*

AJIL	*American Journal of International Law*
ASIL	American Society of International Law
BYIL	*British Year Book of International Law*
DSB	*Department of State Bulletin*
ECSC	European Coal and Steel Community
GATT	General Agreement on Tariffs and Trade
GDR	German Democratic Republic
HR	Hague *Recueil* (*Recueil des Cours de l'Académie de Droit Internationale de La Haye*)
ICJ *Rep.*	International Court of Justice, *Reports*
ICLQ	*International and Comparative Law Quarterly*
ILQ	*International Law Quarterly*
NYT	*New York Times*
OAS	Organization of American States
OAU	Organization of African Unity
OECD	Organization for European Co-operation and Development
OEEC	Organization for European Economic Co-operation
PEP	Political and Economic Planning
UNCTAD	UN Conference on Trade and Development

* Excluding those in everyday use, such as EEC.

Preface

ROGER MORGAN

ON the occasion of Kenneth Younger's retirement from the Directorship of Chatham House, a group of his friends and colleagues have written these essays in his honour. Although Kenneth Younger has always rightly insisted that the Institute's research programme should deal with issues of importance to those responsible for British foreign policy—of whom he has been one—he has always encouraged Chatham House researchers to interpret these terms of reference very broadly, as the allusions to RIIA studies in this book testify. Again, his colleagues have certainly heard him expressing some scepticism about the contributions offered by certain of the newer approaches to the study of international relations.[1] Yet he has also impressed a world-wide circle of friends and acquaintances —to mention only one example, a group of German social scientists at a Chatham House conference a couple of years before his retirement—by his insistence that the methods used to study international affairs must keep pace with the constantly-changing nature of the subject-matter itself. As Kenneth Younger's retirement was due to occur shortly after the Institute's fiftieth anniversary, we felt it doubly appropriate to plan a 'stock-taking' book, surveying some of the major aspects of international studies at the present time. Each contributor has given an assessment of the literature and has indicated subjects for future exploration within his particular speciality, doing so in such a way as to place the relevant research activities of Chatham House in the perspective of international studies as a whole.

---

[1] Cf. his article 'The study and understanding of international affairs' in *International Affairs*, Nov. 1970, p. 150.

The world of learning, influenced here as in other ways by Germanic models, calls this kind of volume a *Festschrift*—and its aim is indeed to celebrate the achievements of Kenneth Younger at Chatham House—but the French term *Mélanges* might be equally apt. The authors were given a free hand to write in their own way about their own branch of research, so as to explain it to specialists in other fields as well as to readers whose interest in international affairs is a more general one. Some contributors have chosen to cast their essays in the form of an argument for or against a particular point of view, while others have preferred to offer more factual surveys of their own special topic, with varying degrees of retrospective attention to its development during the fifty years of Chatham House's existence. These chapters—like the work of Chatham House itself—are also diverse in the sense that some deal with an aspect of area studies and others with a broader international theme.

Inevitably, this volume's coverage of international studies cannot claim to be complete: many readers will be able to point to topics which a fully comprehensive survey might have included. It has unfortunately proved impracticable to cover two areas of research in which Chatham House has in fact been an active pioneer—Latin America and the Middle East. American foreign policy and strategic studies, again, while not the subject of separate contributions, receive attention in the essay on international politics.

The book is a characteristically Chatham House product in the sense that—while each author retains full responsibility for his or her contribution—many of the draft chapters have benefited from discussion among the Institute's research staff. Valuable and much appreciated comments on some of the essays have also been made by Professors Richard N. Cooper, Geoffrey Goodwin, and F. H. Hinsley. Hermia Oliver has once again earned the deep gratitude of all the contributors by her creative and tenacious editorial activity.

The broad scope of these essays reflects the wide range of Chatham House's activities during the twelve-year Directorship of Kenneth Younger, to whom they are affectionately and respectfully dedicated.

London
July 1971

1 Introduction: The Nature of International Studies

ANDREW SHONFIELD

As has been observed before, there is a certain predictable quality about surveys of the results of research. One conclusion that is almost certain to be reached at the end is—that a bigger research effort is needed. Perhaps it is not surprising. 'Quand un vicomte rencontre un autre vicomte, qu'est-ce qu'ils se racontent? Des histoires de vicomtes.' The present volume is no exception—with this proviso, that the needs of research emphasized by many of the contributors is not for more of the same, but for more intellectual overspill from fields other than their own. They point to the weaknesses in the study of international affairs which result from the concentration of effort within the confines of a single intellectual discipline. Political scientists do not absorb the realities of international economic relations into their judgements; and economists reciprocate their intellectual indifference. Too many international lawyers are exclusively concerned with law, failing to see that their subject is of little significance to people who actually have to make decisions unless it is grounded in the hard stuff of politics and the habitual ways of governments.

The problem is aggravated by another feature of international studies which emerges with considerable force from the surveys in this volume. This is the overwhelming importance of the choice of a particular explanatory model within which the particular scholar casts his data and looks for a coherent pattern of behaviour. Professor Bruce Miller, remarking on the curious lack of systematic theoretical discussion of the structure of the Commonwealth as a type of international organization, observes that there has been nevertheless a lot of doctrinal assertions about the nature of Commonwealth relationships which depend on cosy analogies, notably those drawn from family life. The beguiling analogue of the family, he concludes, helped to conceal or obscure questions about the Commonwealth which required analysis in order to discover what was really going on. Professor Hugh Tinker makes a parallel point in his observation that British scholars of Asian affairs have tended to miss out on some of the realities because of their reluctance to think of military rule as a polity forming a legitimate field of political study. Presumably by refusing to give military rule a place in the model of the Asian political system it was felt that one was doing one's bit to make it go away. In the study of contemporary China, John Gittings finds another kind of distortion. He suggests that the conclusions reached by much of the scholarly work in the West have been predetermined by the assumption that American policy in the Far East was of its nature reactive —always responding to moves initiated by other powers with ambitions in the area. An alternative model which endowed American policy with the aim of securing its own power and influence in the area, and doing so in pursuit of national objectives not different in kind from those of its opponents, would produce a very different picture of the forces at work in the Far East. And in Western Europe (see the essay by Dr Roy Pryce) how is the experiment in integration of the Common Market to be described? Some analysts see it as being in a literal sense a drive for supranationality—a series of grand initiatives designed to replace the essential functions of state power, which started off pretty well in 1958 and then went aground in the second half of the 1960s. But there is another model of the process of integration which looks for the relevant facts among the multiplicity of small contacts between nations, many of them contacts that do not directly concern governments, which cumulatively tend towards the result of making independent national initiatives by members of a group of countries on significant matters less and less feasible. Looked at in this way, the performance of the EEC in the 1960s is of a quite different order of importance.

There are different styles of model-making. An interesting development of the postwar period has been the deliberate importation of the economic style into political analysis. B. M. Russett has brought together a collection of such analytic pieces, which apply the artificially sharpened conceptual tools of the economists to international relations, in a useful volume, *Economic Theories of International Politics* (1968). The contributions show how the method can be employed to focus attention on significant issues which have tended to be overlooked or downgraded in traditional studies of international affairs. One finds, for example, that the formal analysis of the 'costs' of international organizations for nations of differing size and interests casts a fresh light on the curious ability of small states in many situations in recent years to act more independently in pursuit of their national aims than their larger neighbours. Thinking of the underlying structure of the bargaining situation in terms that economists use, e.g. in relation to oligopoly or market competition, provides the means of defining the conditions that have to be satisfied in order to answer such fundamental questions as whether a given international system is likely to be stable or unstable. It is not that economists are better at supplying the answers to these questions, but their techniques suggest new ways of doing so.

The power of the model in the study of international relations adds greatly to the danger of being guided in the selection of data and its interpretation by the intellectual conventions of a single discipline. The only point that I would wish to emphasize in the argument that runs so strongly through several of the essays in this book is that it is not just a question of pairing off appropriate disciplines which are at present unnaturally divorced by the guild prejudice of each. The range of relevant knowledge in the study of international relations goes much wider than that. When the lawyers and the political scientists have learned to take a professional interest in each other's work, and have then been joined in the process of mutual education by the economists, there will be a great deal still left out. Reference to two Chatham House studies by sociologists, Ronald Dore's *Land Reform in Japan* (1959) and Emanuel de Kadt's *Catholic Radicals in Brazil* (1970), are a sufficient reminder of how the study of what may seem to be the interstices of politics can illuminate the whole of a political landscape.[1] There is,

---

[1] The process sometimes takes political analysts into the field of social anthropology; W. L. Blythe's suggestive study, *The Impact of Chinese Secret Societies in Malaya* (London, 1969) has opened up a promising field for social anthropologists.

of course, a well-established traditional type of study, of which L. S. S. O'Malley's *Modern India and the West* (1941) is a good example from the Chatham House stable, that sets out to examine social and cultural change as a factor in political processes. The difference is that the modern analyst of societies employs more sophisticated tools of sociological analysis; he may not always see deeper, but he reduces the risk of being guided by an arbitrary impressionistic judgement. It is to be observed that the more remote the place, the more liable we are to discuss the problems of its external relations as if the social structures in which these relations are ultimately grounded can be regarded as both fixed and in some sense simple. That perhaps explains why the insights supplied by sociologists are not by any means always welcomed by the traditional student of international relations.

I recall an attempt at Chatham House during the late 1960s to answer the question whether the military effectiveness of the United States, and hence in the last resort her foreign-policy options, were likely to be reduced by the sharpened social conflict which emerged in the universities and the coloured population at that time. This was one of the occasions when we were—*pace* John Gittings—genuinely trying to take a detached look at some of the underlying forces in the United States shaping American external policies. But we did not get very far. We were frustrated chiefly, I think, by a sense of the inadequacy of our own approach to the problem. It was not merely a lack of relevant fact; we became aware that we did not have a satisfactory method of arriving at systematic judgement on a matter of this kind. Yet the issue is an extremely familiar one for those who conduct or advise on international relations. It is not that the scholars or the policy-makers in practice eschew the making of judgements about the influence of domestic social factors on the foreign policies of states. What happens, rather, is that such judgements are for the most part implicit and therefore tend to go largely unchallenged. The principle of *ceteris paribus* is all too eagerly accepted by scholars who are anxious to get on with the deployment of their own particular bit of expertise. And when that principle becomes visibly untenable, for example in circumstances of overt social conflict, there is a tendency for the shock effect to induce a rush to visions of the cataclysmic—all things are then judged to be in flux. The sociologist's perception is that they were never so orderly or disorderly as they appeared. It is true that so far there has been very little sociological analysis which effectively spells out the connections between social change in a given country and its foreign policy. But at least it should be possible for the sociologists to tell the student of international relations about the characteristic combinations of circumstances to look for in different types of society which signal the probability of accelerated change, and then to supply some indications of the elements in the social structure which are likely to be more fluid than others.

Next, we need to proceed from structures to an appraisal of attitudes, especially of the attitudes of those élites who exercise a strong influence on the ideas guiding the external policies of nations. After the sociologists, the psychologists need to be called in to carry the investigation further in depth. This kind of study is still very much in its infancy. A lead has been given by some of the recent work in historical psychology, notably that of Erik Erickson. His study of Gandhi in mid-career, *Gandhi's Truth* (1970), has shown how this type of speculative investigation using the tools of psychoanalysis can add a fresh dimension to the understanding of a certain kind of political leadership and political conflict—in this instance operating among a high élite group who have left a characteristic mark on the style of Indian politics which is likely to be felt for some time to come. Another author, younger than Erickson and more directly concerned with contemporary history, who has demonstrated what the psychological method can do for the study of politics, is Robert J. Lifton. His empirical investigations of the varieties of spiritual pressure employed on prisoners in communist China, *Thought Reform and the Psychology of Totalism* (1961), and of the inner meaning of the Chinese cultural revolution of the 1960s, *Revolutionary Immortality* (1968), are important contributions to the study of international affairs.[2]

These examples are cited only to suggest possible directions for future work. It is not that psychological insights as a

[2] So in a more oblique way is his detailed study of the effect of the experience of nuclear bombing on a generation of Japanese, *Death in Life* (New York, 1968; Pelican 1970).

constituent of political judgement are a new thing in the study of international relations. One recalls such suggestive works as Hermann Rauschning's *Germany's Revolution of Destruction*[3] in the 1930s. The advance lies in the systematic employment of the methods of psychological analysis. The case is somewhat similar to the work of cultural historians—another field where the contribution to the study of contemporary international affairs has been slight. It has not been thought of as a promising field of scholarship for this purpose, if only because the timespan during which significant artistic and literary influences produce identifiable effects on a public mood tends to be so long. Or better, it *tended* to be long. With the revolution in the technology of communications, the movement of ideas and of cultural influences across national frontiers has been visibly and dramatically speeded up. It is likely to accelerate further. But what difference this may have made or may make in the future to international relations has barely been studied. If, for example, tastes in goods and in packaged ideas of various kinds cross frontiers much faster than ever before, the political processes of European union could turn out to be of a quite different kind from anything that might have been guessed from a study of relations between states in earlier history, in the era before the development of long-range television and other advanced forms of mass communications. One does not have to go all the way with Marshall McLuhan's imagery of the electronic base sustaining a 'global village' to recognize that there is a factor here that could alter the whole notion of a national frontier by making it vastly more permeable to influences from outside than it has been assumed to be hitherto. But so far we are still groping for methods which will make possible the systematic analysis of the impact of different kinds of communications and of the content of what is communicated.

Some serviceable tools of investigation are beginning to come into use, for example the techniques of 'content analysis' of speech and of written communication. These have the advantage that they can be coupled with the enlarged processing power of the computer, making use above all of its capacity to do the tedious work of identifying and classifying more accurately and

3 Engl. trans. London, 1939; German ed. Zurich, 1938, entitled *Die Revolution das Nihilismus*.

much more quickly than any human agent. Of course the business of getting the computer to work on a programme of search and enumeration of significant items still demands all the traditional skills and ingenuities of documentary scholarship. But now a single scholar's capacity to formulate hypotheses about the less obvious meanings of documentary material, which may be suggested by certain patterns of argument or verbal construction, and to subject these hunches to systematic and rapid testing has been enormously enhanced.[4] These computer techniques of searching for the pattern of meaning have the further advantage that they demand explicit statements, and hence greater clarity about alternative interpretations being entertained by the researcher as he proceeds with his investigation.

It is indeed generally true that a common characteristic of the newer disciplines that are now beginning to be applied to the study of international affairs is the pressure for explicitness, both in regard to the assumptions of the scholar and to his expectations. He is asked to say in advance as precisely as possible what propositions he is seeking to have confirmed or denied and what kind of evidence he would regard as establishing probabilities about their truth or falsehood. He must, in other words, identify the structure of the explanatory model that he intends to use for his particular purpose. The same point emerges clearly in a recent American work on *History as Social Science* (1971), edited by David S. Landes and C. Tilly, and produced as part of the Survey of the Behavioral and Social Sciences.[5] It concludes that the characteristic of the 'social scientific historian' is that

he begins where possible with an explicit statement of assumptions, concepts, and hypotheses; and he relies on evidence that is reproduceable, verifiable and potentially refutable. The concepts and

---

[4] Edmund Leach's comment on the influence of the use of computers on methods of analysis is also applicable to this case. 'Traditional taxonomies have necessarily depended on the presence or absence of a small number of "obvious" characteristics. This has meant that a very large number of apparently minor yet possibly significant variables have been excluded from all consideration. Until the coming of computers any other routine would have proved impossibly cumbersome. But now, in the computer era, it is the previously neglected variables which are receiving priority attention' (in D. M. Emmet & A. C. MacIntyre, eds., *Sociological Theory and Philosophical Analysis* (London, 1970), p. 188).

[5] A joint exercise of the National Academy of Sciences and the (US) Social Science Research Council.

procedures employed commonly come from adjacent social sciences such as demography and economics. . . . The study of man abounds in myths that need to be tested against the record of human experience. Demographic and economic history have shown what can be done along these lines; we can expect similar contributions from other branches of history as they begin to address themselves to the theses and problems of the social and behavioural sciences.

Perhaps this sounds rather portentous. But what the demand for explicitness chiefly means is that one is made to be more than usually conscious of the influence exercised over the results of research by what one chooses to look for. One often simply fails to observe certain kinds of fact because one has made a decision in advance that such facts are not the ones that are likely to make causal connections in the context of the particular model that one has selected for one's study. Awareness of this danger is the first need. Unfortunately it does not by itself provide a solution. What might be termed the 'check-list approach' to interdisciplinary study—that is, going through a list of well-established connections between political events and developments outside politics, and ticking off those which might apply in the particular case under study—can just as surely distort the picture of what is happening in periods of rapid change. As Susan Strange shows in her essay, one has to beware of accepting a lot of established conventions about the *kind of relationships* that exist between certain types of economic circumstance, for example, and the social or political developments that are alleged to accompany them, which derive from the interpretation of some earlier period of history. The contemporary historian of international affairs cannot afford the luxury of treating such relationships as constant during a period when so much else is changing unusually fast. It would indeed be remarkable if, for instance, the relationship between a given percentage rise in the national income and an associated change in social behaviour which had been observed at one stage of economic advance were to be the same ten years later on. The point is very obvious—yet it is also very commonly overlooked in the desire of each one of us to stick the label '*ceteris paribus*' on the influences exerted by forces which are not amenable to ready analysis by the methods of our own particular discipline. And the practitioner of the other discipline is not likely to go out of his way to correct us. He will not necessarily see the implications of suggestive data that he may have uncovered on the margins of his own immediate study—or even bother to notice them, unless he has been alerted to the interest of the student of international relations in evidence of discontinuities in certain established patterns of behaviour. He has to be intelligently quizzed; and that can only be done by someone who is sufficiently knowledgeable about the field of the particular specialist to elicit the information required. The contemporary historian has to recognize that part of his role is to be an active broker between disciplines. That is not only intellectually taxing; it is very time-consuming.

In sum, what I am arguing is that the study of international relations is a task for people who are especially attuned to the spirit of the modern social sciences—to the variety of different kinds of insight which they can provide, as well as to their limitations as suppliers of demonstrable truth. It is not for specialist practitioners in any one social science, however skilful they may be in the practice of their own specialisms. It is the capacity to go beyond the familiar framework of ideas set by a particular intellectual discipline which is essential. It is in this sense that the subject reflects what I consider to be a characteristic feature of the social sciences at their present stage of development—the sense that the traditional boundaries between disciplines no longer provide a useful method of intellectual demarcation. The closer one gets to the problems of the real world, the more insistent the need for the genuine interdisciplinary effort; and at the same time the more one departs from the simplifications of explanatory models drawn from a particular discipline, the less determinate are the answers to clear-cut questions. The great debate in the social sciences today is about the degree of indeterminacy that they can tolerate and still be useful to the makers of policy. The original image of the social scientist providing answers of an unequivocal predictive type, like the natural scientist, dies hard. But at least it surrenders to reality more easily when the subject of study is, as in international relations, blatantly interdisciplinary.

In the light of all this, it is ironic to recollect that when Kenneth Younger and I (I was then Director of Studies at Chatham House) were about to give evidence to Lord Heyworth's

Committee on Social Studies in the early 1960s, doubts were voiced by one or two senior members of the Institute. It was surely stretching our pretensions, it was argued, to call the work that we did 'social science'. Indeed, the question was raised whether we were being quite honest in asking for public support for a subject which, it was suggested, was remote from the normal concerns of social scientists. The discussion that we had then about whether international relations studies did or did not truly belong with the social sciences—rather than with the humanities—now seems doubly ironic, in view of the fact that when the Social Science Research Council had been set up, on the Heyworth Committee's recommendation, I was invited to leave my post as Director of Studies at Chatham House in order to become its Chairman.[6] I believe that it was in fact no accident that the kind of person who has a sufficient acquaintance with a number of different social-science disciplines to take charge of a research council of this kind, should be found to be working in the field of international affairs. Academic people may not have thought of us in this way beforehand, but that I suspect was at least partly due to a certain cultural lag in the universities. Once we were there among the other social scientists, no one ever doubted that we were natural members of the family.

The Heyworth Report (Cmnd 2660, 1965) saw us essentially as a sub-category of the study of 'Politics' and commented as follows: 'Much importance is attached to comparative studies, e.g. of constitutional and administrative developments at both local and national level, and to historical studies, e.g. of the principal concepts of politics, of foreign policy, of international relations' (para. 12). Subsequently, the SSRC in its review of *Research in Political Science*[7] (1968), described in more detail how the subject of international relations was seen as fitting in to the collection of disciplines involved in the social sciences:

. . . The subject retains its close links with international history. Thus, on the one hand, in the tradition of political science (or, per-

---

[6] In 1969; I was the second chairman of the SSRC, following Dr Michael Young.

[7] This section of the SSRC report reflected the work of a panel of specialists on international relations, which was set up under the chairmanship of Professor Geoffrey Goodwin (a member of both the Research Committee of Chatham House and, at that time, of the SSRC Political Science Committee), with another member of the Chatham House staff, Miss Susan Strange, acting as rapporteur.

haps more accurately, of political sociology) the study of international relations attempts to discover in the welter of diplomatic events that which is characteristic, typical; its method is usually comparative and its concern is to arrive at valid propositions about the nature of political activity at the international level. On the other hand, international history, either as part of or closely allied to international relations, provides the raw material for the formulation and testing of these propositions; it gives depth and perspective to the study of the present; and above all it can impart the sense of the concrete, of the particular and the contingent in human affairs, which is an enriching experience in itself and a check upon over ready generalisation.

It then went on to remark on how difficult it was

to disentangle many problems of international relations from those of the human situation as a whole. There are problems of world economics, there are social problems, such as those of race, class, and nation, and there are problems within the realm of the natural sciences, such as those of food production, birth control, etc. all of which have a bearing on international relations.

I sometimes wondered, when as Chairman of the SSRC I was responsible for the demarcation between different fields of research, whether the above comment really pointed to a rather more radical conclusion than the authors of the research review suggested. Their argument indicated that international studies consisted of an amalgam of social-science disciplines and subjects, with no single one of them overwhelmingly dominant. The kind of analogy that suggested itself was with Management Studies, a subject which combines economics, sociology, psychology, and much else, and which is treated as having its own distinct and separate character. Initially the inclination was to treat the scientific study of management as if it was a subbranch of economics, the reason being no more than that many of those interested in the former had derived their training and general intellectual formation from the latter. Perhaps the same considerations apply to international relations, and its allotment in the SSRC system to the Political Science Committee reflects little more than the fact that the current generation of university teachers and researchers in international relations in Britain come predominantly out of the politics and modern history schools. This fact has also coloured the research proposals on international relations that have come to the SSRC during the first few years of its existence. It is only fair to say that if it had been otherwise—if many more of the research projects put forward involved the use of psychology, sociology or economics —a differently constituted committee of the SSRC would have been seen to be required in order to judge their merits. I would hope that it will not be long before such an administrative problem arises.

The uses of international studies

It may be felt that the demands that I have suggested should be made on the serious student of international relations are likely to deter rather than encourage scholarship in this field. If it is necessary to have the abilities of a polymath in order to perform effectively in it, where are the recruits to it to come from? Nor will it be possible to attract them by the promise that, as a result of their labours in a multiplicity of disciplines, they will arrive at the kind of scientific truth which can be used for purposes of prediction. On the contrary, as I indicated earlier, the more interdisciplinary the method, the less determinate the answers to problems posed are likely to be. It is necessary therefore to ask in severely practical terms what purpose international studies are supposed to serve.

My answer to that question is that the business of scholars is to provide models of the international system which can be used by practical men of affairs to interpret new events in a way which assists them to make rational decisions. Their decisions may or may not be wise; but the scholar will have done his part if his model contains enough of the significant elements in the situation, together with an account of the probable causal relationships between them, to permit rational decisions to be made. Now one is plainly not thinking of just one scholar and one man of affairs confronting one another. There is a cumulative effort by many minds on the one side and a mass of detailed decisions on the other. Moreover, there are many matters about which the decision-maker is bound to know a great deal more than the scholar. What the scholar is supposed to contribute is a clearer and more systematic way of analysing how the component parts of the system may affect one another in varying sets of circumstances. It is in that sense that a good model, derived in part from information that may be remote from the immediate present, can be of much greater use than any amount of factual data about the current situation.

It may be thought that the role of the scholar described here is not very different from that of any other expert adviser in the field of politics or business. One practical difference which applies to the study of international affairs is that the policy-maker tends to be more easily made aware of the gaps in his knowledge of foreign countries. He is also inclined to accept greatly simplified explanations of the ways in which they operate. The responsibility of the model builder in international studies is therefore especially great. In domestic politics every administrator and politician is to some extent his own expert model maker. He knows how the system works, or he thinks he does, from personal and direct experience. He will also, if he is intelligent, remind himself of obscure factors in the situation on which he will demand precise and expert information. But when he turns to international affairs he usually has neither a chart nor a check-list of questions. In consequence he is more vulnerable to the specialist scholar's tendency to concentrate heavily on information derived from his own specialism, at the expense of other pertinent matter. That is one further reason why the intellectual habits of the multidisciplinary approach to the study of international relations need to be more firmly established than they have been hitherto.

I am not suggesting, however, that there is no place for good scholarly work of a specialist character on some single aspect of international affairs. The contention is rather that the large-scale work of interpretation, which sets out to provide an over-view of the international system and to point to the significant features in it, should be recognized as being of quite a different kind. I have in mind in particular the synoptic studies, of which the *Survey of International Affairs* is a familiar example. They are the characteristic product of an institute of international affairs which aims to make a contribution in the field which the Americans have christened the 'policy sciences'.[8] What such work requires is an intellectual approach which is parallel to that of the administrator himself, an approach which seeks

[8] See D. Lerner & H. D. Lasswell, eds., *The Policy Sciences* (London, 1951).

constantly to formulate problems of research in terms that would be familiar to a person whose business it is to make decisions. And each decision taken is seen, in turn, as an opportunity to test some hypothesis derived from the model of the international system.

Viewed in this way, the wide-ranging demands made on the student of contemporary international relations no longer seem quite so forbidding. They are, after all, the kind of demands that are normally made on the man of affairs. The scholar in this instance needs to adopt something of the tastes and the temperament of the man of affairs. Because he cannot hope to master the detail of every aspect of his field of study, he may have to sacrifice some depth of knowledge in order to achieve breadth. Now this may seem a dire doctrine for scholars. It is not, however, to be mistaken for a general licence for superficiality of treatment. Rather, it points to the conclusion that this kind of enterprise requires the collaborative work of a group of scholars and cannot be compassed by one of them working on his own, however able and learned he may be.

This is not to be confused with the argument developed by Donald Watt that a comprehensive survey of international affairs is, because of its extent, beyond the capacity of any single author. The preference for a working group of people rather than a single individual derives from the multidisciplinary character of the enterprise. The ideal arrangement is for each member of such a working group to have his own area of specialist academic expertise, as well as a sufficient familiarity with the disciplines of his colleagues to permit him to make a critical appraisal of their contributions. The extensive overlapping of scholarly interests and the consequent mutual surveillance should help to ensure the quality of the final product.

I should say that the process here described is a laborious one, involving long arguments and sometimes wearisome explanations of the different approaches being adopted by people deploying different disciplines and types of expertise. It is a much more demanding exercise than the activities of the study groups of professional composition, which have been a standard feature of Chatham House's research activities for many years. The Chatham House formula of bringing in people from the world of public affairs, from the Civil Service, from business and journalism to join in a dialogue with the academic specialists was, and remains, a significant advance on the procedures of most university seminars. How often have I heard an attractive theoretical argument demolished by someone bursting with practical experience of the matter under discussion, who cries out almost in anguish: 'No, it really wasn't like that!' And the effect can be equally telling on the other side, and just as dramatic, when men of affairs who see certain matters with which they are familiar as quite special or even unique have to be persuaded to look at them as part of a larger pattern of behaviour, whose characteristics recur at different times and places with only slight variations in their form. The experts on form and the experts on content are thus forced to learn from one another. Some of the best books that Chatham House has produced have emerged from this process.

However, the demands made on a group of international experts drawn from different disciplines who are called upon to engage in a systematic effort to identify the intellectual limitations of each other's approaches to a common range of problems are far more taxing than this. The experience that I have had which is nearest to this is in the Chatham House group which has been working on a study of the development of international relations in the 1960s. The subject-matter of this group has been deliberately narrowed to focus on the relations among the nations of the Western world. But even so, the variety of different expertise that has been brought to bear on the study by different members of the group—international lawyers, political scientists, financial experts, and trade analysts—has meant that the essential tools of analysis and the common assumptions on which the study is to be based are again and again brought up for re-examination. One recurrent difficulty is to agree on the particular events and the type of data that should be *left out* of the various parts of the study. The merit of this process is that we are as a group constantly being called upon by one or another of our members to think again about the criteria of significance that we are applying to the material under investigation. One becomes intensely aware of the way in which expertise in a particular aspect of international relations, allied to habits of mind formed by long familiarity with certain kinds of information, tends to produce its own special image of the international system as a whole. Perhaps the most important outcome of the discussions of the group is that these implicit images are made public, and modified in the process.

I suspect that our experience in this venture will be found to be characteristic of other synoptic group studies of international relations. Such groups will have to spend much more time on the discussion of theory and methodology than has been usual in the pragmatic atmosphere of Chatham House. This is to be expected, since the nature of the exercise demands that people should not just be left to do their own thing, and explain it afterwards. They have to justify to one another their own canons of relevance. Perhaps, after all, what is required from the next generation of Chatham House scholars is less the abilities of a polymath than a capacity to engage in co-operative research with people whose assumptions and methods of investigation start out by being different from their own. There probably is a quite modest upper limit to the size of a research team of this kind that can work effectively together. This and other operational characteristics of such teamwork will only gradually emerge out of the experience of tackling particular pieces of research. The first step is to recognize that the team rather than the individual is the basic unit for the main body of the research work that needs to be done in order to fulfil the purposes of an institute of international affairs.

2   Human Rights in International Relations

J. E. S. FAWCETT

THE international protection of human rights has been much debated and analysed as a common ideal, as a social and legal structure, as a set of procedures; but the question is seldom asked in this literature why we find the protection of human rights in practice often submerged in the pursuit of quite different objectives, so that protection is not achieved in fact, or may not even have been seriously intended by those ostensibly invoking human rights.

To attempt an answer to this question it is necessary to see first that a consolidated concept of human rights has emerged in the last quarter of a century out of a large number of quite disparate rights and claims, and that this concept has become a political factor of some influence in international relations: as a standard of acceptability of regimes; as a vehicle for the self-determination of peoples or the activism of revolutionary groups; as a ground for justifying foreign policies, predetermined by objectives having little to do in fact with human rights; and as a reason for intervening in the affairs of other countries. These functions of human rights as a political concept are plainly complex, with differing moral bases and often in conflict. To understand them better let us begin with the emergence of the concept in its contemporary form.

I

The international codification of human rights, that is, their reduction to a number of generalized propositions, is to be found in the Universal Declaration of Human Rights (1948) as

extended and elaborated by the UN Civil and Political Rights
Covenant and Economic, Social and Cultural Rights Covenant,
of 1966.[1] Partial and regional codification are also to be found
in the European Convention on Human Rights and the Inter-
American Convention on Human Rights. There are too a large
number of international conventions, some dating back to the
beginning of the century, concerning genocide, racial discrimination, political rights of women, discrimination in education, refugees and statelessness, slavery,[2] forced labour, and
traffic in women. In addition over 120 Conventions have been
concluded under the auspices of the ILO setting standards for
the conditions and remuneration of labour and for protection
of trade union rights, in industry, agriculture, and shipping.
These last have had a large measure of acceptance and success.[3]

But how widely accepted are the UN Covenants and other
general Conventions, and what is their substantive character
and influence? If we take the number of UN members as base,
the proportion of acceptances is not impressive. Only the Genocide Convention and the Slavery Convention (1956) have been
accepted by as many as 60 per cent of the membership, and
the limited convention on Political Rights of Women (1952)
has been accepted by about 50 per cent, while the Convention
on the Elimination of Racial Discrimination has barely attained
25 per cent. However, it would be a mistake to conclude too
quickly that the actual influence of the UN Covenants and
general Conventions is limited to their formal acceptances.
First, the effect of the reduction of rights and claims to short,
general propositions, understandable in any language, is not
to be underestimated. While few are innocent enough to suppose
that Conventions, declarations, and bills of rights, whether
international or national, are in themselves an effective safeguard, experience shows that they can serve as a standard of
achievement, as the Universal Declaration of Human Rights
claimed to be, and as at least a first line of defence. This last
point was emphasized by the subcommission concerned with

---

[1] Each Covenant requires 35 ratifications for its entry into force. Up to the end
of June 1970 there had been only six ratifications: Colombia, Costa Rica,
Cyprus, Ecuador, Syria, and Tunisia had each ratified both Covenants.

[2] See Sir Reginald Coupland, *The British Anti-Slavery Movement* (London, 1933).

[3] See C. W. Jenks, *Human Rights and International Labour Standards* (London, 1960)
and his *Social Justice in the Law of Nations* (London, 1970).

the form of the Nigerian constitution; and in its report it expressly disagreed with the opinion of the earlier Simon Commission (1929) on the government of India that the inclusion of a bill of rights in a constitution achieves little. Indeed, Lord Acton went so far as to say that the Declaration of the Rights of Man was a scrap of paper stronger than all the armies of Napoleon.

A second reason for not placing too much weight on the bare number of acceptances is that the Covenants and Conventions reflect in substance actual human needs, demands and goals, about which there is much common agreement around the world,[4] and they have had much publicity, and have come to be almost customarily invoked in many environments, so that governments are, or feel themselves, less free to disregard their provisions in practice, as the Soviet Union appeared to recognize in the form it gave to its efforts in the UN General Assembly to defend its intervention in Czechoslovakia. It is in fact arguable that the UN Covenants, whether they enter into force formally or not, have in effect displaced the Universal Declaration of Human Rights as setting out standards of achievement, if only for their greater elaboration and their expression of the common thinking of over 100 countries as opposed to less than fifty that adopted the Declaration. Further, many of the provisions of these international instruments have been embodied with little or no change in a number of new constitutions.[5] Their principles are also found repeated in instruments of political organization. Thus, in addition to the UN Charter itself, the Charters of the OAS (1948, Arts. 5, 28–31) and the OAU (1963, Art. II, 1-b, d, & e) and the Statute of the Council of Europe (1949, Arts. 3, 8) give prominent place to protection and development of human rights. The Rome Treaty, despite its apparent dedication to closer political union, has little to say about the social principles that must underlie it.[6] Paradoxically, perhaps, in contrast the North Atlantic Treaty (Art. 2) calls on the parties to strengthen their free institutions,

[4] See E. Schwelb, *Human Rights and the International Community: the roots and growth of the Universal Declaration* (Chicago, 1964); M. Moskowitz, *The Politics and Dynamics of Human Rights* (New York, 1968).

[5] See S. A. de Smith, *The New Commonwealth and its Constitutions* (London, 1964).

[6] Art. 119 (equal pay for men and women) is almost the only reference to the rights and claims familiar in the other international instruments.

to bring about 'a better understanding of the principles upon which these institutions are founded, and to promote conditions of stability and well-being'. Yet, as we shall see, it was the EEC rather than NATO that reacted against the new regime in Greece.

Finally, the distinction between formal acceptance of international conventions and their application in practice is obvious and it would be rash to compare countries in terms of acceptance or non-acceptance without a closer look at the reasons. So, if we take a group of twenty general conventions, of the kind already described, we find that at the end of 1968, for example, Yugoslavia, Norway, and Sweden had accepted 13–15, 10 had been accepted by Brazil, Cuba, Czechoslovakia, Denmark, France, Jamaica, Turkey, and the United Kingdom; Canada, Pakistan, and the Soviet Union had accepted 7, Spain, Portugal, and the United States 4 or less, and Zambia none.

This brief discussion of what may loosely be called the international codification of human rights goes no further than to suggest that its political use and influence can be wider than its legal structure appears to allow, and this because the codes and general conventions have brought many disparate human rights and claims together into focus as a unifying political concept. What are its components?

In the contemporary political concept of human rights, three components stand out: the confrontation of the individual and the state, social claims to higher standards of life and development, and the self-determination of national groups. Let us take them in turn.

Individual and state

When Aristotle spoke of man as a 'political animal' he did not mean that he was a political animal as a successful minister, diplomat, or trade unionist might be described, but that he was a creature living in communities of which the Greek city-state was a type. The rights of the citizen, as a member of such a community and so distinct from the alien stranger, have been designed to protect his life, liberty, and property from interference by others, including the community itself in the shape of the state (*die Freiheit vom Staat*), and to give him freedom of opinion, expression, and assembly to secure his full participation in the life of the community (*die Freiheit zum Staat*). These civil rights and liberties, legally defined and enforceable, have been the natural groundwork of constitutions. But the drafters of the Declaration of the Rights of Man (1789) asserted that, over and above *droits de citoyen*, there were common rights inherent in every human being; and the long history of treaty and diplomatic practice on the protection of aliens can be summoned in support. Indeed the alien as slave, diplomat, trader, immigrant, has contributed much to the extension of civil rights.

Social claims

Another broadening influence has been the emergence of social claims to higher standards of life and development, implying rights that are hard to formulate and even harder to enforce. The protection of labour and the right to work, and community responsibility for health, education, and welfare, are issues of political struggle, resolved only over time and at certain levels of economic growth. The difference between civil rights and social claims, which may be only inchoate rights, was well expressed in the United States Supreme Court:

The very purpose of a Bill of Rights was to withdraw certain subjects from the vicissitudes of political controversy, to place them beyond the reach of majorities and officials, and to establish them as legal principles to be applied by the Courts. One's right to life, liberty and property, to free speech, a free press, freedom of worship and assembly, and other fundamental freedoms, may not be submitted to vote; they depend on the outcome of no elections.[7]

In this classical framework of liberty, it was easy not to look beyond the necessary forms of freedom to the social and individual values it was to serve, to confuse the scaffolding with the house. So many offences against property in this country were capital; a man who stole a sheep could be sure of a fair trial and had the freedom to speak out and write against the law that condemned him, but he was still hanged. Liberal capitalism took over the classical framework, but the pressure of many claims has gone some way in tempering its notion of

[7] Mr. Justice Jackson in *West Virginia Board of Education* v. *Barnette* (1943) 319 U.S. 624.

liberty with that of social justice. The socialist conception of human rights, on the other hand, traceable through UN debates on the Universal Declaration and the Covenants, and with obvious roots in the economic groundsoil of society, goes much further. Civil rights and liberties, it is argued, without a balancing of economic rights and social interest, are at best ineffective and at worst a cheat and a façade for oppression. They are not, on this view, even inherent in the individual, or fundamental; rights and freedoms are rather granted to him by the community, transitionally the ruling class, of a kind that the recognized social objectives can allow and to the extent that these objectives are being attained. But the wheel has come full circle, when, ironically perhaps, it is economic offences in the Soviet Union which are still capital.

Civil rights and social claims began to converge in the first efforts at international codification after 1945, though a distinction was maintained between what came by abbreviation to be called 'legal rights' and 'programme rights', leading to the adoption for the former of the Civil and Political Rights Covenant, and for the latter the Economic, Social and Cultural Rights Covenant. But, despite the frequent characterization of rights in the codes and conventions as 'fundamental' or 'basic', some assumptions about these terms had changed. Rights and prohibitions can be described as fundamental or basic in a number of senses: that they cannot in any circumstances be denied or disregarded; that they express certain generally agreed values that underlie the social order, but may be restricted or disregarded if the public or common interest requires; that, in a legal sense, they are presupposed by the constitution of a country and given the status in that constitution of 'entrenched provisions'. Few indeed are the codified rights or prohibitions which meet the first criterion, the prohibitions of slavery and of torture or inhuman treatment being among them. But the confrontation of individual and state remains in many societies, and there are rights and freedoms protecting him in this confrontation, which are basic in the second and third senses.

The introduction of social claims among human rights,[8]

---

[8] Such as 'the right of everyone to an adequate standard of living for himself and his family, including adequate food, clothing and housing' . . . 'the right of everyone

means that, in so far as they can be treated as rights at all, they are such only in the second sense. To apply the first criterion to them would be almost meaningless, and their possible place in any constitution is well taken in the Constitution of India,[9] which turns such social claims into directive principles of state policy, addressed not to the courts for judicial enforcement but to the legislature to govern its enactments.

The old static order of civil rights, relatively precise and enforceable, has been invaded, then, by the dynamic of social claims, giving human rights drawn from both sources a potent political concept. This can be seen still more clearly in the third component of the concept, self-determination.

Self-determination

The evolution of the idea of self-determination since 1945 is worth attention. The Universal Declaration does not speak of it expressly, but states that: 'Everyone has the right to take part in the government of his country, directly or through freely chosen representatives. . . . The will of the people shall be the basis of the authority of government . . .' (Arts. 21(1) & (31)), and that 'Everyone is entitled to a social and international order in which the rights and freedoms set forth in this Declaration can be fully realised' (Art. 28). Self-determination appears as a right in UN General Assembly Resolution 637 (VII) A (16 December 1952), which states that 'the right of peoples and nations to self-determination is a prerequisite to the full enjoyment of all fundamental human rights' and fully flowers in the UN Declaration on Granting of Independence to Colonial Peoples (1960):[10] 'All peoples have the right to self-determination; by virtue of that right they freely determine their political status and freely pursue their economic, social and cultural development.' This clause unchanged now forms Article 1(1) of both the UN Covenants of 1966. Since it is not excluded from the scope of Article 41 of the Civil and Political Rights Covenant, the right of self-determination may, it seems, rank as an

to the enjoyment of the highest attainable standard of physical and mental health'; 'the right of everyone to education': Economic, Social and Cultural Rights Covenant, Arts. 11(1), 12(1), & 13(1).

[9] See Arts. 37, 38, & 39. Arts. 43, 39(e), 47, & 45 correspond to the Covenant articles just cited.   [10] GA Resolution 1514 (XV).

enforceable right before the proposed Human Rights Committee equally with the other covenanted rights. But to treat self-determination as itself an enforceable human right is to misconceive it in two ways: first, it is a right of a second order, not directly enforceable, but standing behind the rights and freedoms set out in the Covenants and Conventions as a precondition of their full exercise by individuals as members of communities. Secondly, it is a collective right and again distinct from the individual rights with which the Covenants and Conventions as regimes of enforcement are essentially concerned. The collectivities for which self-determination is sought may be established nations, or whole peoples seeking freedom from colonial rule, or groups markedly distinguished from the remainder of the community in which they live by physical characteristics, habitual language, religious belief and practice, or political affiliation. Thirdly, among these collectivities the group is frequently in conflict with the nation, so that a choice may have to be made as to whose self-determination is to prevail; often it is urged that, if a community is not to disintegrate, that of the nation must prevail. To treat self-determination as an enforceable right is at the least impractical.

II

Some political uses of this concept can now be described. First, there has been in the last twenty years an identification of colonialism and totalitarianism with a general denial of human rights, in that each are seen by their very nature as involving such a denial, even though specific rights and freedoms are not in issue. Here colonialism is taken to be a form of rule of a dependent territory primarily for the convenience and benefit of the metropolitan country and its nationals, as distinct from the inhabitants of the territory; and the notion is sometimes used by analogy to discredit the administration of minorities, whether ethnic or religious groups, within a country. A regime can be said to be 'totalitarian', if it has three linked features: largely uncontrolled discretion of the government or ruling party to interfere in the social and economic life of the community; inadequate participation of the people in the making of policy; and coercive methods of dealing with any opposition, marked usually by abnormal powers of the security police or armed forces. Where colonialism or totalitarianism is shown to exist in these forms, it is plain that there must be systematic denial of at least some human rights under them.

The human-rights concept has, then, prompted two main kinds of governmental action on the international plane: first, the expression in various ways of the disapproval of or hostility to a foreign regime, which is manifested by influential groups, national or international; and second, reactions against the regime seen as a threat to national or international security. Under the first, the role of influential groups must be distinguished from that of government, since their objectives may not necessarily coincide and may even be in conflict. So, even if not the government as a whole, influential members of it may be ready to oppose a foreign regime on human rights grounds; or it may oppose, but have other national interests to secure, which limit or prevent practical expression of disapproval or hostility, and yet be still persuaded for electoral or other internal reasons by influential groups at home or abroad to take or join in international action. The latter situation is the commoner.

The second kind of government action also calls for general remark. There is a sense in which the protection of human rights is always a response to a threat or act of aggression, if by aggression we mean the use of coercion or violence against an individual or a group, as well as against a whole nation-state; for the denial of human rights is generally the use of coercion or violence to limit the freedom or common rights of individuals or groups On the international plane the human rights concept helps to fuse this kind of aggression with the traditional notion of aggression by one nation-state against another, so that the systematic denial of human rights in one country may come to be seen as a threat to the security of others.

Practical expression by governments of disapproval of a foreign regime may take several forms, of which two stand out: refusal of recognition, and dissociation, which may be collective.

An example of the first was the non-recognition of the Chinese People's Republic by the United States in part in reliance upon the human-rights concept. In a State Department Memorandum sent to US Missions abroad in September 1958[11] the case for non-recognition was closely reasoned and set out at length. Among the grounds chosen, it was said that on the mainland of China 'regimentation, repression and forced sacrifices demanded of the people, and the consequent extensive popular unrest show that the regime does not represent the will of the people substantially declared'. This echoes the words of Thomas Jefferson, who as Secretary of State in 1792 declared that: 'It accords with our principles to acknowledge any government to be rightful which is formed by the will of the people substantially declared.' President Wilson, in his policies towards Central America, took the principle further in requiring constitutionality of a new government as one of the criteria for its recognition. But the United States later returned to the old principle, and the lack of free elections in the GDR has been insisted on as one of the demonstrations that it is not an independent state. Yet the principle has sometimes faded into an acceptance of 'apparent general acquiescence' of the people, or 'the absence of active resistance': in short, it has been adjusted to other political requirements.

A belief that a foreign government has no popular foundation is distinct from a judgement upon its domestic policies, and it is the latter which is generally the ground of dissociation from an already recognized government. Other governments may reduce or stop cultural contacts and exchanges, or limit trade, or sever diplomatic relations, or exclude it from international organizations to which they belong. It is in collective acts of dissociation that the human rights concept has been most prominent.

Consideration of these collective acts must keep in mind the multiplicity and sometimes confusion of objectives, in which the protection of the rights and freedoms of individuals or groups, directly or indirectly by bringing about a change of regime, may or may not predominate. Further, collective action through international institutions may have constitutional as well as practical limitations.[12] Examples will be taken from Spain, Greece, Aden, Rhodesia, and Vietnam.

[11] *DSB*, 8 Sept. 1958.
[12] See Rosalyn Higgins, *Development of International Law through the Political Organs of the UN* (London, 1967), pp. 118–30; E. Luard, ed., *International Protection of Human Rights* (London, 1967).

III
Spain

Spain was characterized at the San Francisco Conference as a country whose regime had been installed with the help of armed forces of countries which have fought against the United Nations,[13] and the Soviet Union, United States, and United Kingdom declared at Potsdam that they would not support the admission to the UN of the 'present Spanish Government'. In December 1946 the UN General Assembly resolved that 'the Franco Government of Spain be debarred from membership in international agencies established by or brought into relationship with the United Nations'; and recommended that:

if, within a reasonable time, there is not established a government which derives its authority from the consent of the governed, committed to respect freedom of speech, religion and assembly and to the prompt holding of an election in which the Spanish people, free from force and intimidation and regardless of party, may express their will, the Security Council consider the adequate measures to be taken in order to remedy the situation; . . . [and] that all Members of the United Nations immediately recall from Madrid their ambassadors and ministers plenipotentiary accredited there.[14]

The Security Council had in April 1946 appointed a sub-committee of inquiry, which found unanimously that 'the Franco regime is a Fascist regime' and that: 'the facts established by the evidence before the Committee are by no means of essentially local or domestic concern to Spain. What is imputed to the Franco régime is that it is threatening the maintenance of international peace and security and that it is causing international friction.'[15] However, a resolution in effect adopting the report and recommendations of the subcommittee received 9–1 votes with one abstention, the single vote being a veto.

But in 1950 the position changed. The General Assembly, now holding that the establishment of diplomatic relations with a government 'does not imply any judgement upon the domestic policy of that government', revoked the recommendations in the earlier resolution for withdrawal of ambassadors and

---

[13] Resolution: UNCIO Document 1167 I/10.
[14] Resolution 39 (I), recalling an earlier Resolution 32 (I), cast in general terms.
[15] *SCOR*, 1st yr., 39th meeting.

ministers, and debarring Spain from membership in inter-
ional organizations.[16]

Nevertheless, the Council of Europe, on its establishment in
1949, made no place for Spain, nor was she named among
countries recommended for membership in 1950, which included Portugal; but she has for some years had an observer at
the Council.

The admission of Spain to the UN in December 1955 by
55-0-2 votes was part of the 'package deal' on membership, of
which the human-rights concept formed only part of the background, in that by mutual consent existing members suppressed
their objections to the regimes of candidate states, as being
in different ways totalitarian. The membership of Spain was
normal and relatively quiet until 1964, when she came on the
UN scene in a different role as a claimant for Gibraltar, and
not long after as the addressee of recommendations on the
decolonization of her own dependent territories in Africa. In
a series of resolutions[17] the General Assembly called for continued negotiations between the United Kingdom and Spain,
'taking into account the interests of the people of the territory';
and, in implementation of Resolution 1514 (XV), for 'termina-
tion of the colonial situation in Gibraltar', the deadline of
1 October 1969, being finally pronounced.[18] The General
Assembly also found fault with the referendum held in Gibraltar, as contravening an earlier resolution.[19] With regard to
the Spanish territories in Africa, Ifni and the Spanish Sahara,
the General Assembly called for 'an acceleration of decolonization' of Ifni, bearing in mind 'the aspirations of the indigenous
population', and for a continued 'dialogue with Morocco'.[20]
For the Spanish Sahara a referendum was suggested, after
consultation with Morocco and Mauritania, under UN supervision and with 'only indigenous people' participating.[21] In
December 1969 the General Assembly recorded its regret that

[16] Resolution 386 (V) (4 Nov. 1950), carried 38-10-12.
[17] 2070 (XX) (Dec. 1965); 2231 (XXI) (Dec. 1966); 2353 (XXII) (Dec. 1967);
2429 (XXIII) (Dec. 1968).
[18] Resolution 2429 (XXIII).
[19] Resolution 2353 (XXII), invoking 2231 (XXI). The contravention is not
obvious since the latter resolution says nothing about a referendum.
[20] Resolution 2428 XXIII (I) (Dec. 1968).
[21] Resolution 2428 XXXIII (II).

the recommended consultations had not yet been 'possible', and in substance repeated the earlier resolution.[22]

Negotiations on the Spanish Sahara were still continuing in June 1970, the interest in the phosphate deposits being an issue. But Ifni was ceded to Morocco by agreement between Spain and Morocco, the transfer being made on 30 June 1969.

In this record three things stand out: the shifting assessment of Spain in terms of human rights; the recognition that self-determination does not necessarily entail independence; and acceptance of the disposition of a territory, small in population or area, as being still negotiable between states.

The political use of human rights is well illustrated by the evolution of the position of Spain in the UN. The regime, condemned in the early years as a 'Fascist regime', won admission to the UN, and was later able to mobilize support for its claims on Gibraltar by hoisting the flag of colonialism over it. Under this flag the wishes of the people of Gibraltar were brushed aside, and their representatives given a rough passage in the Third Committee. The General Assembly called for their 'interests' to be taken into account, but not their 'aspirations', to which a place was given in parallel resolutions on Spanish territories in Africa. The propriety of placing the people of Gibraltar under a regime which had not essentially changed its character since 1946 was given little attention; nor was the Spanish offer to provide, on the cession of Gibraltar to Spain, a special legal regime for its people, which in some forms at least would have the strange result of discriminating in their favour against the Spanish people. It may be that to have held the referendum in Gibraltar without UN supervision had tactical disadvantages, but its result could not be dismissed as no evidence of the political aspirations of the people. All was left to negotiations between Spain and the United Kingdom, but that the conclusion favoured by the majority in the General Assembly was cession to Spain is shown by the preamble to Resolution 2231 (XXI), in which it is declared that 'any colonial situation, which partially or completely destroys the national unity and territorial integrity of a country is incompatible with the purposes and principles of the Charter'. Resolution 1514 (XV), paragraph 6,

<hr/>

[22] Resolution 2591 (XXIV).

was here invoked. This reads: 'Any attempt aimed at the partial or total disruption of the national security and the territorial integrity is incompatible with the purposes and principles of the United Nations.' This paragraph is plainly aimed against the deliberate division, socially or territorially, of a colonial people, so as to frustrate their self-determination.

But, whatever may be said on other grounds against the persistence of enclaves like Gibraltar, it can hardly be maintained that this enclave is an attempt to disrupt, even partially, the national or territorial unity of Spain. The recognition that self-determination does not necessarily entail independence appears also in a General Assembly resolution[23] adopted virtually unanimously soon after Resolution 1514 (XV), and setting out principles, under which a territory can cease to be non-self-governing for purposes of Article 73 of the Charter. Principle VI includes 'free association' or 'integration' with an independent state. Principles VII–IX, however, set out some fairly stringent conditions which the process of integration must satisfy. In the first place, the territory into which the formerly non-self-governing territory is integrated must itself 'have attained an advanced stage of self-government with free political institutions'. Secondly, the territory integrated must accept integration 'freely and voluntarily' through 'informed and democratic processes'. Thirdly, the people of this territory must be placed in all respects on a basis of political and economic equality with the people of the country into which they are integrated. These Principles were not invoked or applied by the General Assembly either to the situation of Gibraltar or in the cession of Ifni to Morocco. There is no record of any consultation by informed and democratic processes of the people of Ifni about its integration in Morocco, or of any recognition of the needs of the Catholic minority forming a third of the population.

There is, however, an option for retention of Spanish nationality, and provision for the continued recognition of professional qualifications and the maintenance of Spanish cultural institutions.[24]

---

[23] 1541 (XV) (12 Dec. 1960).
[24] Arts. 3, 6, & 7: for text of the agreement of 'retrocession' see *R. de política internacional*, 102 (1969), 337.

We see, then, in this record directive principles, and measures of dissociation from a regime, adopted ostensibly to serve the protection of human rights, whether in Spain or other territories, but progressively distorted by shifting political alignments and objectives.

Greece

The regime which came to power in Greece in April 1967 has been, by the criteria suggested above, totalitarian. But the process by which Greece was compelled to withdraw from the Council of Europe—a measure of dissociation—was a confusion of two different approaches to the protection of human rights, a largely intuitive political and moral judgement of the regime on the one hand, and on the other investigation by adequate standards of fact-finding, leading to proposals for specific changes or reforms. The whole object of establishing a Commission and Court to deal with complaints of breaches of the European Convention on Human Rights was to open a way to the second approach: to substitute close and independent inquiry and a search for acceptable changes in place of abrupt and misdirected condemnation, and to remove the protection of human rights, as far as might be, from political whims and pressures. The Greek experience shows that it may not be very far, for in the end the first approach prevailed. The Consultative Assembly had adopted a resolution in June 1967 condemning the Greek regime; but, notwithstanding the reference of the situation in Greece to the Commission by Denmark, Netherlands, Norway, and Sweden in September 1967, it conducted inquiries of its own in Greece and repeated its condemnation in further resolutions culminating in that of 30 January 1969, in which it found Greece to be in breach of Article 3 of the Statute of the Council of Europe.[25] The Commission report to the Committee of Ministers, finding a number of breaches of the Convention, was based on investigations both in and outside Greece, meeting necessary standards of fact-finding, which the inquiries, reported to the Consultative Assembly, did not

---

[25] 'Every member of the Council of Europe must accept the principles of the rule of law and of the enjoyment by all persons within its jurisdiction of human rights and fundamental freedoms. . . .'

and did not indeed claim to meet: in particular, that allegations of torture or ill treatment must be proved beyond a reasonable doubt, and that on such specific allegations, and on any
other alleged breaches of the European Convention on Human
Rights, the Greek government should be given a full opportunity
to comment, explain or reply. The Committee of Ministers,
faced with the alternatives of following the recommendations
of the Consultative Assembly to move to the suspension and
expulsion of Greece under the Statute of the Council, or of
bringing persuasion and pressure to bear upon the Greek
government under the Convention to alter and improve its
methods, chose the first. Greece took the obvious course of
withdrawal. This result may have given moral satisfaction to
the Council of Europe, but it achieved little for the protection
of human rights in Greece. It was in fact the EEC which,
despite the lack of any particular preoccupation in the Rome
Treaty with human rights, took the strongest action against the
Greek regime. The EEC suspended financial aid to Greece in
September 1967 and in an official communiqué on 16 April
1970 its Commission stated that it was:

following the development of the situation in Greece with growing
concern. The development of the recent trials in Athens and the
constant arrests of particularly well-considered figures have increased
this concern. These various events do not seem to announce the
return to a normal democratic way of life which is awaited with
increasing impatience by European public opinion. The repeated
infringements of the Rights of Man and of the Citizen are causing
the Commission to *reconsider the already very difficult functioning of the
Association Agreement between Greece and the European Community*. The
Commission deeply deplores this situation, for, more than ever
before, it considers that the full and complete participation of the
Greek people in the efforts towards European integration is still
infinitely desirable.[26]

Aden

The subordination of regard for or protection of human rights
to other political purpose is also shown in the UN handling of
the situation in Aden. In December 1966 the General Assembly

[26] *Europe* (Agence Internationale d'Information pour la Presse), no. 551, 16 Apr.
1970.

adopted a resolution (2183 (XXI)) which committed the UN to intervention in the political struggle in Aden, which was only doubtfully its duty, and which gave only secondary consideration to the protection of human rights there, which was its duty. The Secretary-General was requested to send a special mission to determine, in consultation with the United Kingdom government and the Committee of Twenty-four, not only 'the extent of UN participation in the preparation and supervision of elections', but also 'practical steps for the establishment of a central caretaker government'. But over 'reports issued by various international humanitarian organizations (Amnesty) on the maltreatment of political prisoners' it expressed concern at 'the continuation of military operations against the people of the territory'. Yet the Committee of Twenty-four was able to carry a motion by 14–7–3 votes that it refuse even to accept for consideration evidence tending to show Egyptian support for acts of violence in the territory; and the UN made no response to confirmed reports by the International Committee of the Red Cross of the use of toxic gas, probably mustard gas, against civilians in the Yemen campaign, despite its resolution adopted in December 1966, condemning in general terms the use of toxic gases.

Links, real or artificial, between the protection of human rights and responses to aggression can be traced through the intricacies of international action in Rhodesia and Vietnam.

Rhodesia

The drafters of the UN Charter would doubtless have been much surprised if they had been told that the first application in history of mandatory international sanctions would be, not to deter or contain an obvious aggressor, but to secure the self-determination of a political minority—for this is the condition of the African people in Rhodesia, a majority in numbers but a minority in terms of political representation and power. But was this denial of self-determination and other rights a threat to the peace? This obvious precondition of any collective action under Chapter VII of the Charter was established only gradually by the Security Council. It had earlier said of the practice of apartheid in South Africa that it 'disturbs the peace', and in the first of its four resolutions[27] in Rhodesia after UDI, it was silent on the issue of a threat to the peace. In the second the situation in Rhodesia was said to be such that its 'continuance in time constitutes a threat to the peace'; the other resolutions, however, make a clear and express determination of a threat to the peace in the sense of Article 39 of the Charter. It must be remembered that such a determination by the Security Council is a matter of prediction not of proof; and that it is directed primarily, not at the apportionment of blame or the designation of the possible aggressor, but at the removal of international tension and the avoidance or limitation of action likely to provoke the international use of force, regardless of who initiates it. There was ground for seeing a threat to the peace in the Rhodesian situation in this sense in the Rhodesian threat to expel immigrant workers, the vulnerability of the Kariba Dam, and the infiltration into Rhodesia of armed irregulars and their support by other countries. But it is possible to detect in international action, whether taken or proposed, against regimes in Southern Africa a half-articulated identification of the denial of human rights with aggression. The idea takes an extreme form in the anarchist doctrine, as crude as it is disingenuous, that all organized society is violent. But, as Abraham Lincoln observed that freedom must be given to the slave to secure the freedom of the free, there is a widely and justly held belief that oppression can be contagious and that a totalitarian regime in one country can be a threat to the security of others.

Vietnam

The identification of the denial of human rights with aggression can be seen, though in a more complex form, in the patterns of intervention in Vietnam. One aspect is the characterization by the United States of the infiltration from North Vietnam and its support to 'hostile activities . . . aimed at the overthrow of the Administration in the South',[28] as an armed attack in the sense of Article 51 of the UN Charter even before February 1965.

[27] 216 (12 Nov. 1965); 217 (20 Nov. 1965); 221 (9 Apr. 1966); 232 (16 Dec. 1966).
[28] US State Dept. Memo. (4 Mar. 1966) in *DSB*, 28 Mar. 1966, p. 474. The expression quoted is taken from the report of the International Control Commission made in 1962, the Polish member dissenting.

Among these hostile activities are mentioned 'kidnapping and assassination of civilian officials—acts of terrorism that were perpetrated in increasing numbers'. The totalitarian threat seen by the United States is further emphasized by the reference in the Memorandum to the SEATO Treaty and to the 'United States understanding, expressed at the time of signature, that its obligations under Article IV, paragraph 1,[29] apply only in the event of *Communist* aggression'. There is some analogy, then, between the characterization of North Vietnamese policy and methods on the one hand, and of the Rhodesian regime on the other, as threats to security beyond their own territories.

Another aspect is the invocation of self-determination and other human rights by all the participants in the Vietnam conflict to justify their actions.

These invocations pose dilemmas. We are all for the rights of the child, but what if he is taught to throw hand-grenades? Does the policy of 'waste', the obliteration of villages and the pollution of his natural environment, unparalleled in the history of war, make his cause just; or do the systematic cruelties perpetrated by the Vietcong against their own fellow countrymen justify every reprisal? It is easy to state the dilemmas. The difficulty is that here, and often with the actions of guerrillas or other revolutionary groups elsewhere, in Uruguay, Quebec, or Northern Ireland, we have passed below the minimum of social order and stability which the codes and conventions of human rights presuppose. The European Convention on Human Rights was in great part a reaction against cruelties and oppression in Europe, which had been resisted by partisans and maquisards as well as the regular forces of war. Many countries are back in this situation, and here the invocation of human rights is not a means of their protection, but is simply a political instrument to fortify national policy or denigrate opponents.

IV

Contemporary writing and discussion about the international protection of human rights, both official and academic, is in danger of being too laudatory of institutions, too uncritical of

[29] 'to act to meet the common danger in accordance with its constitutional processes.'

practice, and too much preoccupied with forms and procedures.[30] Satisfaction with the codes and conventions of the last two decades must be tempered by the thought that they may mark less the beginning of new advances than the end of an era. But their impact has not been small and they set standards by which it can be seen that no community, whatever its political structure or assumptions, has yet succeeded in fully reconciling the demands of civil order and social justice.

The study of human rights and their place in international relations should leave doctrine and procedures for a time and concentrate on the political factors, national and international, which limit the exercise of generally recognized rights and freedoms, and which defeat or distort their international protection.

[30] Exceptions are the publications of the International Commission of Jurists, and, e.g. R. J. Dupuy, 'La Commission Européenne des Droits de l'Homme', *Ann. françaises de droit international* (1957), 449; T. Burgenthal, 'Domestic status of the European Convention on Human Rights', 13 *Buffalo Law R.* (Winter 1964) 354, and other articles by the same author; D. J. Harris, 'The European Convention on Human Rights and English criminal law', *Criminal Law R.* (Apr. 1966) 205; C. G. Morrisson, *The Developing European Law of Human Rights* (Leyden, 1967); M. Moskowitz, *The Politics and Dynamics of Human Rights* (New York, 1968); Anna P. Schreiber, *The Inter-American Commission of Human Rights* (Leyden, 1970).

3 International Law and the UN System

ROSALYN HIGGINS

THE definition of international law as rules applicable between states has always been a partial one. Certain categories of individuals, in limited circumstances, have long been within the reach and protection of international law[1] and in recent years it has come to be recognized that even entities which are not fully sovereign may from time to time engage in transactions which are governed by international law.[2] A change of attitude has also taken place in the years since the second world war; there has grown an appreciation that law is more than rules. 'Rules' is in effect a shorthand way of referring to the accumulated trend of past decision. But international law performs many functions, which go beyond the application of rules. Communication and the limitation of options are high among those functions.[3] But perhaps nothing has had greater impact upon the development of international law than the evolution of the United Nations and its family of agencies. It is hard to exaggerate the significance of international organization for international law.

[1] For example, international law provides direct benefits for individuals under the European Convention on Human Rights and the UN Covenants on human rights; and the Nuremberg Tribunal confirmed the principle that an individual has direct responsibility under international law so far as military conduct is concerned. The Calley trial in the US has turned on the Nuremberg principle that the carrying out of an order by a superior to behave contrary to the laws of war is no legal defence, even though it may mitigate punishment; see also S. Horowitz, 'The Tokyo trial', *Internat. Conciliation*, 465 (1960); K. K. Woetzel, *The Nuremberg Trials in International Law* (London, 1960); E. Jiménez de Aréchaga, 'Treaty stipulations in favour of third states', 50 *AJIL* (1956) 338; C. Parry, 'Some considerations upon the protection of individuals in international law', 90 *HR* (1956) 635, and C. A. Norgaard, *The Position of the Individual in International Law* (Copenhagen, 1962).

[2] e.g. Rhodesia was, prior to UDI, a party to GATT.

[3] This point is developed by Richard Falk in *The Status of Law in International Society* (Princeton, 1970; espec. in chs. I & XV).

Broadly speaking, the UN has had three main functions concerning law: it is an originator, an applier, and a developer of international law. Of course, these functions overlap each other to a very real extent. For example, it is often by 'applying' law that law is in fact 'developed'. But, for the sake of discussion, I have in this essay tried to disentangle these three threads. The relevance of law to the UN cannot be appreciated without having all these threads. And we shall see that, whereas much of the rhetoric is in terms of the UN and 'obedience' to international law, this is a very limiting way of looking at the question. The ways in which law is made and applied are inseparable from the degree of compliance which its norms secure. And further, international law is not, in any event, merely a set of 'rules to be observed'; it has other forms, other functions.

The UN as originator

In the first place, the UN system brings with it a whole new internal structure. There exists a complicated network of administrative tribunals, career appointments and pension arrangements, rules of procedure and co-ordinating machinery.[4] To master these internal matters can be a lifetime's work.[5]

The very subject-matter dealt with by the UN has led to the development of entirely new areas of international law. Because of the reality of political and technological developments, and because of the quasi universal character of the UN it has been the natural forum for the emergence of international legal standards on such topics as outer space,[6] peaceful coexistence, the sea-bed. And because it is at the UN that world opinion can most conveniently be mobilized, certain current issues—such

---

⁴ See e.g. the Judgments of the UN Administrative Tribunal, in the series AT/DEC/; S. E. Werners, *The Presiding Officers in the UN* (Haarlem, 1967); J. Hadwen & J. Kaufman, *How UN Decisions are Made* (New York, 1962).

⁵ See e.g. the writings of C. W. Jenks, including *The Proper Law of International Organizations* (London, 1962); *International Immunities* (London, 1961); 'Some constitutional problems of international organizations', *BYIL* (1946) 11–72. See also the writings of Suzanne Bastid, including 'Statut juridique des fonctionnaires des Nations Unies', in Ned. Studenten Vereniging vor Wereldrechtsorde, *The UN: ten years' legal progress* (1956), 145–65, and 'Les tribunaux administratifs internationaux et leur jurisprudence', 92 *HR* (1957) ii. 343–514.

⁶ See GA Resolutions 1348 (XIII); 1472 (XIV); 1721 (XVI); 1802 (XVII).

as hijacking,[7] pollution,[8] guerrilla warfare,[9] and expropriation, to name but a few—come to that body for legal attention. Frequently, for political reasons that will be readily appreciated, the legal aspects are dealt with at a superficial or generalized level, but the rudiments of legal developments are at least present.

In certain areas the General Assembly deliberately acts as a law development agency. It may set up specialist subcommittees, issue reports, seek the views of governments, and then draft a resolution for approval by its members. This was the manner in which the Assembly sought to clarify and update the law on the expropriation of aliens' property.[10] Again, the culmination of such work may be the opening, by the Assembly itself, of a draft convention for signature and ratification. Thus two draft Covenants on human rights opened for signature in 1966 represented eighteen years of work by the Third Committee, and were an attempt to develop international law and to make binding as between parties certain of the provisions enumerated in the Universal Declaration of Human Rights.[11] Where it is not possible (usually because the area of political consensus is limited) to enumerate legal principles in a form sufficiently detailed for an international treaty, a solemn declaration is sometimes substituted. This was the pattern followed in respect of the work on peaceful relations between nations. There are occasions when the legal issues are too complex and too significant to be handled within the Assembly; the initial preparatory work (perhaps spreading over a period of years) may be done within the normal UN framework, and then an international diplomatic conference convened, under UN auspices, to prepare a convention. This technique is being used with regard to the uses and exploitation of the deep seabed,[12] and was used for the conferences on different aspects of the law of the sea.[13] Nor is it uncommon where the work originated with the International Law Commission. Under the terms of Article 13 of the Charter, the Assembly is entrusted

[7] GA Resolution 2645 (XXV).   [8] GA Resolution 2657 (XXV).
[9] GA Resolutions 2674 (XXV); 2675 (XXV); 2677 (XXV).
[10] GA Resolution 1802 (XVII).   [11] GA Resolution 217 (III).
[12] GA Resolutions 2749 (XXV) & 2750 (XXV).
[13] 1958 Geneva Conventions on the Territorial Sea and the Contiguous Zone; on the High Seas; on Fishing and Conservation of the Living Resources of the High Seas; and on the Continental Shelf.

with taking action for the codification and progressive development of international law. To this end it established the International Law Commission, a body of individually elected
experts. The Commission chooses its own topics for codification, and presents a report—and sometimes draft articles—to
the Assembly. Some of these, when the principle is approved
by the Assembly, clearly necessitate the convening of a diplomatic conference. Thus the 1961 Convention on Diplomatic
Relations stemmed from work done by the International Law
Commission, as did the 1963 Convention on Consular Relations.[14]

The General Assembly will, from time to time, elaborate
and clarify existing principles of international law. Thus it
confirmed the legality of the Nuremberg principles (Resolution 95 (1)), and also drew up the draft code of offences against
the Peace and Security of Mankind.[15]

There has, of course, arisen a considerable operational
corpus of international law within the framework of the UN.
Functionalism has been relevant to international law as to
other aspects of institutionalism. Perhaps the major example of
this functional development of international law is to be found
in the field of peace-keeping. The Charter itself has something
to say about the use of force by the Organization; but in
operational terms an entirely new law has developed around
the fossilized framework of Chapter VII.

It was originally intended that not only should the main
responsibility for keeping the peace lie with the Security Council (Art. 24), but that the main onus should fall upon the
Permanent Members. Agreements were to be reached at the
initiative of the Permanent Members (Art. 43), who were then
to invite other UN members to contribute forces under arrangement with the Security Council. The details of command were
not worked out, but the terms of the Charter clearly stated that
there was to be a Military Staff Committee (Art. 47) and that
this was to be composed of representatives of the Permanent
Members. UN military action was envisaged in circumstances
where the Security Council had determined that there was a
threat to the peace, breach of the peace, or act of aggression
(Art. 39), but where its directives to one or more of the parties
had been ignored. Under the terms of the Charter, the Security

[14] A/CONF/25/12.   [15] 49 *AJIL* (1958), spec. suppl. 19.

Council is then entitled to decide upon economic and diplomatic sanctions (Art. 41), and if need be upon military enforcement measures (Art. 42). It was always envisaged that the veto should obtain in respect of these measures.

In the event, things have worked out very differently. The reasons are too well known to be recounted at any length here.[16] The early postwar fight between the Soviet Union and the United States (and the competing ideologies which underlay this fight) made impossible any agreement upon the composition, control, and purposes of a UN force to enforce peace. In so far as their numerical majority allowed the West to improvise on peace-keeping, they did so; and advantage was also taken of the opportunity (of keenly debated legality) of providing a residual peace and security role for the General Assembly. The more important of these innovations was that UN forces should—after the sole exception of the Korean experience—no longer be directed to enforcing the peace. Political realities dictated that henceforth UN military operations should be of a 'policing' kind; that is to say, with the consent of the warring parties and, particularly, that of the host state on whose territory the UN force was to operate. There has, over the years, developed a common expectation, amounting to a norm of law, that the consent of a 'host state' is necessary, Chapter VII of the Charter notwithstanding. A further legal convention has developed that the Security Council and the General Assembly can only recommend military action, but may not compel members to participate. Over the years a standard status-of-forces agreement has been evolved. This agreement, which governs relations between the UN and the country on which the force is stationed, has come to contain, with small variations, certain basic principles. High among these is the inviolability of UN premises and the immunity of UN forces from legal suit for actions in the course of duty. Detailed arrangements are invariably made for the handling of any civil offences which any UN forces may commit, and these agreements provide for the freedom of movement of the visiting force.[17] Again, the legal convention has grown that UN forces have only small

---

[16] But see D. W. Bowett, *UN Forces* (London, 1964) and Alan James, *The Politics of Peace-keeping* (London, 1969).

[17] See Higgins, *UN Peacekeeping*, i: *The Middle East* (London, 1969), pp. 373–84, 508–11, 563–5.

arms, which may be used only in self-defence (though in the Cyprus operation self-defence has been interpreted to include defence of installations). UN peace-keeping actions have all necessitated the development of claims procedures, and here too a new body of law has developed.[18]

This area of international law has been well rehearsed. There have been some distinguished monographs on the relationship between law and action, and a cluster of valuable books on the topic.[19]

The UN as applier

For some, of course, there is little to say about the UN as an applier of international law. Those who pride themselves on realism, assert quite simply that the UN is a political body which pays precious little heed to law. Indeed, the argument often runs that the UN is now dominated by Afro-Asians who care only to promote their own obsession with racialism, and that international law is cynically ignored. An elaboration of this theme suggests further that the big powers are immune from the restraints of international law, and cite it only when its terms operate to their particular advantage. To study the UN puts one, in the eyes of the 'political realists', into the category of a 'do gooder'; and to study international law and the UN confirms one as a fantasizer of the most regrettable sort.

The degree to which there is any truth in this perception of UN and legal studies depends, of course, on one's knowledge of the UN and one's views as to the nature of international law. Scholarship has shown, for any who care to avail themselves of it, that no one group or bloc of states has a monopoly of power in the UN.[20] Not only are most of the groups not mono-

---

[18] This procedure was to be particularly important in the Congo venture.

[19] See Oscar Schachter, 'The relation of law, politics and action in the UN', 109 *HR* (1963), ii. 169–256; Lincoln Bloomfield, *International Military Forces* (Boston, 1967); Bowett, *UN Forces*; A. Burns & N. Heathcote, *Peacekeeping by UN Forces* (London, 1963); Norweg. Inst. Internat. Aff., *Peace-keeping: experience and evaluation*, ed. Per Frydenberg & others (Oslo, 1964); Ruth Russell, *UN Experience with Military Forces: political and legal aspects* (Washington, 1964); D. Wainhouse, *International Peace Observation* (Baltimore, 1966); Higgins, *UN Peacekeeping*, 3 vols. (vol. iii in preparation) and 'UN peacekeeping: the political and financial problems', *World Today*, Aug. 1965.

[20] T. Hovet, *Bloc Politics in the UN* (Harvard, 1960); R. E. Riggs, *Politics in the UN: a study of US influence in the General Assembly* (Urbana, Ill., 1958).

lithic, save perhaps on one or two issues, but they lack the necessary numbers to procure two-thirds of the votes of the General Assembly, the required majority on 'important' questions. Of course, alliances of groups may be in a position to acquire that majority; but only on the cases in which world opinion is indeed overwhelmingly ranged on one side. And it also has to be remembered that the General Assembly can make recommendations, but can effect no decisions (save on internal and budgetary questions). The Special Assembly, in the summer of 1967, provided clear evidence that no power, or bloc, is able to impose its will upon an unwilling membership at large. Resolutions on the aftermath of the June War, proposed in turn by the Soviet Union, Yugoslavia, and the Latin Americans all failed to be adopted. In short, popular mythology notwithstanding, the General Assembly is nobody's poodle.

As for the Security Council, the so called Big Five do, of course, have the veto. It was clearly intended from the outset that military enforcement action by the UN under Chapter VII should only take place where there was agreement between all the big powers; and the necessary corollary, given the power of veto, is that enforcement action was not intended against any of the big powers themselves. To be immune from UN enforcement measures is not to be equated with immunity from international law. It is not to be assumed that international law and military sanctions are one and the same thing. Action under Chapter VII is one type of sanction available in one very specific area of international law. Both military activity and a centralized sanctioning process are in fact very uncommon in the law of nations. The big five powers are, in legal terms, subject to the same prohibitions concerning the unilateral use of force as the smaller nations, even if the threatened sanction is different. (In fact, the sanctions of enforcement against all transgressions under Chapter VII are more apparent than real; not since the Korean war has the UN called for collective military action.) The big powers are still subject to the restraint of the criticism of their allies, and of public opinion—domestic as well as international—with the findings of the UN feeding back, in a free society, into the evidence cited by local opposition. The pressure brought upon the United Kingdom and France to withdraw from Suez provides a clear example.

But, it will be contended, the superpowers at least can engage in actions that are clearly contrary to the UN Charter—the invasion of Czechoslovakia, the attempted invasion at the Bay of Pigs—and get away with it. It is at this point that the discussion must turn to the nature of international law. To perhaps the majority of international lawyers, and certainly to the majority of laymen international law provides rules and standards; and the breach of them does no more than point to the limitations of international law as an effective legal system. But for a smaller group of international lawyers, whose thought has been influenced by the sociological approach to international law,[21] international law is not so much the accumulation of past decisions (rules) but the identification of community expectations as to behaviour or decision-making in the present and future. For such lawyers, the emergence of a pattern whereby big-power interventions within their own sphere of interest are tolerated, means not so much that there are repeated breaches of the rule of non-intervention, but that community expectation about non-intervention has changed. International law, they would argue, has now so interpreted and refined the notion of non-intervention as to imply at least that the international community will not actively prohibit military action in a superpower's sphere of influence. The condemnation in speeches in the UN of both the Czech invasion and the Bay of Pigs is evidence that the old prohibition has not been totally thrown over. The failure of UN organs to press condemnatory resolutions to the vote is evidence that nations' understanding about what the big powers may or may not do, in normative terms, is in process of change. In other words, the present position is not so much that an international-law prescription against intervention is ignored as that the prescription is no longer operative in the field of the superpowers' spheres of interest.

It is, of course, a commonplace (but no less the true for that) to assert that in any event collective military measures are far from being the only sanction of international law. A state may have it within its power to perform an act that is contrary to international law, and may wish to do so; but foreign offices are geared to compliance with the law and decisions will have

---

[21] Exemplified by the work done under the leadership of Myres McDougal and Harold Lasswell at the Yale Law School.

to be taken at high level for a course to be followed which is known to be illegal. And, in taking this decision, a government will have carefully to weigh the short-term advantage which it perceives against the long-term costs—and these will include the knowledge that reciprocal action or reprisals may ensue and that damage has been done to the very fabric of international law on which the defaulting state may itself wish to rely at some time in the future.[22]

The UN 'applies' international law in a multitude of decisions. In so doing it makes our understanding of law the more specific. Oscar Schachter has spoken of this as the conversion of 'soft law' into harder, more precise law.[23] If the decision of the organ which passes the decision is widely supported, it has probative value as evidence by the parties of their legal obligations; and the repetition of a stream of similar decisions provides the foundation for custom.[24] We have already spoken, under the head of the UN as originator, of the deliberate reference to, and elaboration of, the law in the passing of declaratory resolutions on legal themes. Law is also applied when the Security Council endeavours to settle disputes which come before it. This writer wrote elsewhere:

The central problem remains that members of the Security Council are not prepared to assume the political consequences of sitting in judgment on fellow members that are parties to a dispute. So far as the parties to a dispute themselves are concerned, it is a commonplace that they use international law as a means of furthering their political case. If law is not a figleaf to cover disagreeable political realities, it is a tactical device, a weapon in the armory of rhetoric. But one must also be sure to see the other side of the coin. The other side of the coin is that reference to legal principle, whether that of the Charter or of general international law, ensures that partisan states will at least have to justify their views on grounds that are acceptable to others. International law is the common language.[25]

International law, then, can be a method of communication as much as 'rules'. It is fairly rare for the Security Council to be

---

[22] Louis Henkin, *How Nations Behave: law and foreign policy* (New York, 1968).
[23] 58 *AJIL* (1964) 960.
[24] See Higgins, 'The development of international law by the political organs of the UN', *Proc. ASIL 1965*, and 'The place of international law in the settlement of disputes by the Security Council', 64 *AJIL* (1970) 3.
[25] Higgins, in 64 *AJIL* (1970) 1–18.

required to pronounce directly on legal claims as such. An exception was its 1951 resolution on freedom of passage through the Suez Canal. Egypt claimed that she was at war with Israel, and therefore entitled to shut the Canal to her shipping under the 1888 Constantinople Convention. Israel, however, noted that there had been no armed hostilities between the two countries since 1949, at which time an armistice, intended to lead to peace, had been signed. The Security Council faced the substantive issues directly, and found that no claim of a belligerent right was permitted under the Armistice. But this type of case of law appliance is unusual. It is much more common for the Council or the Assembly to be presented with a dispute in which there is much merit in the legal argument of both sides— the main problem lying in determining which arguments were preferable. Thus, with regard to Gibraltar, the United Kingdom points to the legal principle of self-determination; while Spain rests her case on title to territory, and the invalidity of title obtained by force. No matter how much a decision by a UN organ may seek to sidestep the legal arguments being advanced, by implication one party will feel favoured by the outcome as against the other.

This is not, one hastens to add, tantamount to saying that all UN decisions are thoughtfully conceived statements of law. Where the UN is fulfilling its declaratory role (such as in the Assembly resolutions which emerged from long years of work on peaceful coexistence, or on sovereignty over natural resources) its legal pronouncements are apt to be carefully arrived at, even if deliberately at a somewhat high level of generality. When the UN is applying law incidental to a decision, its use of the law may be very much more dubious. For example, the Security Council has effectively decided, without any real legal analysis of an immensely complicated problem, that Jordan has a title in East Jerusalem more valid than that of Israel. It may or may not be correct as a legal proposition: but the Security Council has produced no legal supporting evidence.

In fact, does reference to international law make the settlement of a dispute less likely because the law is an inflexible tool? The answer to this clearly depends upon one's perception of law. If by the term 'international law' one means the alleged, automatic interpretation of a fixed set of rules, then the answer may well be yes. But if one views law as composed of matching normative opposites,[26] then it is a very much more flexible tool. Its role in the Security Council is multidimensional. It is a common method of communication. In diplomatic terms, it narrows the options available.

One further point: it is, in fact, rather unusual for the UN to decide which of two parties has the preferred legal case, because, in turn, it is reluctant to categorize one party as the 'wrong-doer'. Rather, it usually prefers to address its injunctions to all parties alike, finding that this makes it more possible for the parties to heed its calls. It is only in the most recalcitrant cases—such as South Africa and Portugal—that the UN has chosen directly to demand compliance by named states. It is apt to do this only when in effect it doubts profoundly that such compliance will be forthcoming.[27]

One of the main organs of the UN is the International Court of Justice. The function of the Court (Art. 38 of its Statute) is to decide in accordance with international law such disputes as are submitted to it. In formal terms, it is to apply international law to particular cases; but in reality, the application of general principles to specific situations inevitably becomes part of the process of law creation. Not that any decision by the Court 'makes law' in the sense that it binds all members of the UN. A judgment of the Court is binding only upon the parties immediately before it. None the less, it is superficial to argue that judgments of the Court are irrelevant to the understanding and development of international law, because pronouncements of the Court are treated by nations as authoritative, and are taken as a correct interpretation of the present state of international law. For the same reason, though the Court does not regard

---

[26] To say that there is a rule of international law prohibiting aggression, though true, may not be helpful. It is analytically more useful to note that international law prohibits aggression but permits self-defence; that it recognizes territorial sovereignty but allows some extraterritorial jurisdiction; that it declares the freedom of the seas but prohibits certain acts thereon; and so forth. In other words, much international law is composed of a series of matching pairs of opposing claims (what state A claims is aggression, state B insists is self-defence), and it is between these that the decision-maker must make a choice in the light of all the circumstances and agreed objectives. This conception of 'matching normative opposites' has been elaborated by McDougal in 'Some basic theoretical concepts about international law: a policy oriented framework of enquiry', 4 *J. Conflict Resolution* (1960) 337.

[27] The point is made by Schachter (n. 23 above).

itself as bound by precedent, in fact it does considerably rely on its own prior judgments and opinions. The need for consistent and perceived expectations, which are at the heart of any legal system, could hardly dictate otherwise.

The Court adjudicates upon disputes between states; and it gives advisory opinions upon questions put to it by certain UN organs or other international organizations. In strictly formal terms, advisory opinions are not legally binding; but they, too, stem from the most distinguished Court of international law, and in so far as they are indications of the law, they carry high moral persuasiveness. Further, they *do* still create community expectations about what is legally required behaviour in future comparable circumstances.

It is difficult to generalize about the Court's law-making role. The Court as a whole has perhaps been cautious, if not conservative; though it has at all times had upon its bench individual judges who would have had it be more bold and innovatory. Its substantive law development has necessarily been limited by the fact that its jurisdiction is optional, and that preliminary objections as to jurisdiction may be made, and perhaps sustained. States which are parties to the Court's Statute may declare at any time that they recognize as compulsory *ipso facto*, and without special agreement, in relation to any other state accepting the same obligation, the jurisdiction of the Court (Art. 36(2)). This optional acceptance of the Court's jurisdiction is subject to reciprocity, and reservations, which also operate reciprocally, are also permitted. These reservations may relate to the subject-matter, or designate a period of time. It will be seen that these limitations permit of many preliminary jurisdictional objections when an attempt is made to settle a dispute before the Court. As a considerable number of preliminary objections have been found compelling, the Court has lacked the opportunity to deal with the merits of the case, and to elaborate the law in those areas.[28]

Whereas, in the United States legal system, it is possible to speak of the Supreme Court as the 'Warren Court', or now the 'Burger Court', and to trace marked attitudes of the Court

---

[28] On preliminary objections see G. Abi-Saab, *Les exceptions préliminaires dans la procédure de la Cour internationale* (Paris, 1967) and I. F. I. Shihata, *The Power of the International Court to Determine Its Own Jurisdiction* (The Hague, 1965).

during the period of a particular presidency, a comparable pattern does not emerge for the International Court. In certain cases—for example, the case of *Reparations for Injuries*, the *South West Africa (Voting) Case*, and the *Case of Certain Expenses*, the Court has gone well beyond what was strictly necessary in terms of finding a legal rationale on which to rest its decision. Striking legal development occurred in each of these (as it did in the *Nottebohm* and *Norwegian Fisheries Cases*). But in yet others—*South West Africa Cases* (1966), the *North Sea Continental Shelf Case*, and the *Barcelona Traction Case*—the Court has held back when, on the same criteria, legal development or innovation would have seemed called for.[29] In another cluster of cases—*Peace Treaties Case* (2nd phase), *Rights of Passage Case*, *Northern Cameroons Case*—the conservatism of the Court seems very much more necessary, other legal options being much less readily available. The literature on this, and on all questions concerning the Court's jurisdiction, is excellent;[30] the high promise of Sir Hersch Lauterpacht's classic *The Development of International Law by the International Court* (1958) has been upheld by subsequent works.

The criticism is not so much that the Court has been conservative as that it has been inconsistent. It is often argued that the introduction of policy considerations into the judicial process makes for uncertainty. Yet there is little in the Court's jurisprudence (protesting as it does that its function is to apply, and not to make law) which leads to any great feeling of predictability. Policy factors clearly played a major part in the United States Warren Court; yet that Court was not lacking in legal direction or in an adequate degree of certainty in its legal processes. It is this writer's opinion that this clarity of direction is

[29] See e.g. Higgins, 'Certain aspects of the *Barcelona Traction Case*', 11 *Virginia J. Int. Law* (1970), and L. F. E. Goldie, 'The *North Sea and Continental Shelf Cases*—a ray of hope for the International Court', 16 *NY Law Forum* (1970), 327–77.

[30] R. P. Anand, *Compulsory Jurisdiction of the International Court of Justice* (Bombay, 1961); H. Briggs, 'Reservations to the acceptance of compulsory jurisdiction of the International Court of Justice', 93 *HR* (1958), i. 229; E. Hambro, 'Jurisdiction of the International Court of Justice', 76 *HR* (1950), i. 125; Jenks, *The Prospects for International Adjudication* (London, 1964); S. Rosenne, *The Law and Practice of the International Court* (2 vols., Leyden, 1965), 'The advisory competence of the ICJ', 30 *R. de droit int.*, 10 (Geneva, 1952), and *The Time Factor to the Jurisdiction of the ICJ* (Leyden, 1960); Sir H. Waldock, 'Forum prorogatum or acceptance of a unilateral summary to appear before the International Court', 2 *ILQ* (1948) 377 and 'Decline of the optional clause', 32 *BYIL* (1956), 244.

unlikely to come to the International Court until either one or two of its members assume an unspoken leadership of the Court (and there have been signs of this in the last few years) or until the Court evolves for itself a philosophy of the place of policy in the judicial process.[31]

How important is the limited jurisdiction of the Court? Certainly comparatively few countries accept the Court's jurisdiction, and most of those who do enter some substantial reservations. Western Europe, by and large, accepts the Court's jurisdiction; and so does much of the 'old' Commonwealth and the United States—the latter though with a reservation which some deem to negate the very acceptance.[32] A proportionately fewer number of the new countries, whether of Africa, Asia, or the Caribbean, accept the Court's jurisdiction; nor do the communist nations. Full and detailed analysis, both of the factual situation and of the reasons for it, exists. C. Wilfred Jenks's *The Prospects for International Adjudication* (1964) is a classic of our time, and there have been spirited arguments by Asian scholars explaining the way in which the body of international law is perceived as Western in origin, and protective of Western interests and values.[33] The communist countries, while permitting nationals to sit upon the bench, do not otherwise use the Court, their political philosophy rejecting third-party adjudication. Conventional wisdom deplores this state of affairs, and urges a greater acceptance of the Court's jurisdiction.

This seems to me to be of little importance. There is little evidence that the Court is a suitable instrument for resolving many of the conflicts which are typical in today's world. The judges, by their very emphasis on the exclusiveness of legal considerations alone, reject the relevance of related social sciences to their own decision-making,[34] and it is arguable that there is a very small cluster of disputes suitable for such handling. Indeed,

---

[31] 'The place of policy in the international judicial process', 17 *ICLQ* (1968) 58.

[32] The so-called Connolly amendment, by which the US exempts matters within its own domestic jurisdiction—as determined by itself.

[33] See Anand, *Studies in International Adjudication* (Delhi, 1969); Abi-Saab, 'The newly independent states and the scope of domestic jurisdiction', *Proc. ASIL 1960*; J. J. G. Syatauw, *Some Newly Established Asian States and the Development of International Law* (The Hague, 1961).

[34] See e.g. Judge Fitzmaurice's statement that 'social, humanitarian and other' factors, even when they underlie a legal case, are 'for the political rather than the legal arena' (*ICJ Rep. 1962*, p. 466).

in spite of the excellence of the literature of the Court,[35] there has been remarkably little scholarly writing (whether by lawyers or not) concerning what types of disputes are most likely to be resolved by what forms of settlement. There is little evidence to support the lawyers' assumption that more third-party adjudication would serve the common good. At present all too little is understood about what factors in decision processes must readily affect different types of conflicts. Research is urgently needed in this area, and it can clearly proceed only on an interdisciplinary basis.

The Court issues a majority judgment. But judges whose reasoning is different (though they reach the same conclusion) may attach separate opinions, whilst those who disagree with the conclusions of the majority may append dissenting opinions. It is not uncommon for the separate and dissenting opinions not only to be large in number, but for their length to dwarf the declared judgment of the Court. The impact of the Court's judgment is thus diluted. This may occur not only when there is a marked division of opinion among the Court's members, but even when, as in the *Barcelona Traction Case*,[36] there is an overwhelming majority in favour of the Court's judgment.

A great difficulty has also arisen in relation to the joining of preliminary objections to the merits. From time to time it is felt by the Court that it can not deal with a preliminary objection to its jurisdiction without going into the merits of the case, either as to law or as to fact. In such cases the Court will (if it dismisses any other preliminary objections which have been advanced) attach such an objection to the merits thus to be dealt with in a subsequent case. One sees, of course, the advantage and sense of so doing. Yet it may occur that, after a long case on the preliminary objections, protracted litigation on the merits may ensue, only for the case ultimately to be dismissed on a preliminary objection joined to the merits, the merits never being pronounced upon by the Court. In the 1966 *South West Africa Cases* the problem was particularly acute because the Court, in a hearing on the merits, rejected the applicants' *locus standi* on a point that appeared to have been

---

[35] See above, n. 30.
[36] *ICJ Rep*. (Belgium *v*. Spain) *1970*.

rejected in the case on the preliminary objections.[37] In the *Barcelona Traction Case* the standing of the applicants was dismissed after some years of litigation on the merits. Little research has been done on this question, both as a technical problem and as a factor which will undoubtedly influence governments in their decision whether to accept the Court's jurisdiction.

The Court is composed of some fifteen members, elected directly by the Security Council and the General Assembly in accordance with the provision of the Court's Statute. Article 8 provides that the General Assembly and the Security Council shall proceed independently of one another to elect the members of the Court, and Article 10 (1) lays down those candidates who obtain an absolute majority of votes in the General Assembly and in the Security Council shall be considered as elected. Of this direct voting, by political bodies, Shabtai Rosenne has written in his unsurpassed *The Law and Practice of the International Court* (1965):

On the one hand, the system of nomination and election of judges is in practice designed to reflect political considerations. . . . On the other hand, the depoliticized treatment which the Court is called upon to give to the matter referred to in the exercise of its judicial competence is reflected in the irremovability of the judges and their unaccountability for their judicial actions. . . . If political factors momentarily enter into play at the time of the election of the judges, once elected the Court is granted every facility to maintain the proper degree of judicial independence (i. 165).

Article 2 of the Statute provides that the Court members shall be elected regardless of their nationality on the basis of their technical qualifications. Furthermore, Article 9 stipulates that not only should the persons elected individually have high qualifications, but the body as a whole should represent 'civilization and . . . the principal legal systems of the world'. The degree to which this latter injunction has been heeded can be seen by the present composition of the Court, which is composed of judges from Pakistan, Lebanon, Mexico, Senegal, France, the Philippines, the United Kingdom, Sweden, Poland, Nigeria, the United States, Dahomey, Spain, and the Soviet

[37] This writer—among others—has criticized that judgment in 'The International Court and South West Africa: the implications of the judgment', *International Affairs*, Oct. 1966.

Union. Russia, the United States, and Poland have been represented at all times.

There are those (who know little of the Court) who assert that a judge's vote must necessarily be influenced by his nationality. In so far as the implication is that governments bring pressure to bear upon judges of their nationality, the charge can categorically be rejected. Individuals can, of course, feel—without any pressure being brought to bear—in a difficult position vis-à-vis their own governments. The relationship of an ad hoc judge to the government which nominated him is obviously difficult in this regard. But full judges do not normally expect office at the hands of their national government. Seniority brings independence in its wake. Even this being said, the personal factor remains paramount. Judges Fitzmaurice of the United Kingdom and Jessup (the former US national on the Court) have less in common than, say, Judge Jessup with Judge Takana (the Japanese jurist who formerly sat on the Court).

Article 31 (1) of the Statute stipulates that judges of the nationality of a party before the Court are entitled to sit in a case before the Court. This right rests upon the assumption of the judicial independence of the Bench. At the same time, in order that justice may also be seen to be done (and at the risk of permitting an apparent inconsistency) provision is made for the appointment of an ad hoc judge when one of the parties to a case does not have a judge of its nationality upon the bench.

There has been comparatively little literature upon the question of partiality of the judges—partly because there so clearly has not been bias in the sense of conformity by judges with the desires of their own national governments, and partly because it is considered 'bad form' to discuss this question at all. This writer believes that neither the law nor the judges of it are 'neutral'. Contemporary international law reflects certain values, and judges (like all of us) bring their own value preferences to bear in interpreting the law. These value preferences in turn stem from legal philosophy, social outlook, and personal inclination: and to a small, but not determining, degree nationality may be relevant in shaping these.

The issue of partiality arises in various contexts. Certainly judges have shown that they are prepared to vote against their own governments when these appear before the Court in litigation. The record so far as judges ad hoc are concerned is perhaps less comforting: but the sample is so small that few conclusions may be drawn. Further, it may be that a country which has appointed a judge ad hoc does have the better legal case in any given litigation, and the judge ad hoc is certainly entitled so to vote. In the 1966 *South West Africa Cases* Judge Sir Zafrullah Khan was asked to step down on the grounds that, before becoming a full member of the Court, he had agreed to be judge ad hoc appointed by the applicants, Ethiopia and Liberia. That he stood down seems unfortunate—not only because precedent indicates that he should not have done so,[38] but because his action gives strength to the proposition that ad hoc judges may be assumed to be partisan. In the recent advisory case on South West Africa which was before the Court,[39] requests were made by South Africa for Judges P. D. Morozov, Sir Zafrullah Khan, and Padilla Nervo to stand down on the ground that, when members of delegations to the UN in the past, they had shown hostility to South Africa. The request has been refused—rightly, because it is unacceptable to give substance to the myth that persons of intellect are incapable of playing different roles within different institutions. As a member of a UN delegation, a man speaks as his government orders him. As a judge, he exercises his independent judgement.

Criticisms have also been made of the length of time involved in judicial proceedings. The Court has become very sensitive on this matter (e.g. in their opinions on the *Barcelona Traction Case* several of the judges felt compelled to address themselves to this) and has insisted that its own deliberations and drafting are done at all due speed. The delays are due, asserts the Court, to the requests of parties before it for more and more time in which to present their case. And if they desire more time, says the Court, it is not for the Court to say no. Certainly it is true

[38] Judge Charles de Visscher was nominated ad hoc judge by Belgium in respect of both the *Borchgrave Case* (v. Spain) and the *Water from the Meuse Case* (v. Netherlands). In both cases he sat on the Court in his subsequent capacity as an elected judge of the Court.

[39] The Security Council asked the Court: 'What are the legal consequences for States of the continued presence of South Africa in Namibia, notwithstanding Security Council Resolution 276 (1970)?'

that the length of proceedings is due to requests by the parties for the extension of time periods originally allotted, and that the sheer bulk of their memorials and counter-memorials makes such requests difficult to refuse. At the same time, one may be driven to wonder whether the sovereignty of the parties before the Court really necessitates allowing the time factor to run on such a loose rein, and whether in the future the Court will not have to be prepared to take a tighter hold over the length of proceedings. Their very length is perhaps a disincentive to the use of the Court; and where it is one party which presents extremely lengthy memorials it may be that the other party— for reasons of finance if no other—may be put at a disadvantage. This may be particularly so where one party is considerably wealthier than another—and the respective positions of South Africa on the one hand, and Ethiopia and Liberia on the other, is a case in point.

The UN as developer

In 1963 Chatham House published this author's *The Development of International Law through the Political Organs of the United Nations*. This book attempted to provide a detailed study of UN practice in the key areas of statehood, domestic jurisdiction, the use of force, recognition and treaty law. This it did within the framework of a particular thesis: namely, that

The United Nations is a very appropriate body to look to for indications of developments in international law, for international custom is to be deduced from the practice of states, which includes their international dealings as manifested by their diplomatic actions and public pronouncements. With the development of international organizations, the votes and views of states have come to have legal significance as evidence of customary law. Moreover, the practice of states comprises their collective acts as well as the total of their individual acts; and the number of occasions on which states see fit to act collectively has been greatly increased by the activities of international organizations. Collective acts of states, repeated by and acquiesced in by sufficient numbers with sufficient frequency, eventually attain the status of law. The existence of the United Nations—and especially its accelerated trend towards universality of membership since 1955—now provides a very clear, very concentrated focal point for state practice (p. 2).

In 1963 this view was more unorthodox than perhaps it appears today. Not only did orthodox legal opinion perhaps doubt the very capacity of political organs to make law, but it sharply distinguished between the practice of UN organs and customary international law.[40] It was thought that a further distinction was to be made between 'the examination of examples [of law] from debates and resolutions, rather than with the elucidation of principles and rules'.[41]

Some non-lawyers, too, had a less integral view of the nature of law making, and a more conservative outlook on the methods by which norms evolve. It was thought that 'doubt is in order concerning the fundamental premise of the book: that the legal practice of the UN is a source of customary international law and therefore binds all members of an international society'.[42] Even if this was so in non-controversial fields, it was argued, it was not true elsewhere.

In nine years the intellectual climate has changed, and I think such views no longer represent the majority opinion. I believe it is now generally accepted that UN political organs can, in certain circumstances, 'make law'. There has been a wealth of literature on the contribution of UN political bodies to the formation and change of international law.[43] The literature—as well as events—would seem to have confounded the view that international law promulgated by UN bodies can only bind members with their consent. For example, Dr. Ingrid Detter, in an impressive survey which covers the UN specialized agencies as well as the UN itself, provided persuasive evidence that, at least in 'primary' acts (those related to the operation of the organization itself), there is a considerable area of practice in which express consent is no longer required. In the case of 'operative' acts (those more concerned with the aims of organizations) there is a greater tendency by states to require certain formal safeguards. But even here, and especially in the

---

[40] See n. 41.

[41] Sir Francis Vallat, then Legal Adviser to the Foreign Office, made all three of these points in a review in *ICLQ* (1963).

[42] Alan James, in a review in *International Affairs*, Apr. 1964.

[43] e.g. O. Y. Asamoah, *The Legal Significance of the Declarations of the General Assembly of the UN* (The Hague, 1966); Lino Di Qual, *Les effets des résolutions des Nations Unies* (Paris, 1967); E. Yemin, *Legislative Powers in the UN and Specialized Agencies* (Leyden, 1969); J. Castaneda, *Legal Effects of UN Resolutions* (New York, 1970).

case of the technical agencies, the unilateral features of action by the organization are often coming to assume a greater significance than the safeguard.[44]

But what of those 'operative acts' of an organization, to use Dr. Detter's terminology, where a state explicitly denies that it is bound? Where this occurs in what we might call the regulatory area, the state's protests can, in legal terms, avail it naught. Article 25 of the Charter makes it obligatory of members to carry out the decisions of the Security Council. The Security Council does have, in this limited area, a very real law-developing power.[45] Not only are UN members bound by such a decision but—and especially because of the difficulty of reaching a decision in spite of the veto—community expectations are created. A related question arises. Are decisions of the Security Council non-reviewable? Can a member of the UN decline to give effect to a decision under Chapter VII of the Charter on the grounds that, for example, the International Court should first review the legality of the decision? South Africa has in effect taken this attitude over Rhodesian sanctions, contending that there is no threat to the peace, and thus enforcement measures are not permissible. She suggested that the World Court be asked for a ruling on this point. It seems to me that both the Charter and the preparatory negotiations indicate that in the area of peace and security compliance is vital, and all states come under an immediate obligation to comply with decisions taken under Article 25 of the Charter. In this sense the Security Council is engaged in 'law-making'.

Even outside of the regulatory area, Alan James would seem to be wrong about states not being bound without their consent. Things just don't always work in this purist way. For example, mere recommendations to establish subsidiary bodies entail financial consequences which are legally incumbent on all members, whether they voted for them or not. The time has come to acknowledge—and it is widely acknowledged in the United States, though much less so in Britain—that legal consequences can flow from acts which are not, in a formal sense, binding.

[44] *Law Making by International Organizations* (Stockholm, 1965).

[45] I have developed this theme in 'The UN and lawmaking', *Proc. ASIL 1970*, and 'The place of international law in the settlement of disputes by the Security Council', 64 *AJIL* (1970) 1.

Nor does the lack of a legislative competence in the Assembly mean that it is incapable of law development. The resolutions and declarations of international organs, repeated with sufficient frequency and bearing the characteristics of *opinio juris*, can establish a general practice recognized as a legal custom. Propositions that were novel in 1963 have commanded wider support today; and in recent years several books analysing the scope of the regulatory of law-making power of the UN and its agencies have been published. Both scholarship and the facts negate the claim that the sole basis of legal obligation in international organization is that of consent.

What part should the study of international law and international organization properly play in research institutes of foreign affairs? It is interesting in this respect to compare Chatham House with two similar bodies in the United States: the Brookings Institute and the Council on Foreign Relations. Brookings has, in the last decade, had the permanent services of some of the most distinguished scholars of the UN—Ruth Russell,[46] H. Field Haviland Jr.,[47] Arthur Cox,[48] Ernest Lefever,[49] Larry Fabian,[50] and Robert Asher.[51] The specifically UN work which they have done for Brookings has been within the Foreign Policy Studies programme. Significantly, perhaps, they do not have, and have not had, an international lawyer on their staff, and have not commissioned work from international lawyers. Of those mentioned above, Ruth Russell has been most closely associated with the world of international law, and is both a regular participant at legal gatherings and well known to international lawyers. The Council on Foreign

[46] See n. 19 above and her *The UN and US Security Policy* (Washington, 1968) and (with Jeanette Muther), *A History of the UN Charter* (Washington, 1958).

[47] Author (with Daniel Cheever) of *Organizing for Peace* (London, 1954) and *American Foreign Policy and the Separation of Powers* (Camb., Mass., 1952); (with others) of *Vietnam after the War: peacekeeping and rehabilitation* (Washington, 1968); and editor (with F. O. W. Wilcox) of *The US and the UN* (Baltimore, 1961).

[48] Author of *Prospects for Peacekeeping* (Washington, 1967) and (with K. Mathiasen) *UNITAR, proposals for program, budget and organization* (Washington, 1965).

[49] Author of *Crisis in the Congo* (Washington, 1967), *The Limits of UN Intervention in the Third World* (Washington, 1968), and *Uncertain Mandate, politics of the UN Congo operation* (Baltimore, 1967).

[50] Author of *Soldiers Without Enemies* (Washington, 1971).

[51] Author of *Development Assistance in the Seventies* (1970), *Grants, Loans and Local Currencies, their role in foreign aid* (1961), and (with others) *The UN and Economic and Social Cooperation* (1957), all publ. in Washington.

Relations has, like Chatham House, placed a smaller emphasis on the UN and international law. Ernest A. Gross, a renowned practitioner of international law and formerly a member of the US Mission to the UN, has had a long association with the Council (though not as a member of the staff), participating in study groups and writing *The United Nations: structure for peace* (1962). Charles Yost, immediately prior to his ambassadorship to the UN, wrote *The Insecurity of Nations* (1968) for the CFR. And from outside the staff Louis Henkin wrote for the Council his admirable book *How Nations Behave* (see n. 22). But, other than the brief appointment of Charles Yost, the Council has had no permanent member of the staff dealing with the UN, and no international lawyer.

Chatham House, too, till 1963, had no one in this field. This writer has since then attempted to represent these fields within the Institute. But, of course, staff membership is, for all institutes, only a very small part of the story. The former Director of Chatham House, Kenneth Younger, has had a long association with the UN. He was from 1950 to 1951 Minister of State at the Foreign Office, and represented Britain at the UN during the Korean war and at the time of the famous Uniting for Peace Resolution. He is Chairman of the Board of Trustees of UNITAR (UN Institute for Training and Research) in New York. The present Director of Studies, James Fawcett, who is Vice-President of the European Commission on Human Rights, is an international lawyer who is especially knowledgeable about human rights[52] and about international monetary and financial law.[53] Indeed, he was General Counsel of the IMF from 1955 to 1960. It is reasonable to say that Chatham House plays its full part at international conferences and symposia dealing with UN legal and political questions.

Chatham House's two journals have also included a fair number of articles dealing with the UN and/or with international law. *The World Today*, for example, has included articles on legal aspects of space, the law of the sea, the Soblen case, peace-keeping, Rhodesian sanctions and the UN Charter,

[52] See his *The Application of the European Convention on Human Rights* (Oxford, 1969).
[53] See 'The IMF and international law', *BYIL* (1964) 32–76; 'Trade and finance in international law', 123 *HR* (1968), i. 215–30. He has also written widely on the legal problems of space and conservation of the environment.

the workings of the General Assembly—to name but a few. There are also regularly articles on substantive topics which are on the agenda of the UN and of direct concern to it, such as South Africa, Cyprus, international telecommunications, disarmament, the Middle East, and so forth.

International Affairs has in recent years had a major book review section on international law and international organizations, as well as the occasional article on UN or legal themes, whether on UNCTAD, Gibraltar, or South West Africa.

It is not so commonly realized that the *British Yearbook of International Law* is published under the auspices of Chatham House. But though its editorial board is, in formal terms, a sub-committee of the Institute, it has a high—indeed almost total—degree of autonomy. It is very much a lawyers' law journal, and this is to be expected. What is perhaps more surprising is the way in which it has so often failed to provide legal guidance on contemporary issues of international relations. True, there have been a couple of valuable articles on the Rhodesian problem. But it has been virtually silent on the present Middle East problem, and had nothing whatever to contribute to the debate on the Suez intervention of 1956. By contrast, the *American Journal of International Law* has had full coverage of the legal controversy surrounding Indo-China (the American Society of International Law, whose journal it is, has published two volumes on this); and indeed, just about every controversial action of the United States government has been scrutinized in terms of international law. The ability of the American Journal to do this rests partly on the fact that it is a quarterly, whereas the *British Yearbook* is an annual. And certainly there has been better coverage of this sort in the *International and Comparative Law Quarterly*, though in no way comparable with that of the *AJIL*. But it is, I am convinced, much more a question of disposition, reflecting an attitude as to what is relevant to international law. It is sometimes said that the *AJIL* is of transitory value, whereas the less contemporary articles of the *BYIL* are of lasting value, and a higher quality. Without wishing to discuss specific articles, I find this argument unconvincing. The absence of systematic contemporary analyses in the *BYIL* is unresponsive to the needs of the legal community which it serves.

In both *International Affairs* and *The World Today*, and rightly so, articles on international law have been included where they are relevant to a contemporary problem of international relations. Institutes of international affairs are properly interested in international law not as a separate discipline, but as an integral part of the study of international affairs. There have not been, and neither would one expect there to have been, in either of the Chatham House journals articles on the more recondite aspects of international law. The way in which institutes include international law in their programmes rests on certain assumptions, however. It is assumed that international law is indeed a relevant component of international decision-making, and that the total 'power politics' theory of international relations is unacceptable. Undoubtedly certain problems of communication still do exist between the disciplines, but by and large institutes of international affairs have perceived (even if individual members have not), that international law is more than a set of ineffective rules against the use of force. International law is not solely about 'rules' (that is to say, the trend of past decisions), but also about contemporary community expectations. Rules are not 'applied' automatically or neutrally by judges or other decision-makers: rather, these decision-makers are frequently faced with two matched, opposing legal norms (aggression/self-defence; title to territory/right to self-determination) and most choose between them—in the light of the facts and of international community policy. Those institutes of international affairs which employ international lawyers, or publish books on contemporary international law, have, with varying degrees of self-realization, accepted this functional approach to law. It is far from certain that international lawyers, at least in this country, have done so themselves. I believe it true to say that law here is still regarded primarily as rules, and as neutral rules applied by an 'objective' judge. Foreign Office legal advisers, of course, have long recognized the relevance of policy to international decision making; but their vantage point (understandably and wisely) is national and not transnational, and their intuition is not matched by any substructure of theory as to the place of policy.

It seems to me self-evident that any specialist in international law writing on contemporary issues should perceive the relationship of his own tools and skills to others also relevant to the problem. In the United States both international lawyers and political scientists are far more prepared to accept the relevance of the other discipline in functional terms, and to attempt to keep up with some of the literature. The Yale Law School has, as full professors of law, distinguished scholars whose initial disciplines were economics, psychiatry, the social sciences. The Board of Review and Development of the American Society of International Law also has the social sciences and economics represented. There is nothing comparable in this country. An Oran Young and a Ruth Russell will keep abreast of contemporary writing on international law, especially in the field of theory; and a Richard Falk, a Myres McDougal, a Michael Reisman will all be familiar with the social science journals and the great debates occurring within the related disciplines. There are all too few British international lawyers or British political scientists who have this familiarity with writings in each others' fields. How many British international lawyers regularly read *World Politics* or the *Journal of Conflict Resolution*, or even *International Organization*? All of these serve the student of international law and institutions well. *World Politics* has relied with great success at the editorial level on an interdisciplinary approach within Princeton University; and the co-operation of such persons as James Rosenau, Richard Falk, Cyril Black, Oran Young, etc., has been to the intellectual advantage of all concerned with the social sciences. *International Organization* too has successfully straddled the disciplines, dealing with law, politics, and alternative methodologies in both of these. But for the moment there is not, this side of the Atlantic at least, a perception of international law as a social science.

There are enormous strides to be made in this country towards knowledgeable interdisciplinary co-operation, and it is to be hoped that the next generation of international lawyers will attempt this task—and by so doing, will break the vicious circle that now exists, and will encourage scholars in international relations to examine more seriously the relevance of international law to their own problems.

4 International Economic Relations I: The Need for an Interdisciplinary Approach

SUSAN STRANGE

WHAT international studies needs today—and needs more than money or research institutes and possibly more than even teachers and students—is some radical desegregation. At present, these studies are too often divided by artificial, man-made barriers—those separating international economics from international politics, and those separating both from international law. These barriers need to be overthrown, broken up, and done away with. Here and there, as in the study of international economic law, beginnings have been made. But much more re-integration needs to be done, quickly and from all three sides. The study of international affairs has already suffered serious damage—some of it may even prove permanent—as a result of this practice of intellectual apartheid. It is time it went.

The Afrikaners in this situation—I am tempted to say 'in the woodpile'—are the economists. It is they who do most to preserve the barriers and who are so reluctant to rub shoulders with others whom they seem to regard as second-class academic citizens. In the last forty years, since the Great Depression, we have seen a great boom in the popular demand for economics. It has spread throughout the universities, into commerce and industry, and even, finally, into government departments and the schools. And the longer the boom has gone on, the further divorced has the bulk of economic science become from its origins in political economy. With the exception of a handful of 'liberals', professional economists resent and reject trespassers in their professional preserves as bitterly as any Dixiecrat fuming about Eleanor Roosevelt.

But the barriers have also been preserved and strengthened from the other side. There have been many Uncle Toms on the political and diplomatic, and sometimes on the legal, side of international studies who have been content with their restricted role, content to stay in blissful ignorance of what the other half was up to, and who were happy to dismiss as 'technical' and 'specialist' matters of trade and payments which were of just as deep political concern as the terms of an alliance or the delineation of a frontier. And—to pursue the provocative analogy a little further—just as established institutions and processes which are not quick enough to change with the times are apt to find themselves outflanked by new and more militant groups and methods, so the established institutions and processes of international studies are in constant danger of being outflanked by new groups of experts approaching the subject from fresh directions. The fashionable attention to strategic studies, to area studies in all their infinite variety, and now to international business studies is not accidental. In these new territories the barriers between the economic and the political, if they exist at all, are lower than in the general field. And in consequence these studies do not accord so much status or influence either to the Afrikaners in economics or to the Uncle Toms in political science.

On the whole, I would judge the record of Chatham House during the last decade in this respect to have been rather creditable. It has consciously maintained a catholic breadth of interest in the economic no less than the political dimensions of international affairs. In doing so it has followed faithfully the pioneer work done in earlier years—for example by Sir Keith Hancock in the Commonwealth *Surveys*, in which the two dimensions were most effectively and elegantly combined. Its dual interest has been well reflected in its research programmes, as in its publications and its meetings—though it is significant that economists as a group make a rather more substantial contribution as authors, speakers, and participants and advisers, but constitute only a rather small minority of the Institute's subscribing membership. If Chatham House has erred, it has been by being rather too diffident to proclaim its almost unique situation as a neutral and non-partisan meeting-ground. As such, it stands not only between the worlds of government, business, finance, and the universities, between government and opposition, between the bureaucrats and the press, but it can also claim in some degree to stand neutral between the divided (and elsewhere segregated) academic disciplines of politics and economics.

If I repeat here a view that I have expressed before (and for which I have since found there is more support than I had imagined), I beg the reader's pardon.[1] But it is necessary to explain my further contention that the idea of 'economic relations' as a discrete, discernible, and definable sphere of human activity—and therefore as a separable segment of international studies—is an absurdity. Economic Man was knocked firmly on the head by Peter Drucker as long ago as 1939.[2] But the parallel concept of the Economic State has survived for far too long. And so has the notion that international affairs can be divided into two neat boxes labelled 'economic' and 'political'. It is this apartheid which has done a great deal of damage to the balanced development of international studies.

The non-concept of economic relations

By way of illustrating the point, let me start with the problem of definition. We may assume that an economic relationship exists around an economic activity. An 'economic activity' may be held to embrace consuming; producing or processing; buying or selling; broking; and borrowing or lending. Leaving out Robinson Crusoes and peasant households subsisting in primitive isolation, each of these activities brings at least two parties into an economic relationship. But it is seldom if ever a *purely* economic relationship—and under the influence of social anthropology and the newer behavioural studies, even economists no longer claim that it is. Every economic activity only exists in a social framework of law and custom, in a particular political order and in a particular social structure. If this is true of economic relations between individuals, it is even more true of the economic relations between states. States are never complete strangers to one another, linked only by an economic

---

[1] See *International Affairs*, Apr. 1970.
[2] *The End of Economic Man* (New York & London, 1939). The title was perhaps rather better than the content. To contemporary eyes, Drucker's *Concept of the Corporation* (New York, 1946) is in some ways of greater interest.

bargain, as individuals may sometimes be (if rarely). States are sufficiently few in number and sufficiently long-lasting that behind each economic bargain struck with another state there lies a complex web of historical association, political and strategic conflict or co-operation, and social and cultural sympathy or antipathy. No practising policy-maker would ever pretend for a moment that this web had no influence on the pattern and development of international economic relations.

Thus none of the activities in which states indulge are purely economic. Equally, all activities have a necessary and unavoidable economic aspect. Even in the most emotional international situations, in matters of life-and-death, allies weigh the cost of co-operation, and enemies the cost of continuing the conflict.

The interaction of politics and economics in international relations, of the economic aspect and the political aspect of the international system, goes on all the time. The interaction is necessarily understated, if not completely ignored, by political scientists who construct purely political theories and by economists who construct purely economic theories about the 'international system'. These over-simplifications may be useful for pedagogic purposes and as a convenient intellectual shorthand. Their shortcomings do not matter much when the influence of the supposed international political 'system' on the supposed international economic 'system'—or vice versa—is more or less static, or when it is changing only very slowly. The political factor in the economic system or the economic forces within the political system can then be safely taken for granted. But when one of the two main dimensions of the international system starts to register rapid and radical change, then the nature of its influence over—and its interaction with—the other dimension needs careful reassessment. Then, the shape of the resulting international political economy is so altered that existing theories, political and economic, evolved for an earlier relationship between economic forces and interests and political authorities and interests no longer fit and are apt to mislead. The recent rapid expansion of the international economy is such a change requiring new efforts at political-economic analysis.

(The phenomenon is perhaps more easily recognized on a national scale than on an international one. In the past, when the political and economic aspects of a society shifted their relationship to one another—like land masses on either side of a geological fault—it was either because the political framework for the economic system was transformed (as, for example, by the French or Russian Revolutions or by Afro-Asian emergence from colonialism), or because the economic system began to outgrow and put new strains on the political one (as, for instance, in the post-Napoleonic period of English industrialization or when, after 1951, Kuwait experienced a rapid growth in oil output and revenues). It is at these times that the old assumptions about the political framework for economic activity are called in question and have to be thought out anew, often producing new political theories and economic ideologies.)

To put the point in another way, many people would agree that the answer to the question 'whither international society?' depends in large part nowadays on whatever technological developments may be anticipated for the foreseeable future. Whether these may lie in the exploitation of outer space, of the sea-bed, in the further development of transport and communications systems, or of sources of power and energy—or, indeed, of the means of human nutrition and contraception—they are all bound to have some significant effect, directly or indirectly, on the international political economy and relations between states.

That is to say, the shape of the future political relations between states, the areas of administrative management and operative enterprise that states are prepared to abandon or to relinquish to international agencies, the problems on which they will or will not seek international agreement, will depend in the next generation less on the compatibility of their ideologies or on the similarity of their constitutional structures than on the demands of an economic and communications system based on a rapidly changing technology.[3] For alongside the accelerating pace of technological change (and indeed closely related to it as cause and as effect) is the accelerating pace of change and growth in economic structures, economic techniques

---

[3] This is not quite the same as convergence theories. The suggestion is not that dissimilar politics and hostile ideologies will become less dissimilar and less hostile, but that the things on which they will be obliged to seek agreement, willy-nilly, will be decided increasingly by economic and technological change.

—another form, after all, of technology—and economic capacities for production, distribution, and finance. The steady expansion of the international market, and the growth of international production to cater to the market, and equally of international finance to cater to the international producers, has inevitable effects on the internal tasks and policies of individual national governments, as well as on their external relations with one another.

These are facts of modern life with which we are all familiar. But their implications for international studies have not so far been fully thought through. They seem to me to be far-reaching and to go well beyond the question of what needs to be done inside the restricting box labelled 'international economic relations'.

To give one example, some of the detailed attention now being paid by political science to party structures and psephological trends in specific countries is grossly overdone, and, indeed, somewhat old-hat. It would be more important, certainly, for an understanding of the dynamic forces shaping, say, French foreign relations to examine attitudes and policies towards the operations of international business in France[4] than to know about recent changes in the French Socialist Party. John Dunning's two studies in foreign investment (1958 and 1970) are more important to the study of British foreign relations than, say, David Butler's studies of British elections.[5] And it is precisely for this reason that Andrew Shonfield's study of *Modern Capitalism* (which concerns the political influences that have moulded selected national economies) rightly belongs in the Chatham House list, helping to add and gain acceptance for (as Wilfrid Knapp recently noted)[6] an important new dimension to the traditional view of international studies.

More positively and precisely, I would suggest that the analysis I have tried briefly to outline indicates clearly three task areas in which those already interested in the study of international economic relations ought to extend and increase their efforts, whether of teaching or research or both. In each some

[4] See e.g. Robert Gilpin's *France in the Age of the Scientific State* (Princeton, 1968).

[5] D. E. Butler & M. Pinto-Duschinsky, *The British General Election of 1970* (London, 1971).

[6] 'Fifty years of Chatham House books', *International Affairs*, special issue, Nov. 1970 (p. 146).

preliminary work has been done, but much more remains to be done.

Development of theory

The first of these task areas—and in my view much the most important—lies on the theoretical frontiers of the wider subject of international studies. It seems to me to follow clearly from the situation I have described that if international studies are not to be left high and dry—desiccated and of less and less popular interest—and if they are to seem to non-specialist outsiders to have some direct bearing on the dilemmas of the contemporary human condition, then a determined effort has to be made to look for coherent explanations of the changing behaviour of governments, international organizations, and other actors in the international political economy at this period of rapid change and transition. Academics call this 'the development of theory'. The alternative description of 'a search for coherent explanations' deliberately suggests the necessarily tentative nature of any theories that may be developed.

At the present time the search has been pursued only in a few unrelated directions. These have been taken not quite at random but often in response to specific political aspirations. First, a goal has been discerned and embraced with the political emotions; only later has the search begun for some ideological backing to justify it rationally and to the intellect. A third stage is reached when the extreme statement of this crusading ideology has stimulated the development of less partisan antitheses, often more balanced and cautious and less dogmatic than the original thesis.

One such direction is in integration theory. The impetus this received from the movement for European union is unmistakable; and it has been reinforced more recently by the interest of developing countries in the imitative possibilities open to them of discriminatory combinations for common commercial advantage. The outstanding contributions here have been those of Ernst Haas, whose initial study, on *The Uniting of Europe 1950–7* (rev. ed. 1968) was followed up by *Beyond the Nation State: functionalism and international organization* (1964). For the later period, the material of Haas's books has to be supplemented by

Miriam Camps's *European Unification in the Sixties* (1967). A large part of both books, unavoidably, is historical and descriptive but the distinguishing feature of both is that interacting political and economic forces are dealt with together and without discrimination. Moreover, in both the need to draw conclusions and suggest explanations is not shirked.[7]

The main contribution from the international economists has undoubtedly been Bela Balassa's *Theory of Economic Integration* (1961), which goes far to illuminate the economic process. But it is so divorced from political realities that its conclusions cannot easily be applied to the sort of questions that arise in real situations—as, for example, those facing states like Malaysia and Singapore, or the three members of the East African Common Market, or the five members of the Central American Common Market. On these, more light seems to me to have been shed by area specialists, for instance by Michael Kaser in *Comecon* (rev. ed. 1967), by Joseph Nye in *Pan Africanism and East African Integration* (1966), by Arthur Hazlewood in *African Integration and Disintegration* (1967), by Miguel Wionczek in *Latin American Economic Integration: experience and prospects* (1966), and by Sidney Dell in *A Latin American Common Market?* (1966).

What is now needed is an up-to-date bridge-building book linking the political and economic, something of the general scope and range of Professor Hawtrey's *Economic Aspects of Sovereignty*, which was first published in 1930 and which now inevitably appears a trifle dated and unsatisfying—even, in the light of subsequent discussions, a little superficial. The nearest approach I have seen to it is Chapter 3 of Charles P. Kindleberger's *Power and Money* (1970), which briefly discusses the minimum attributes of national sovereignty.

Another direction, not unrelated to the first and somewhat overlapping with it, concerns the development of international organization—the general area of functionalism. This again started with an emotional political concern with the growth potential of international administration and decision-making and was pioneered by David Mitrany, who was committed to

---

[7] One might also mention Leon Lindberg's *The Political Dynamics of European Economic Integration* (Stanford, 1963), Amitai Etzioni's *Political Unification* (New York, 1965), and Uwe Kitzinger's *The Challenge of the Common Market* (Oxford, 1962).

a belief in the ultimate triumph of practical, rational inter-
nationalism over traditional, irrational nationalism. This faith
was expounded particularly in *The Progress of International
Government* (1933) and in *A Working Peace System* (1946).
Mitrany's work is a good example of the seminal influence of
a theoretical hypothesis; even if it is later rejected, it serves to
stimulate a series of contradicting, modifying, or qualifying
amendments to the original which themselves slowly build up
into a more coherent explanation of known facts about international organization. Selecting rather drastically from the
large and growing literature on international organization, I
would mention William Diebold's *The Schuman Plan* (1959) and
Pat Sewell's work on UN aid programmes, *Functionalism and
World Politics* (1966). Much of this ever-growing literature,
however, is tediously descriptive and the general standard of
textbooks on international organization—especially economic
organization—is abysmal. The lawyers are perhaps the dreariest
of culprits. No wonder many university students think it is such
a boring subject, requiring only the acquisition—and later
regurgitation—of a large mass of uninteresting, unrelated facts.
This is why Inis Claude and his much-revised *Swords into Plowshares* (1964) still stands out like a beacon in a dark landscape.
His chapter on the functional approach is well worth re-reading
even by those (like myself) who do not altogether agree with it.

It may be that one useful point of departure for the neglected
task of comparative and theoretical analysis and the construction of international organization theory has been found in the
study of decision-making as developed by the political scientists.
This method, it will be recalled, was most strikingly used by
Robert Dahl in *Who Governs?*, a study of the real nerves and
sinews of political power in local government in New Haven,
Connecticut. The *Anatomy of Influence*, edited by Robert Cox
and Harold Jacobson, to be published shortly, is a recent
attempt to apply these methods to a group of international
organizations, including the IMF and the GATT. It suggests
that this may be one way to develop the basis for theory and to
enliven the subject.

By comparison with functionalism, games theory and conflict
analysis have been much less fruitful of new enlightenment in
international studies. It is not so much that games theory is

demonstrably untrue as that it is—by its own confession—restrictive. It consciously forces the untidy chaos of reality into a procrustean bed of oversimplification. For example, the player's concern with the game and its outcome is assumed to be equal and static, whereas—as any close observer of children is well aware—there is in fact a very wide variation both between individuals and between the same individual's behaviour at different times and moods and in different groups and environments. A good deal of history suggests that states are not too different in this respect.

Similarly, some other branches of recent economic theory, notably bargaining theory, market theory, cost-benefit analysis, and other developments mostly used in advanced business schools are inclined to make very exaggerated claims about their relevance to an understanding of the international system.[8] Certainly, one may detect analogies between oligopolistic behaviour in the market and the behaviour of great powers in international diplomacy—but it would be dangerous to overlook the fact that there are also rather important and significant differences. The practical difficulty is that this literature has—as Professor Geoffrey Goodwin remarked in a recent paper[9]—'strong proselytizing overtones' and its preachers have plentiful resources. Consequently, he concludes (rightly, I think) that although the work of applied economists and economic historians is likely to add more to our understanding, yet it is important that the economic theorists should be heard and read, so that when necessary they can be gently but firmly contradicted. Their presence in the field is in itself an indication of the poverty of international studies as at present pursued and of the consequent dearth, from the political-science side, of theoretical explanations that seem helpful and relevant.

Economics in the making of foreign policy

The second task area comprehends the very extensive field of foreign-policy analysis; and the study not just of the policies and attitudes of single states but also those of groups of states,

[8] The best collection is to be found in Bruce M. Russett, ed., *Economic Theories of International Politics* (Chicago, 1968).

[9] 'Economics and International Politics', a contribution to a symposium to be published in 1973.

whether or not these take a formal, constitutional, and organized form or not. In both these fields a more sophisticated emphasis needs to be put nowadays on the place of the economic factor in the policy-making processes, not in isolation from other factors yet subject to more searching scrutiny than it is often given.

At present, although foreign-policy studies constantly refer —as they cannot avoid doing—to the trade policies, the balance-of-payments problems, the monetary concerns or the investment interests of states, this is often done in an airy, off-hand manner, as if the weights to be attached to these economic considerations were a given fixed quantity in the process of national decision-making that did not vary and could therefore be taken for granted.

But in actual fact, remarkably little is known about the predominant motivations of foreign economic policy-making— much less than, say, about defence and strategic policy-making. European resistance to the United States doctrine of multilateral trade is one example. Some American writers are inclined to attribute this to ideological heresy and cultural backwardness. Others explain it in materialist terms as due to a hard-headed defence by protective measures of one kind or another against the threat to domestic producers from competitive American imports. Yet others give decisive weight to the Europeans' overriding concern with different and often conflicting political objectives. Which of these actually predominated in any particular set of negotiations, no one has very seriously tried to establish. One could comment similarly on the motivation of such important decisions as that taken to set up an OECD out of the remnants of OEEC; of the Soviet opposition to economic reform in Dubček's Czechoslovakia; or the deciding reasons for the prolonged post-Imperialist concern of Britain with the security of Malaysia—or indeed of Hong Kong. On these and innumerable other questions, the analysis of the *actual processes* of national decision-making, where economic considerations are inextricably tangled up with political considerations, still tends, too often, to be very superficial.

In the same survey of the subject, Geoffrey Goodwin discerns 'five striking lacunae' in the area of foreign-policy analysis that merit early attention. In each, 'an important economic consideration has obviously had a real bearing on policy-making, yet has attracted surprisingly little attention so far from the main body of international studies'. These five lacunae were: the threat to economic solvency represented by large and/ or persistent payments deficits; the interaction of monetary policy on foreign policy; the political implications of creditor-debtor relations; the motivations of 'economic penetration' of weaker states by stronger ones; and, finally, the political importance to be attached to the growth of international business. 'The plea', concludes Goodwin, 'in all the five cases mentioned is not so much that they merit further exploration—though they do—but rather that the studies that are already available should be more closely integrated in our foreign policy analysis' (p. 38).

The other facet of this second task area, the analysis of economic factors in group relationships, is covered in part by the studies of economic integration and of the development of international economic organizations already mentioned.[10] But it is not wholly covered. There is an infinite variety of kinds of associations of states, from alliances to the loose grouping of those who share in practice certain common customs or standards. In most varieties of association, the formality of organization is often the least important factor deciding the behaviour patterns of the group. And where this formal organization is not present, no less than where it is, there is a need in international studies to give more careful and balanced attention to the economic factor. The Council on Foreign Relations sought to do just this with the series it commissioned under the overall title of Atlantic Policy Studies.[11] American concern with the Atlantic alliance is natural enough, and it is obviously easier to get money from the foundations for study programmes with an immediate relevance than for those where this is less evident. Yet even to understand clearly the urgent problems of the Atlantic alliance, it would surely help if more comparative work had been done on other alliance groups. On the first world war

[10] This phrase 'international economic organizations' is used for convenience. It is, of course—like 'international economic relations'—an inexact term. All international organizations have an economic side to them, and none is exclusively economic either in purpose or in operation.

[11] As well as Henry Kissinger's reappraisal of the political and military aspects of the alliance in *The Troubled Partnership* (New York, 1965) and Miriam Camps's *European Unification in the Sixties* (London, 1967), the series included Richard Cooper's *Economics of Interdependence* (New York, 1968) and Bela Balassa's *Trade Liberalisation among Industrial Countries* (New York, 1967).

one recalls only Salter's still valuable *Allied Shipping Control* (1921); on the second there is Richard Gardner's *Sterling–Dollar Diplomacy* (1969 ed.) and the official British histories by Medlicott and by Hancock and Gowing.[12] On the Soviet alliance system there is the work of Kaser and P. J. Wiles's *Communist International Economics* (1968); John Gittings's *Survey of the Sino-Soviet Dispute* (1968) is valuable, but great gaps remain.

As an example, on the specific question of organizing allies in the conduct of economic warfare almost no serious work was done between Medlicott's two volumes of the British official war history and the recent and very illuminating study by Gunnar Adler-Karlsson of the Western strategic embargoes.[13]

The aftermath of war and the politico-economic consequences of peace settlements are other important topics which have been neglected in recent years. Since the Keynes–Mantoux[14] debate of the interwar period, little work has been done on the reparations question—and even here, when they were interested, the economists' concern has centred mainly on *how* the new adjustment was made, not on the validity or otherwise of punitive reparations as applied between developed states in a market economy.

Another middle-ground subject that once attracted great academic attention but has done so less of late is that of economic imperialism, or, more broadly, the relationship between dominant and penetrated economies. There is no lack of polemic; and the raw material is not scarce. But attempts at serious analysis—either of motivation or consequence—seem to have been confined to historical studies in the rather different circumstances of the pre-1914 world.

It is not, in short, that we have no theories or hypotheses about these recurrent patterns of relations between groups of states in each of which the economic factor is of very central importance, but that those we have and which are ultimately used by policy-makers are insufficiently subjected to analysis and testing by academic study. Nor, though individual studies,

---

[12] Medlicott, *The Economic Blockade* (London, 1952–9, 2 vols.) and 'Economic Warfare' in RIIA, *The War and the Neutrals* (1956) (*Survey 1939–46*); W. K. Hancock and M. M. Gowing, *British War Economy* (London, 1949).

[13] *Western Economic Warfare: a case study in foreign economic policy* (Stockholm, 1968).

[14] See Keynes's *Economic Consequences of the Peace* (London, 1919); Etienne Mantoux, *The Carthaginian Peace, or the economic consequences of Mr Keynes* (London, 1946).

contemporary or historical, of situations involving one or other of these common relationships are quite plentiful, is there very much attempt to seek enlightenment through comparative methods. This paucity is, of course, one of the main consequences of the fragmentation of international studies. We are all too scared of the specialist next door to risk being caught trespassing on alien ground.

The aim both of universities and of research institutes like Chatham House concerned with the vigorous development of international studies should be to do everything in their power to provide more and better opportunities for the acquisition of dual qualifications. We need economists with a grounding in history and politics; political scientists at home with statistical methods; international relations specialists familiar with the intricacies of banking and finance; international lawyers familiar with company or antitrust laws of several different countries —the list of permutations and combinations of qualifications that would be not only academically enlightening but commercially marketable is a very long one indeed. Duality of qualification is now increasingly common and increasingly in demand in commerce and industry today. It is becoming more and more common in other professions such as engineering, medicine, and law. Social scientists should be the first to overthrow outworn restrictions and the last to be hidebound by custom and convention. They should be at least as innovative and flexible as the world outside the universities.

In practice, this means making many changes to reverse the trend towards greater and greater specialization that has so dominated the whole educational system from the bottom of the secondary schools to the top of the postgraduate departments for over a generation. The basic principle should be proclaimed by all those engaged in international studies—economists, lawyers, political scientists—that it is never too late to learn; that undergraduates, graduates, and junior lecturers should always have the means made available to them to acquire familiarity with the tools and methodological processes of another discipline. In fact, with modern methods and machines there are few scholastic gaps, however great, that cannot with determination be made good more quickly today than ever before. And it is absurd, wasteful, and in the long run self-destructive for university departments of international politics or economics to keep out good students on the grounds of their lack of specialist qualifications. It is arguable that history is at least as important a foundation for understanding international economic relations as mathematics. But it is still more difficult to get into international economics courses without the one than without the other. And it is we who will suffer if these changes are not made. But *revenons à nos moutons*.

Politics in the making of economic policy

The third task area is the obverse side of the coin: the addition of the political factor to studies in international economics—what Kindleberger calls the politics of international economics. His first pioneering shot at a comprehensive treatment of the subject in the second part of *Power and Money* identifies the main areas of international economics—trade, aid, migration, capital, corporations, payments, and the monetary system—in which a political dimension exists and influences policies of states, and, therefore, international economic relations. Brief to the point of seeming hurried and sketchy, Kindleberger still attacks an immensely broad range of topics with clarity and courage, and the result is stimulating and illuminating.

Yet in the pioneering attempt to present an all-azimuths view, St Paul the Economist can sometimes be seen kicking against the pricks of his own political commonsense. As an example, he starts off by castigating the doctrine of mercantilism as 'puerile political nonsense'—but then almost at once has to admit that while some mercantilist behaviour by governments may be due to irrational miserliness, it could also be that, in political terms, the instinct to build strong gold reserves makes sound sense. Given the nature of the international political system—and this is something economists nearly always find hard to accept—strong reserves may be needed (as he says) 'for strength or power to protect the country against famine or the sudden need of supplies in wartime' (p. 198). Or, it could be added, they may be desirable in more normal times to guard against the danger of a sudden and otherwise damaging deficit in the balance of payments and of a threat to the national exchange-rate. As he himself later says, a country's exchange rate is not a number but is for each country 'an emblem of its importance in the world, a sort of international status symbol' (p. 204).

His comments on the study of international monetary questions are characteristically pungent and provocative. 'The difficulty', he observes, 'is that economists know no political science and the political scientists know nothing about them at all' (p. 227). But though there is something in this, it is a little too sweeping and simple to be much help. And on closer consideration, there is more to it than mutual ignorance.

In the first place, the literature on international monetary relations is badly unbalanced, in that some areas and questions have been almost over-cultivated while others have been grossly neglected. And secondly, study of the subject suffers more, I think, than other aspects of international economic relations from internal difficulties, in that the different bits of the subject have often been studied in isolation from each other. There is a consequent lack of the broader overview that the non-specialist discovering a new subject inevitably looks for. Thus the literature contributed from the economics side is not only very extensive but is also very skewed to certain topics of apparently greater interest—notably international monetary reform, adjustment processes, and exchange-rate questions.

The third weakness is that international monetary relations is an area in which economic historians, with a few notable exceptions, have not taken a great or consistent interest. And the literature is noticeably poorer for this indifference. There are a few very good books—but there are also large areas of *terra incognita* between them. For example, in the interwar period, there is Ragnar Nurkse's report for the League of Nations, *International Currency Experience* (1944), but really no other historical analysis directed specifically at the monetary aspect of the period. There is F. Garelli's book, *La coopération monétaire internationale depuis un siècle* (1946), but nothing I can think of in English. For the middle period there is Stephen Clarke's excellent study, *Central Bank Cooperation, 1924–31* (1968), but nothing comparable to it for the rather important period of the middle 1930s. W. R. Brown's *The International Gold Standard Reinterpreted, 1919–34* (1940) stops short of the important tripartite agreement of 1936. The best of the general surveys is Arthur

Lewis's *Economic Survey, 1919–39* (1949). The pre-1914 period is better served with studies by Imlah, Bloomfield, and the original reflections of Karl Polyani.[15] But the postwar period, considering the heightened interest in the subject today, is astonishingly under-cultivated. A possible explanation is that not only is it too recent to overcome the professional inhibitions of the economic historians, but also there is (thanks to the secretive traditions of central banks) a particularly wide gap between practitioners and academics, and from the late 1940s onwards the main policy decisions have neither invited nor attracted much public discussion. This is a partial explanation why, after fifteen years, no one has written an adequate sequel to Gardner's *Sterling–Dollar Diplomacy*, the narrative of which ends with the Havana Charter in 1948.

Nor, for that matter, is the neglect made good by related work which approaches the subject from the organization side. There have been the European Payments Union, the Bank for International Settlements, and the Monetary Committee of the EEC as well as the Fund itself. The literature on these bodies varies from thin to tangential. For example, Robert Triffin did attempt a political analysis of the EPU in *Europe and the Money Muddle* (1957), but it was incidental to his main theme. And on the BIS there has been very little except its own annual reports and the reverential Princeton Essay by Roger Auboin, *The Bank for International Settlements, 1930–55* (1955). On the Fund, Shigeo Horie's cautious study *The International Monetary Fund* (1964) is now very out of date, and though the Fund's recently published three volumes[16] of chronicle, analytical essays, and documents are extremely valuable, they are written by Fund officials and therefore are not wholly impartial. This is true even of the extensive contributions (here and elsewhere) of Joseph Gold, who presents monetary issues with admirable legal clarity but also manages in doing so to extract some of the political juice. Compare, for example, Gold's monographs on Special Drawing Rights with Stephen Cohen's recent *International Monetary*

---

[15] A. H. Imlah, *The Economic Elements in the Pax Britannica* (Harvard, 1958); Arthur Bloomfield, *Short-Term Capital Movements under the Pre-1914 Gold Standard* (Princeton, 1963); Polyani, *The Origins of Our Times* (London, 1945).

[16] *The International Monetary Fund, 1945–65: twenty years of international monetary cooperation* (Washington, 1969), i: *Chronicle*, by J. K. Horsefield; ii: *Analysis*, by Margaret G. de Vries & others, ed. Horsefield; iii: *Documents*, ed. Horsefield.

Reform 1964–9 (1970), which deliberately sets out to add the political dimension.

Some of the works of a general character, it is true, include material that could be called international monetary-diplomatic history. But again, because of the fragmentation of the subject as written up by economists—and this covers the bulk of the literature—the number and variety of these general works is sadly limited. Generations of students have now used Brian Tew's *International Monetary Cooperation 1945–75* (10th ed., 1970) and no short introductory book has appeared to compete with it. Of the longer works, W. E. Scammell's *International Monetary Policy* (1961) and Dominique Carreau's *Souveraineté et coopération monétaire internationale* (1970) are both unmistakably written by lawyers; they have the virtue of careful scholarship and textual precision, but both have managed to exclude any sense of political concern or of underlying conflicts of national interest. This sense of the political dimension of international monetary questions is at least attempted in Sidney Rolfe's *Gold and World Power* (1966) and in Francis Cassell's *Gold or Credit* (1965), though neither are aimed primarily at academic readers and it is well sensed in Fred Hirsch's *Money International* (1968), which is also well written and lively and no less authoritative than the deliberate textbooks such as Kindleberger's *International Economics* (1970) or the late Sidney Wells's shorter book (1969) of the same name. A more specific alternative than either is Leland Yeager's *International Monetary Relations, theory, history and policy* (1966).

The best-tilled corner of the field is still, of course, that devoted to the policy issues of international monetary reform, both of the Fund and of its specific rules (e.g. on exchange-rate stability). There is by now really too much of this and the new reader is well advised to select ruthlessly. A taste of Triffin is essential; he is the prophet and sage of the subject. It might be either *Gold and the Dollar Crisis* (1960) or *The World Money Maze* (1966). The rest may best be sampled from Fritz Machlup and Burton Malkiel's systematic arrangement of the main proposals in the Princeton University publication, *International Monetary Arrangements: the problem of choice*[17] or in the selections

[17] Published in 1964 by the International Finance Section of Princeton University, the subtitle is *Report on the deliberations of an International Study Group of 32 economists.*

found in Herbert Grubel's *World Monetary Reform, plans and issues* (1963), which has extracts from Stamp, Bernstein, Harrod, Machlup, Roosa, Meade, and Rueff. (What a pity that Bernstein's fierce individualism has kept him in economic consultancy, where he has never had time for the kind of political economic overview that he could write.) There are other useful collections of selected samples—for example, R. E. Caves and H. Johnson's *Readings in International Economics* (1968) or Lawrence Willett and Thomas Officer's *The International Monetary System* (1969).

The related question of payments adjustment is mostly approached in response to the special problems faced by the United States in the past decade. There was, for instance, the famous Brookings report of 1963[18] and more recently Raymond Mikesell's *The United States Balance of Payments and the International Role of the Dollar* (1970). The main general theoretical work is James Meade's *The Balance of Payments*.[19] Only quite recently have attempts been made to deal with the problem as a political question. Henry Aubrey's awareness that this had been neglected is apparent from his Princeton Essay (No. 71), *Behind the Veil of International Money* (1969), and is also apparent in Robert Aliber's *Choices for the Dollar* (1969), and in my own *Sterling and British Policy* (1971). As Richard Cooper brings out very clearly in the *Economics of Interdependence*, the expansion of international production, marketing, and finance has created new problems of domestic economic management, and these are especially acute in the monetary field. The interaction between governments and markets is therefore subject to particularly rapid change, change which is highly relevant to the contemporary problems of international monetary collaboration and co-ordination. Too little attention as yet has been given to either side—to the political instruments of government and to the institutions and techniques of the market. A. T. K. Grant's *The Machinery of Finance and the Management of Sterling* (1969) has, so far as I know, no parallel on the management of the dollar, though Max Iklé's recent *Die Schweiz als internationaler*

---

[18] W. S. Salant & others, *The United States Balance of Payments in 1968* (Washington, 1963).

[19] *The Theory of International Economic Policy*, i: *The Balance of Payments* (London, 1951); ii: *Trade and Welfare* (London, 1955).

Bank und Finanzplatz (1970) is particularly useful for the author's first-hand experience of central bank operations. (A pity other central bankers and officials have not followed his lead.) The field is left to the financial journalists, such as Henry Brandon, Paul Ferris, and Ian Davidson, who are sometimes over-anxious to avoid gravity.[20] Paul Einzig is a valuable and original exception. Any author who can write both the first general survey of a phenomenon as contemporary as *The Euro-dollar System* (rev. ed. 1967) and a historical study as professional as *The History of Foreign Exchange* (1962) is necessarily a rather rare bird.

So much for one of the main areas of international economics. For the other main areas—trade, aid, and investment—the reader is referred to Caroline Miles's essay. Although I think it will be clear enough that both of us think of these areas as so highly interrelated that it is somewhat artificial to treat them separately, it has been necessary on practical grounds to do so in this book since one essay on the whole field of studies in international economic relations (however it might be defined) would have been much too long. Two parallel ones would have risked repetition. Fortunately it happens that, as colleagues, the main emphasis of our respective interests in the subject has tended to be complementary.

Before concluding, one more general point of a more practical nature on this third task area of the politics of international economics should be added. There is one branch of international economics in which by now a serious attempt to produce a synthesis of the political and the economic elements has become both conscious and deliberate. It is that of development economics—the study of the problems and policies, domestic and external—relating to economic development in poor countries. As one development economist summed it up:

Modern economics has acquired its high degree of rigor at the expense of narrowing the questions it asks. But economic development is necessarily concerned with larger questions, and it must be viewed as a social study that cannot be reduced to a matter of pure

---

[20] Henry Brandon, *In the Red: the struggle for sterling 1964–6* (1966); Paul Ferris, *Men and Money: financial Europe today* (1968); Ian Davidson & Gordon Weil, *The Gold War, the secret battle for financial and political domination from 1945 onwards* (1970), all published in London.

technics. Development economists must consider an unusually wide range of factors, even if some of the relevant factors do not lend themselves to quantification or to the precise analysis that characterizes other branches of economics.[21]

The point here is that the broadening process, of which development economists are themselves now well aware, needs to be carried at least as far in the other main areas of international economics. Problems and policies relating to international trade, to international production, to the international monetary system, and to the movements across national frontiers of labour, technology, and capital also need similar treatment, as aspects of international political economy, not just of international economics.

It is only necessary to state the objective to see how far we have yet to go. But ultimately, as I think we are slowly coming to see, we have to work for a single, coherent, and comprehensive study, a merger or reunion of international political and economic theory, of foreign-policy analysis (the economics of international politics) and of international economics. Within this unitary field of study there would have to be proper scope given to international lawyers and to economic historians no less than to those already engaged in international politics and international economics. It is to be hoped that these conventional academic distinctions will tend, henceforward, to melt, instead of to harden, and that the identity of interest between specialists will come to be more important than the variety of their starting-points.

We need to conceive of a single discipline of international studies embracing the economic aspects and consequences of (primarily) political relationships and the political dimensions of (primarily) economic relationships between states and other actors in the international politico-economic system. It is true that in many universities this will sound like a distant Eldorado, far easier to imagine than to attain. But then nothing happens without imagination and conception. And the experience of—for example—some of the research departments of international organizations like the EEC or the IMF, in which there are strong 'political' motives for getting on with a job in hand,

---

[21] G. M. Meier, *Leading Issues in Economic Development* (New York, 1970), p. 91 n.

does offer encouragement; the disciplinary divisions there are strikingly less evident than they are in academic circles. At least in the newer universities and less hidebound academic institutions, and wherever a little room can be made for experiment and initiative, the first steps should be taken with courage and with hope for the future of international studies.

5 International Economic Relations II: Business and Trade

CAROLINE MILES

Introduction

In the previous essay, Susan Strange has argued forcefully for the removal of the barriers that segregate the different disciplines at work in the field of international studies, shutting away lawyers, political scientists, and economists into separate air-tight compartments. Some at least of these barriers are surely crumbling already, but I agree that a further strong push is desirable. However, I would put even greater stress on another point she raises without developing at length, namely the need for more analytical studies of the actual processes of decision-making in international affairs in all sorts of contexts, from small groups of countries to large multilateral institutional settings. Investigation of what goes on in bodies where governmental and private interests are both directly involved, such as the Organization of Petroleum Exporting Companies and the International Air Transport Association, would be of particular interest to students of international relations.[1] For such work, the historian's sense of judgement is required as well as specialist skills.

Indeed, I would go further and suggest that the Namierian technique might be applicable to some subjects. Biographical studies of the 200 or 300 actors who have constantly reappeared on the European-Atlantic economic stage since 1945 might help to explain why, on occasion, events took the course they did:

[1] Edith Penrose's important work *The Large International Firm in Developing Countries—the international petroleum industry* (London, 1968) and J. E. Hartshorn's *Oil Companies and Governments* (London, 1967), deal with a closely related subject, the relationships between private multinational companies and national governments.

why the European Free Trade Area emerged so quickly after the breakdown in 1958 of Britain's negotiations with the Common Market, for example, or why OECD's Working Party III became so important. The intellectual and personal alliances and conflicts of the relatively small number of people who have been continuously involved in this particular set of international relationships—primarily concerned with economic matters—are worthy of study in themselves, as is the way in which many individuals have been at one time servants of their national governments, and at others international civil servants, politicians, academics, and members of the fourth estate.

Following on Susan Strange's survey of the literature on monetary relations, this chapter deals with two more aspects of international economic relations—multinational business and trade. A preliminary survey of the ground will help to place these topics in their proper setting.

International business is one of the fastest growing areas of international studies. The powerful impact of multinational corporations on the world economy, and the extent to which analysis of their objectives and methods of operation is compelling a rethinking of traditional approaches to trade and payments problems, together with their seeming uncontrollability, underline the importance of the subject. At present, many writers emphasize the uncontrollability point, and this tends to inhibit informed discussion, even at private meetings and conferences, as the actors concerned—the executives of multinational corporations—feel, naturally enough, that they are being got at, and sometimes prefer to substitute public-relations froth for serious consideration of their problems. However, there are grounds for supposing that the situation is improving, not least because of increasing academic interest in the subject, manifested in a number of books mentioned later in this essay.

As an area for research, international business is both interdisciplinary and pragmatic. Data obtained from case-studies of actual circumstances and operations are essential for the establishment of testable hypotheses that can enrich our understanding of complex new forces in the world economy. Chatham House is clearly in a position to make a contribution to this work, not least by bringing together the interested parties, and its potential is considered in the next section.

As for trade policy and international trading relationships, their analysis along politico-economic lines, as opposed to the purely economic theoretical and statistical analysis of trade, seems a bit stuck in the doldrums, though there is no lack of volume of output. The classical theory of trade as an exchange of goods taking place between two countries with different factor endowments, distorted only by customs duties and—perhaps—by fixed exchange parities, is plainly no longer tenable. Regional economic integration, pervasive government subsidies, a host of other 'non-tariff' barriers,[2] and the significance of the multinational corporations are but a few of the new and still only partly understood variables that have to be incorporated in an adequate theory, along with tariffs, which cannot be ignored just because they are now rather low.

Above all, what appears to be emerging is a sense that the factors determining the flow of trade among countries and groups of countries—rich and poor and West and East—are so different in kind that the old international negotiating techniques of tariff bargaining are no longer relevant. What seems to be needed now is a code of practice. Some elements of such a code are already embodied in the GATT rules: the most-favoured-nation clause itself (though it could be argued that this is now more honoured in the breach than in the observance), tariff-binding arrangements, and the ban on the use of quantitative restrictions except under certain closely defined circumstances. However, a major shift in approaches and techniques of trade negotiation is necessary to get away from tariff bargaining and produce a multilaterally acceptable and enforceable code of behaviour.

The issues raised by the special position and problems of the less-developed countries in the world trading community are taken up in the section on trade. But international commercial policy is only one aspect of the role of transfers of resources in promoting economic development. On the vast subject of aid, a major factor in international politics as well as in international economic relations, all I propose to attempt here is to make a few suggestions about areas for future study in which Chatham House might play a useful part.

Current thinking on aid, and more widely the role of

---

[2] A recent GATT survey is said to have listed more than 800.

international assistance of all kinds, is summed up in the report of the Pearson Commission, *Partners in Development* (1969). Over-simplifying grossly, one could say that in the twenty or so years during which development aid has been disbursed, the main discovery has been that economic assistance is much more —very much more—than just a matter of providing capital. Successful development—by which is meant not merely an enrichment of the nation-state, but an improvement in the distribution of wealth and the employment opportunities open to its population—requires an internal revolution in individual habits and modes of thinking, in the educational system, given the need to absorb modern technology, and frequently in methods of administration. All this takes time, and a second important insight is that development is a slow process. Japan has taken fifty years to emerge as a modern industrial state; Mexico and Turkey are moving ahead also about fifty years after their initial revolutionary periods, while many Latin American countries are still making uncertain progress despite the fact that industrialization and modernization began around a century ago.

Sociologists, anthropologists, political scientists, and his-torians are all contributing, along with economists, to this understanding of the complexity and variety of the develop-ment process. Many of the more profound insights come from the proteans who cannot clearly be identified with any one discipline, such as de Tocqueville in *L'Ancien régime et la révolution* (1856), and nearer our own time, Max Weber, Tawney, and Myrdal.[3] Amongst the enormous contemporary literature I will do no more than mention a few works by economists—Rostow's *Stages of Economic Growth* (1960), Hirschman's *The Strategy of Economic Development* (1958), and Andrew Shonfield's *The Attack on World Poverty* (1960).

It is now generally agreed by donors and recipients alike that international economic assistance can play a vital role in the development process, though there is a continuing Marxist critique which claims that all aid is exploitation. To quote Pearson:

[3] Weber, *The Protestant Ethic and the Spirit of Capitalism*, trs. T. Parsons (New York, 1930); R. H. Tawney, *The Acquisitive Society* (London, 1921); Gunnar Myrdal, *Asian Drama, an inquiry into the poverty of nations* (London, 1968).

Although external resources as a whole have only financed some 15 per cent of the investment of developing countries, and foreign aid probably only about 10 per cent, their contribution to the transfer of technology and to the breaking of bottlenecks, especially foreign exchange shortages, has been very important. Except for oil exporting countries, all fast growers have had substantial inflows of foreign resources . . . [though] foreign aid has not always stimulated economic growth. This is not surprising since it has been given for many purposes besides that of promoting development.[4]

Most research into the problems of development, including studies of the impact of aid, must be undertaken in the recipient countries. However, universities and institutions in aid-giving countries can and are making a major contribution, both by providing research workers and facilities for projects overseas— as does the Institute of Development Studies at Sussex, for example—and by looking at topics concerned with the role of donor countries. Two topics of this kind where Chatham House might make a contribution are an examination of the co-ordinating mechanisms of the donor countries and a historical study of the evolution of the British aid programme.[5]

Multilateral aid-giving and co-ordinating institutions, principally the UN and its specialized agencies, have been the objects of many studies. But so far no serious attempt has been made to evaluate the performance of the main co-ordinating body for bilateral aid programmes (which still account for between 80 and 90 per cent of total aid), the Development Assistance Committee of the OECD. This Committee has now been operating for ten years, during which time it has had a fair measure of success in handling a number of contentious problems, including the definition of aid and the measurement of the 'aid' content in various types of capital transfer, the harmonization of aid terms, and, recently, the elaboration of a scheme of non-reciprocal generalized preferences for developing countries, initiated by a resolution of the first (1964) UNCTAD Conference. The time seems ripe for a full study of its work.

Bits and pieces of the history of the British aid programme already exist. There have been studies of the Colonial Development Corporation, the marketing boards, education in the

---

[4] *Partners in Development*, p. 14.
[5] A third, discussed in the section on trade, is a study of UNCTAD.

'new' Commonwealth countries, and so on. As yet, however, there has been no comprehensive investigation of the evolution of the aid programme as a whole, through the difficult years of transition from Empire to Commonwealth down to the present, when the tendency seems to be to loosen the old ties still further, not least by placing greater emphasis on multilateral aid. Such a study, besides pointing to the changes in British attitudes towards the less-developed world, could also illuminate the problems of the shifting relationship between donor and recipient, from parental—or perhaps magisterial—to partnership.

International business

Although the history of foreign manufacturing operations goes back about a century, and the history of world-wide banking, trading, transport, and mining operations much further, the academic study of multinational business[6] and its implications for international relations is a recent development. Up to about twenty years ago foreign direct investment was regarded as but one of the many components of the international flow of capital. Only in a few countries, notably the United States, was any serious attempt made even to measure its size, and the who's, how's, and why's of international business received little or no attention.

Serious study of the motives and methods of operation of companies with extensive foreign operations began in the 1950s, largely in the United States, and concentrated on American business abroad. This inevitably meant that, apart from the very special and politically delicate subject of the extent of US dominance in the Canadian economy,[7] most attention was given to the activities of American corporations in less-developed countries, especially in Latin America. The second American invasion of Europe had hardly begun,[8] except in the United

---

[6] Some students question the use of the adjective 'multinational', but as a way of describing a business that shapes its policies and takes its major decisions in a larger framework than that of the nation-state, even though its headquarters is firmly located in London, The Hague, or the state of Delaware, it is a useful term.

[7] *Foreign Ownership and the Structure of Canadian Industry*, Report prepared by Task Force on the Structure of Canadian Industry (Ottawa, 1967).

[8] The first wave of invasion came around the turn of the century. See F. A. McKenzie, *The American Invader* (London, 1902).

Kingdom, where John Dunning's important pioneering work on the impact of American investment on British industry appeared in 1958.[9]

During the past decade multinational corporate activity in the Atlantic area as well as in the less-developed world has become a growth area for research, teaching, and—given the large political content of the subject—polemics. The emphasis is largely on American corporations, partly because they are most numerous, most important in terms of flows of transactions, and most aggressive, and partly because the research industry on the topic is still largely American-based, in the business schools and at MIT. There is, however, a growing interest in the subject in Europe, particularly in Britain which is, after the United States, the main headquarters for corporations operating internationally.

As is so often the case in new growth areas of intellectual activity, the boundaries of the subject are ill-defined, and while the economists predominate, as elsewhere in the field of international economic relations, they do not have the virtual monopoly of the subject that they possess in trade or finance, for example. Political scientists and sociologists, amongst others, have also entered the field, with important results, and some of the more or less emotional political journalism (e.g. J. J. Servan-Schreiber's *Le Défi américain*) that has been directed towards the uncovering of American challenges and similar burglars under the bed has at least served the valuable purpose of pointing to topics on which it might be desirable to endeavour to establish a basis of fact.[10]

In broad terms, three main lines of approach to the subject-matter can be distinguished. Each of them throws up different topics for further study and empirical research, and each of them suggests different areas of interest and overlap with the wider subject-matter of international relations as a whole. They

---

[9] *American Investment in British Manufacturing Industry* (London, 1958).

[10] One interesting example of such a response is a recent paper by Robert Rowthorn in collaboration with Stephen Hymer, *International Big Business 1957–67, a study of comparative growth* (Cambridge, 1971). The authors set out to put the 'American challenge' into perspective, by an econometric analysis of the growth-rates of US and European firms. They concluded that over the period studied Continental European firms had grown faster than American (or other 'Anglo-Saxon') firms, and that, on balance, the 'American challenge' was declining rather than growing.

are first, what can shortly be characterized as the balance-of-payments aspect, second, the impact of multinationals on domestic economies and the responses induced, and third, the study of the multinational corporation as an operational system with a domain overlapping the jurisdictional boundaries of many nation-states. Like all analytical divisions this one is somewhat artificial and leads to difficulties, but it seems helpful to look at the present state of knowledge under these three headings before trying to peer into the future, and especially to the potential gains from a greater integration with other facets of international relations.

What I have called the balance-of-payments aspect of international business continues to be a central concern of most economists and, above all, of governments, though other social scientists may be tempted to dismiss it as boring. The conceptual and technical problems involved in interpreting the actual statistics are formidable, as was illustrated by the controversy aroused by the Reddaway report on the effects of overseas investment on the British balance of payments,[11] the outcome of a study commissioned by the Confederation of British Industry. Reddaway was concerned with the impact on the UK balance of payments of a marginal change in UK corporate investment abroad, and he concluded that restrictions on capital exports, though of benefit to the UK balance of payments in the short run, would in the long run make the problem worse. Hufbauer and Adler reached broadly similar conclusions in a study of American overseas manufacturing investment undertaken for the US Treasury.[12] A related question of great importance, on which the American and British governments, for a start, are endeavouring to provide some figures, is the significance of the flows of goods between the various branches and subsidiaries of multinational corporations in international trade. The United States government has estimated that about a quarter of total American foreign trade is accounted for by inter-company transactions.

Host countries—the recipients of investments made by

[11] *Effects of UK Direct Investment Overseas*, by W. B. Reddaway (with S. J. Potter & C. T. Taylor). *Interim Report* (Cambridge, 1967) and *Final Report* (Cambridge, 1968).
[12] G. C. Hufbauer & F. M. Adler, *Overseas Manufacturing Investment and the Balance of Payments* (Washington, 1968).

multinational corporations—also have cause for concern about the balance-of-payments effect of these investments. On the one hand there is an initial inward flow of foreign exchange, assuming, that is, that the investment is not financed by local borrowing as it may well be in certain countries and circumstances. On the other, however, is the prospect of a continuous and growing outflow of dividends and royalties to the foreign parent, and payments for component purchases, which may or may not be offset by exports. The ways in which governments try to protect themselves from the consequences of this sort of situation are discussed subsequently.

The balance-of-payments impact of multinationals is only one source of worry for 'host'-country governments. Others derive from the activities of the multinational within the state. They include fears about its impact on domestic economic policies for employment, welfare, regional development, etc., fears about losing control of advanced technology, and the possibility that multinationals—by virtue of their better employment opportunities—will absorb an undue proportion of advanced scientific skills, fears about foreign dominance of key industrial sectors—e.g. computers—and fears that multinationals will hamper the growth of domestic firms by starving them of capital and other resources.[13] Finally, where investments by US-based multinationals are concerned, there are the problems and tensions arising from the extraterritorial activities of the US government in pursuance of its anti-trust policies and restrictions on trading with the enemy.[14]

Whether or not these fears have a basis in fact, they reflect a strong intuitive feeling that the multinational corporation has got out of control and that national sovereignty is threatened. The corporations themselves naturally enough tend to play down this feeling as much as possible, emphasizing the importance they attach to behaving as good citizens of the countries in which they are located, and the way in which they operate within a national legal, fiscal, and administrative framework just like any purely domestic concern. However, even if one

[13] For detailed analysis see e.g. Jack N. Behrman, *National Interests and the Multinational Enterprises* (New York, 1970), C. P. Kindleberger, *American Business Abroad* (New Haven, 1969), and C. Layton, *European Advanced Technology* (London, 1969).
[14] Behrman, chs. 7 & 8.

accepts such pronouncements as being made in good faith and considers many of the fears exaggerated, it is impossible to ignore the fact that the multinational corporation does ultimately take its major decisions—about plant location and product structure, for instance—from a supranational viewpoint, and that conflicts are inevitable.[15]

Possible responses by 'host' countries range from willing or at least resigned acceptance to an outright ban on foreign entrepreneurial activity. In Europe, Holland is at one end of the scale and France was, three or four years ago, very nearly at the other, though the French government has now adopted a much more liberal attitude. Between the two extremes various countries have adopted more or less effective controls, usually of an ad hoc nature rather than embodied in formal legislation, for example insisting on domestic shareholdings, and obtaining undertakings from companies to behave in such a way as to minimize the balance-of-payments problem, for instance by buying components locally and exporting an agreed proportion of output.

Most of these measures really only nibble at the edges of the problem—that is, if one accepts the thesis that there is a problem, and that multinationals need to be 'controlled' in some way. The International Chamber of Commerce, not surprisingly, does not accept it, preferring to talk in terms of 'establishing a climate where the interests of corporation and host country can be harmonised', calling on international companies to behave 'as good citizens of the host country', and making efforts to allay the fears of, and opposition to, foreign investment and international companies generally present in varying degrees in all countries.[16]

Professor Harry Johnson, in a paper prepared for the British North-American Committee, goes even further, arguing that policy discussion should be concerned with 'the limitations that governments should impose on themselves and their interventions in business if their countries are to reap the full benefits

[15] A recent example is Ford's decision to relocate the manufacture of its Pinto engine from the UK and Germany. It is estimated that this will mean a loss of £30–40 m. a year in the export earnings of Ford UK.
[16] S. E. Rolfe, *The International Corporation, with an epilogue on 'rights and responsibilities'*, a report prepared for the Internat. Chamber of Commerce (Paris, 1969). The quotations are taken from the epilogue.

that the international corporations can bring them'.[17] This approach, unlike the ICC's, recognizes the existence of conflicts that cannot be defused by good intentions, but it seems unlikely to gain wide acceptance, deplorable though this may be from the point of view of economic logic.

Many of the tensions and conflicts that arise between governments and multinationals stem from the incompatibility of the two systems of the nation-state and the corporation. Until recently it could be argued that the most interesting literature on the multinational corporation as a system was to be found in the histories of individual companies. The last volume of Charles Wilson's *History of Unilever* (1967) and D. C. Coleman's admirable study, *Courtaulds, an economic and social history* (1969) are two excellent examples. But such studies, illuminating though they are, especially on such matters as corporate strategies on cartels and international competition policy,[18] relate to the past and often to the more remote past. Professor Coleman's work, for instance, stops at 1940–1. A most useful recent general study of the techniques of operating a multinational business is *The Strategy of Multinational Enterprise* (1970) by M. Z. Brooke and H. L. Remmers. This is based on lengthy interviews with senior executives from over eighty companies, and covers such matters as the variety of existing structural relationships, companies' differing financial policies and practices, their motives for going abroad, and their reactions to foreign environments. Another recent work that should be mentioned is R. E. Caves's article 'International corporations: the industrial economics of foreign investment'.[19] This theoretical paper, which does not include any descriptive material, is significant because it is concerned with the economic motivation of enterprises investing abroad, arguing that the further exploitation of a position of oligopoly is highly significant.[20]

Trade unions, as well as governments, are now beginning to

[17] H. G. Johnson, *An Overall View of International Economic Questions facing Britain, the United States, and Canada in the 1970s* (London, 1970), p. 12.

[18] See, besides the two studies quoted, W. J. Reader, *Imperial Chemical Industries, a history*, vol. i (Oxford, 1970), which contains some fascinating material on the international armaments industry from 1870 onwards.

[19] *Economica*, Feb. 1971.

[20] This hypothesis is based on a number of empirical studies, including S. H. Hymer's unpublished thesis 'International Operations of National Firms—a study of direct foreign investment' (MIT, 1960).

react to what they see as the excessive and untrammelled power of the multinational corporations.[21] The chemical workers and the metal workers already collaborate internationally to some extent in pressing the subsidiaries of multinationals to standardize working conditions and pay, and there have been a few token strikes and other demonstrations of support for fellow-workers in other countries. In Europe, the proposed legislation to permit the establishment of a European Company is expected to include some provision for workers' representation, along the lines of existing German company legislation, though this may not have much immediate impact as it is doubtful whether companies will make use of the legislation unless they are given more powerful fiscal incentives than appear to be contemplated at present.

What of the future? Where research is concerned, there is a strong case for continuing to exact contributions from as many different disciplines and institutions as possible. But this does, of course, raise questions of co-ordination and organization of effort, if resources are not to be wasted in unnecessary duplication of work and if the widely dispersed students of the subject are to retain a picture of the whole. Appropriately enough, the business schools, London and Manchester in particular, are taking a strong interest, and they have the advantage of a freshness and breadth of approach lacking in many more conventionally organized university departments.

More empirical work is needed if we are to enlarge our understanding of the forces at work within and around the multinational corporation which lead to the developments that are ultimately observed. But such empirical work, to be fruitful, badly needs a theoretical structure to throw up relevant questions, and as research cannot get very far without the co-operation of the companies themselves, it is desirable to engage them in this preliminary activity of problem-posing. To do this successfully one must create conditions in which the dialogue between researchers and subjects can build up over time, and it is here that Chatham House would seem to be uniquely well placed to establish the right atmosphere and an appropriate dose of political realism.

---

[21] See C. Tugendhat, *The Multinationals* (London, 1971). Chatham House is planning a study on trade union reactions to multinational companies.

International trade

During the past twenty-five years, developments in international trade policy have been dominated by three objectives. Two of them, both largely American inspired, date from the immediate aftermath of the war, and have achieved a very considerable measure of success, though the extent to which they are in conflict has become increasingly apparent in the last few years. They are the aim of creating a liberal world-wide multilateral trading system, and the objective—as much political as economic—of building a united Europe. The third, which emerged towards the end of the 1950s, concerns the ambition of the less-developed countries to obtain special commercial treatment to take account of their special circumstances.

The literature on all three aspects of the subject is extensive. Apart from theoretical work on such questions as the economic effects of tariffs, quantitative restrictions, the regulation of trade in particular commodities, and customs unions, there have been many statistical studies of the impact of particular policies that have been or might be adopted by a country, a group of countries, or the world trading community. But few attempts have yet been made to look at international commercial policy issues and consider historical and institutional developments in the round, giving full weight to political circumstances and attitudes as well as to economics, though amongst the handful of studies that we have are some works of outstanding interest and importance.

What follows is not offered as a comprehensive guide to the literature, but simply as pointers to some of the more interesting books on the subject of international trade policy that have appeared in the last twenty years. I then offer some suggestions as to topics and areas for further work.

To take multilateral commercial diplomacy first, the standard history of the beginnings of the postwar system is Richard N. Gardner's *Sterling–Dollar Diplomacy* (1969), to which Susan Strange has already referred. On GATT itself there are two books, Gerard Curzon's *Multilateral Commercial Diplomacy* (1965) and Karin Koch's *International Trade Policy and the GATT, 1947–67* (1969). Both provide some useful insights into the behaviour of certain countries in certain circumstances, though neither of them describes any major negotiations in detail. Professor Curzon's book, as will be evident from its date, stops well short of the Kennedy Round of 1964–7—which some regard as the apotheosis of GATT—and Professor Koch's gets to it but not through it. We do, however, already have one book about the Kennedy Round written by a member of the American negotiating team, Ernest Preeg,[22] and several shorter pieces, among them a valuable analysis of the results and lessons of the negotiations by Finn Gundelach, who was Deputy Director-General of GATT at the time.[23]

Amongst the numerous works on European economic integration dealing *inter alia* with its commercial policy aspects the outstanding contribution is Miriam Camps's *Britain and the European Community, 1955–63* (1964). This work is a model of the application of an essentially political analysis to the study of what was at base as much an economic as a political episode in history, the establishment of the EEC in the late 1950s and the evolving relationship between the Community and the main European non-member, the United Kingdom. Other works on postwar European developments that deserve mention are William Diebold's two books on the early years of OECD and the beginnings of the ECSC.[24] The history of European trade liberalization in the 1950s has not yet been fully explored, but it is to be hoped that more light will be thrown on it in the study of international economic relations in the 1960s, planned and edited by Andrew Shonfield, now under way at Chatham House.

The sheer size of the UNCTAD conferences, with their hundreds of resolutions, thousands of delegates, millions of words of documentation, and minimal results appears to have overwhelmed the economic and political analysts and the historians. No full-length study of the actual course of either the 1964 or the 1968 conference has yet appeared. The issues were summed up in the report (*New Directions for World Trade*, 1964) of a conference of economists organized by Chatham House in September 1963 to consider guidelines for an international

---

[22] *Traders and Diplomats* (Washington, 1970).
[23] In Frans A. M. Alting von Geusau, ed., *Economic Relations after the Kennedy Round* (Leyden, 1969).
[24] *Trade and Payments in Western Europe, a study in economic cooperation 1947–51* (New York, 1952) and *The Schuman Plan* (New York, 1959).

policy on world trade that would take into account the problems and requirements of the less-developed countries, in the
hope that their findings might be relevant to the first UNCTAD
Conference. Non-specialists who want to know what the arguments are about will find the report useful, though it is more of
an economists' book than most of the others cited.

Looking back over the postwar years, the mid-1960s appear
to mark a watershed in international commercial relations.
Between de Gaulle's first veto on British entry into the EEC, in
January 1963, and the conclusion of the Kennedy Round in
June 1967 a number of questions about future trading relationships and the institutional framework within which negotiations
are conducted were raised. The US Trade Expansion Act of
1962 which, by enabling the American administration to offer
deeper and broader tariff cuts than had hitherto been possible,
provided the impetus for the Kennedy Round, was one indication of new thinking. Others included the adoption, early in
1965, of a new Part IV of the GATT, admitting the principle
of non-reciprocity in bargaining with less-developed countries,
UNCTAD I, held in 1964, and the various proposals for an
'Atlantic' or 'industrial' free-trade area, first mooted around the
time of the initial (1961–3) British negotiations with the Six,
and revived as the Kennedy Round drew to a close.[25]

The fundamental issue that underlay all these initiatives, and
which is still unresolved, is the future of non-discriminatory
principles in world trade, and indeed the actual meaning of
the concept in a situation where tariffs and tariff bargaining,
although still of importance, are no longer the main area for
international negotiations. To be rather more specific, one can
identify five major areas of policy debate. (1) Is the most-
favoured-nation principle in danger of disappearing—and if so,
should efforts be made to save it? (2) Does the Common Market,
as it is at present or if enlarged, present a serious protectionist
threat and if so, what can be done about it? (3) How important
are non-tariff barriers, and how can they be lowered?[26] (4)
What part does and could trade play in accelerating economic

[25] See B Balassa, *Trade Liberalisation among Industrial Countries* (New York, 1967)
and H. G. Johnson, ed., *New Trade Strategy for the World Economy* (London, 1969) for
statements of various proposals and calculations of their potential economic effects.
[26] For a descriptive analysis of some of the more important non-tariff barriers see
R. E. Baldwin, *Non-Tariff Distortions of International Trade* (Washington, 1970).

development, and what should both developed and less-developed countries be doing to ensure that its contribution is maximized? (5) Is there a need for greater integration of countries' trade and financial policies, with the aim of minimizing the adverse effects of changes in either set of policies on the development of the international economy as a whole, and if so, how best can it be achieved?

In all these areas, the debate between the free-trading liberals and the mercantilist, protectionist social policy-makers goes on. The liberals argue that the adverse consequences of freeing trade, such as loss of jobs and balance-of-payments difficulties, should be taken care of by other measures, such as an adjustment-assistance programme or exchange-rate adjustments, while those concerned with the welfare of a single nation or group of nations hold that trade liberalization, while it may be desirable *per se*, often conflicts with other policy objectives and is not always the first priority.

A common thread in many of the debates is the adequacy of existing institutional mechanisms for handling commercial-policy questions. Summing up a conference on economic relations after the Kennedy Round, the Director of the institute that organized it wrote of

the necessity of re-examining the institutional framework for trade negotiations and discussions. . . . It would be neither feasible nor realistic to consider new bodies or a brand new organization for trade matters. As the world, however, grows increasingly interdependent, and issues of trade, aid, economic policy and monetary questions become increasingly intertwined, an effort for more inter-agency cooperation, better coordination, and a framework for intensified discussion is called for. This may well be the essence of future policies after the Kennedy Round . . .: to develop the framework for dealing with the issues as they present themselves in a world which has evolved far beyond the inadequate structures devised to cope with them.[27]

Where existing institutions are concerned, there have already been several studies of the GATT, as I have indicated.[28] But, as

[27] Alting von Geusau, pp. 18–19.
[28] In addition to the works mentioned on pp. 97–8, Gardner Patterson's *Discrimination in International Trade* (Princeton, 1966) is worth consulting, especially on the issues raised by the less-developed countries' participating in trade and on the arrangements governing trade in textiles.

I have also pointed out, there is as yet nothing on UNCTAD or, more broadly, on the less-developed countries as a force in the politics of international commerce. Studies of the reasons for their dissatisfaction with GATT and the genesis and development of UNCTAD, including an analysis of the two major conferences held so far, would add considerably to our understanding of the interrelationship between politics and economics in the formulation of commercial policy. They would admittedly be ambitious undertakings.[29]

However, the central reason for doubting the capabilities of existing institutions is that the nature of the problem has changed. What is now needed is not an international market place, policed but not controlled, where free bargaining can take place, but a framework within which new codes of international behaviour governing such matters as non-tariff barriers, adjustment-assistance measures, trade in the products of advanced technology—usually involving governments more or less directly, as sellers or buyers—and policies to be adopted towards less-developed countries can be worked out.

As far as research and thinking on policy matters is concerned, what seems to be needed at this stage is not so much a blueprint for a new organization—which may not, indeed, even be necessary—as studies of individual problem areas. Although much is said and written in general terms about the importance of adjustment-assistance measures, for instance, there has been no full-length study of them since the ILO publication of *Unemployment and Structural Change* (1962). This is still well worth consulting, but needs bringing up to date by taking account of the experience of the last ten years, during which several countries (and the EEC) have introduced adjustment-assistance measures of one kind or another with varying degrees of success. A further example of a particular problem area which would surely repay a down-to-earth policy based study is the rules, or rather lack of rules, governing international trade between governments and the private sector.

[29] A recent study by I. M. D. Little & others, *Industry and Trade in Some Developing Countries* (London, 1970), sponsored by the OECD Development Centre, should be noted in this context. It is based on seven country studies, and puts the case for liberalization by both developed and developing countries, arguing that excessive protection for infant industries in the latter has resulted in a maldistribution of resources and uncompetitiveness.

In drawing attention to these mundane subjects, I do not wish to seem to ignore the wider and more immediately serious problems connected with the future of world trade, of which the one giving greatest cause for concern must be the threat of a new wave of protectionism in the United States. I am, however, confident that this danger, and the ways in which it might be met, will receive plenty of consideration from students of many disciplines and persuasions, and I therefore felt that it would be useful to draw attention to some relatively neglected areas in which there is work to do. Yet another is East–West trade, and the problems of accommodating socialist countries within a 'market' system.[30]

At the time of writing, the terms for Britain's entry into Europe are known but the political decision has yet to be taken. If we join, it will be urgently necessary to look again at the many commercial policy issues that will arise, both within and outside the Community, given certainty about terms and timetable. If we stay out, it will be even more urgently necessary to examine the alternatives left to us. Either way, the next year to eighteen months is bound to be a crucial period for the international economy as a whole. It is to be hoped that the working group recently established within the OECD[31] can come up with some new thinking on the politics as well as the economic problems before the international community that can help to chart a course for the world economy in the future.

[30] There is a useful paper on Poland's participation in the Kennedy Round in the volume edited by Alting von Geusau.

[31] To review the state of world trade and to form proposals on such matters as non-tariff barriers and trade in agricultural products that are to be discussed at a future international conference.

6 Contemporary History and the 'Survey of International Affairs'

D. C. WATT

T H E *Survey of International Affairs* with its accompanying volume of *Documents* is one of the longest established of Chatham House's contributions to the study of international relations. It first appeared in 1925, as the *Survey of International Affairs 1920–3*, with a slim volume *The World After the Peace Conference* intended as a prologue but in fact published a year later in 1926. A Preface by the Institute's Honorary Secretary, G. M. Gathorne-Hardy, to the latter volume explained that it was intended among others for those 'whose ambitions go no farther than to desire a sound and impartial historical orientation in the troubled era in which they are compelled to live'.

In the Preface to the *Survey 1920–3*, Gathorne-Hardy stated the purpose of the annual *Surveys* to be the provision of 'carefully checked' printed material for 'political leaders and publicists' whose speeches and articles he described as being 'the main factors in moulding public opinion on foreign affairs'. To guide the *Surveys* the Institute had at its disposal the services of Arnold Toynbee, fresh from his dismissal by a purblind London University. In his introductory note to that volume, Mr Toynbee, as he then was, laid down the main lines which successive editors, whose names include those of Peter Calvocoressi, Coral Bell, and Geoffrey Barraclough, have faithfully followed. The *Survey* was to cover international affairs, not foreign affairs of the British Commonwealth or human affairs in general. For the purposes of the *Survey*, the object studied was defined as relations between states save where 'the status or internal condition of a country was itself an international affair' (p. vii).

The first two volumes were written entirely by Arnold Toynbee himself. By 1925, however, the pattern had suffered its first break. Two volumes and a *Supplement* covered that year. The first, by Toynbee, covered *The Islamic World since the Peace Settlement*. The second was edited and largely written by C. A. Macartney and the future Mrs Toynbee, Miss V. M. Boulter, with a couple of anonymous contributions on 'The Far East' and 'The Traffic in Opium and other Dangerous Drugs'.[1] The *Supplement* provided a chronology from 1920–5.[2] The following year the annual volumes were resumed, with independent contributions on inter-allied debts, the United States and the Permanent Court of International Justice, and the International Steel Cartel by R. J. Stopford, Dr Hersch Lauterpacht, then a humble assistant lecturer at the London School of Economics, and M. S. Berkett. This pattern was to continue, with V. M. Boulter's name being added as Toynbee's assistant, until 1938 and the onset of the second world war entirely destroyed it.

By the mid-1930s the problem of covering one year's events within one volume was already beginning to escape even Dr Toynbee's control. The year 1935 demanded two volumes, one entirely devoted to the Italo-Abyssinian war, a volume in which, for once, the objectivity of the *Survey* was singularly lacking.[3] The following year (1936) could again be contained within one volume, albeit a considerably fatter volume than those of the 1920s or early 1930s. Its successor, 1937, again required two volumes—the second devoted to the civil war in Spain.[4] For 1938 no less than three volumes were projected. But work on the second and third volumes could not be completed until 1945.[5] Increasingly through the 1930s outside contributors were called in, to write major sections of the annual *Surveys*. A considerable section on world economic problems was contributed each year by Harold Hodson, succeeded in 1936 by Allan G. B. Fisher. Other

[1] *Survey, 1925*: vol. i was published in 1927; vol. ii, by C. A. Macartney & others, appeared in 1928. All the *Survey* and *Documents* volumes were published in London by O.U.P.

[2] *Supplement: Chronology of International Events and Treaties 1920–5* (1928), compiled by V. M. Boulter, London, 1928.

[3] *Survey, 1935*, ii: *Abyssinia and Italy* (1936).

[4] *The International Repercussions of the War in Spain, 1936–7* (1938).

[5] *Survey, 1938*, i (1941); ii: *The Crisis over Czechoslovakia, January to September 1938*, by R. G. D. Laffan, rev. by V. M. Toynbee & P. E. Baker (1951); iii, by R. G. D. Laffan & others (1953)

contributors included H. R. Hubbard on the Far East,[6] Katharine Duff on 'The American Continent' (*1936*) and the Spanish civil war,[7] Harold Beeley on Palestine and the Mediterranean,[8] David Mitrany on America (*1938*, i). And the entrustment of volumes ii and iii of the 1938 *Survey* to R. G. Laffan, of the Queen's College, Cambridge, showed that the problems facing anyone who attempted seriously to survey international affairs on a global scale were beyond even a mind as wide-ranging and an energy and powers of application as formidable as those of an Arnold Toynbee.[9]

Work on the *Survey* proper was not resumed until after the second world war. It was to be resumed on a different scale and by a different hand. Professor Toynbee, as he now was (a professorship had been created for him in 1926 by the munificence of Sir Daniel Stevenson), was no longer directly concerned as editor. By now well advanced in the writing of his monumental *A Study of History*, his surplus energies were absorbed by the direction of a mammoth series on the period of the second world war—some ten volumes in all with contributions by more than a score of different authors.

Professor Toynbee's successor was Peter Calvocoressi. In his initial volumes, and indeed throughout the volumes he edited, covering the years 1947–53, the reader may detect a conscious effort to return to the original concept of the *Surveys* as set out in the prefaces to the volumes for *1920–3* and *1924*. In the place of Professor Toynbee's ever more luxuriant prose, increasingly encrusted with the historical insights of a mind that ranged freely (his critics said too freely) across some twenty-one civilizations and some thirty to forty centuries of history, recorded in almost as many languages, the new editor deployed a lean and accurate prose style, controlled in a manner which held it well within the emotional range of which its author was later to reveal himself capable.

The new format, or rather the return to the original, was successful. Calvocoressi produced no less than five volumes before he decided to move on to other literary and academic

---

[6] *Survey*, *1934*, pp. 628–91; *1935*, i, pp. 299–339; *1936*, pp. 876–938; *1937*, i, pp. 145–323; *1938*, i, pp. 493–571.

[7] *Survey*, *1937*, ii, 42–114 & *1938*, i, 260–386.

[8] *Survey*, *1936*, pp. 702–47; *1937*, vol. i, pp. 543–607; *1938*, vol. i, pp. 414–92.

[9] He was, at the time, also engaged on his *Study of History*.

work. He was aided by a succession of research assistants; and, as in the 1930s, very substantial contributions were made by others, notably by F. C. Jones of the University of Bristol writing on the Far East, by George Kirk on the Middle East and by R. G. Hawtrey on European Economic Co-operation.[10] Two separate, spectacularly controversial, volumes were contributed on the Middle East from 1939–50 by George Kirk, a historian.[11] But the furore these volumes created made Chatham House unwilling to repeat the experiment.

The volume for 1954 was written by Coral Bell, who had assisted with the volume for the previous year. Thereafter there followed a disastrous lacuna before a successor to Professor Toynbee could be found and appointed and before he could approach the problem of the *Surveys*. That successor was Professor Geoffrey Barraclough. To attempt to catch up the time that had elapsed before he began work on the *Survey*, he engaged and trained a team of research assistants, and extended his volumes to cover two or more years at a time. The volumes produced under his editorship retain the distinctive impress of his personality, that of one of the most distinguished of English medieval historians who had by deliberate choice turned to the contemporary field and abandoned that of Barbarossa.[12] So rapid and so extended a conversion (Toynbee had had several years of the Foreign Office's Political Intelligence Department and a good deal more to carry him over the bridge from Byzantium to Versailles), made for a still different approach from that of previous *Survey* editors. Like Professor Toynbee in 1936, Professor Barraclough was appalled by the manners and mores of the great powers. His dislike of the manner in which the Republican administrations of the 1950s exercised American power was matched only by the distrust he felt for the *bona fides* of both the Soviet Union and the new crystal gazers of the Kremlinological profession. The most notable passages in his final volume are those in which he singles out for his readers' respect and admira-

[10] F. C. Jones in *Survey*, *1947–8*, pp. 268–346; *1949–50*, 316–54, 443–65; *1951*, pp. 338–435; *1952*, pp. 301–93; *1953*, pp. 188–278; *1954*, pp. 235–82. George Kirk in *1957*, pp. 250–91; *1952*, pp. 191–229. R. G. Hawtrey in *1947–8*, pp. 63–89; *1949–50*, pp. 94–118, 324–33; *1951*, pp. 90–101.

[11] *The Middle East in the War* (1952); *The Middle East 1945–50* (1954).

[12] His first volume of essays on contemporary history, *History in a Changing World* (Oxford, 1955), was published shortly before his appointment.

tion the skill with which Harold Macmillan steered the precarious craft of world peace through the perilous waters that followed the break up of the 1960 Paris Summit conference.[13]

It was at that stage that the present editor took over, after an apprenticeship almost entirely devoted to the field of contemporary history, including the production of two pamphlets and the first draft of the report of a Study Group for Chatham House.[14] And it was in the course of his editorship that it became plain that the problems which faced any would-be editor of an annual *Survey* had become incapable of resolution and that some other format would have to be found to satisfy the purpose to which the *Survey* had come to be committed.

These problems fall into two very different categories. On the one hand the nature of the academic profession and the role of Chatham House had changed very considerably under the influence of university expansion and a parallel through even more rapid cost inflation. The accident of Professor Toynbee's career had given Chatham House the illusory appearance of pursuing its own academic career structure. It was clear, as the 1960s opened, that to make that illusion a reality was beyond Chatham House's limited financial resources. The various rather under-endowed professorships were therefore swept away and the research staff came to include an increasing number of part-time appointments, among which the editorship of the *Survey* was now to be included. Those responsible for the new appointment apparently felt that Chatham House's increasingly strained resources could no longer be mortgaged for the production of the *Survey*. Had another Arnold Toynbee presented himself, no doubt they would have felt differently. But it seems universally agreed that the age of giants is over.

A part-time editorship presented a new range of problems. Was the editor to become simply the co-ordinator of a sizeable group of contributors writing on individual subjects? Or was he still to attempt to impose upon each individual volume the stamp of a single approach—a task which would involve, even where outside contributors were employed, lengthy discussion

---

[13] *Survey, 1959–60*, pp. 559–63.
[14] *Britain and the Suez Canal* (1956); *Documents on the Suez Crisis* (1957); *British Interests in the Mediterranean and Middle East; report of a Study Group* (1958).

of the individual contributions and, possibly, their rewriting?
The whole ethos of the *Survey*, as it had grown over the thirty-
five years since its first volume had appeared, made the first of
these alternatives unthinkable. But the magnitude of the work
involved in the alternative imposed delays which caused the
annual *Surveys* to fall even further behind the advancing frontier
of the present. And with the publication of the volume for 1962
delayed until 1970, it was clear that a new approach had to be
found.

The problems, which had thus stretched the task of the editor
of the *Survey* beyond the capacities of the only system of editorship which was felt to be within Chatham House's inflation-
eroded resources, were not confined to the *Survey*. But the scope
and approach of the *Survey* were to make them different in kind
rather than degree from those faced by comparable international
publications. There are in fact some five or six other comparable
enterprises in the West, the *Annual Register* and the now-defunct
Chambers' Yearbook in Britain, *L'Année politique* in France, *The
United States in World Affairs* in America, and *Die internationale
Politik* in West Germany.

Of these the *Annual Register* antedates the Chatham House
Surveys by at least two centuries.[15] It is, of course, only in part
concerned with international affairs and is Britannocentric in
its approach. It is the work of a multiplicity of hands, each
working to a rigid timetable and within very narrow limits of
space and time. The source materials used are therefore almost
entirely the reports in the British quality press. An indispensable
tool of reference, it is in no real sense a competitor of the *Survey*
as a work of history. Its merits lie particularly in the quality of
its contributors, who come in the main from the ablest talents
of the upper Establishment. The same could not have been said
of all the contributors to the *Chambers' Yearbook*; which may go
some way to explain its demise.

If the *Annual Register* is Britannocentric in the main, its
insularity of approach is small beer compared with the Franco-
centricity of *L'Année politique*. This yearbook is produced by a
small group of French scholars. Its merits are those of the French
language and intellectual tradition. Succinct and compact of

[15] *The Annual Register of World Events* has run from 1758 and is currently published
by Longmans.

statement, and even more so of comment, it is usually meticulously fair and accurate. It is however unmistakably and irremediably French in outlook and interests, as indeed its full title, *L'Année politique, économique, sociale et diplomatique en France*, makes abundantly clear. Its account of affairs external to France is seen, therefore, entirely through French eyes and in the light of French national interests. No effort is made to cover subjects which lack a French interest or content.

The United States in World Affairs[16] does for its theme what *L'Année politique* does for France. In format it is however very different. For many years now it has been the work of a single hand, that of Richard P. Stebbins, writing mainly on the basis of reportage in one or two of the top quality American newspapers. It carries illustrations and cartoons and is written with a lightness of touch that makes it the easiest of reading. As its title suggests it is basically an account of American external relations. And like *L'Année politique*, it is admirably up to date.

The closest parallel to the *Survey* is the West German volume, *Die internationale Politik*, produced by West Germany's equivalent to Chatham House, the Forschungsinstitut der Deutsche Gesellschaft für Auswärtige Politik, and published in Munich. It is interesting therefore to note that it is nearly as far behind as the *Survey*. The volume for 1963 was, it is true, published some three years before the date expected for the comparable volume of the *Survey*. But the price of this was the prolonged delay in the appearance of the volume for 1959–60. The West German series has also abandoned any attempt to impose an editorial unity upon the individual volumes, save in so far as a general agreement as to the appropriate approach exists between the various contributors. The approach is, in fact, piecemeal. And the generally high quality and insight of the individual contributions reflects the high level of scholarship of that part of the German academic community upon whom the editors feel free to call.

What differentiates the *Survey* in practice from these other series is the presence of two factors. Firstly, the accident of Professor Toynbee's long direction of the series and the association up to the beginning of the 1960s of the editorship with the Stevenson Research Professorship in International Relations of

[16] Published in New York for the Council of Foreign Relations.

the University of London established and maintained one assumption: that the writing of the *Survey* was an exercise in the writing of history, and that it should therefore aim at satisfying those canons of historical judgement and literary merit to which all British historians, whether their fields of study lie in classical, medieval or modern historical studies, subscribe and attempt to aspire.

The second factor was laid down in the preamble to the deed establishing the Stevenson Chair:[17]

> Whereas the Founder, being desirous of furthering amity and good understanding among all nations, and being persuaded that the study and teaching of history as hitherto practised in this and other countries have not been conducive to this end, that on the contrary in practically all countries the teaching of history and the class books used in them have had a strong nationalistic bias, creating among the peoples from childhood onwards a spirit of antipathy, ill-will and even hatred of other peoples, and being convinced that the teaching of history internationally, and, as far as practicable, without bias, would tend to substitute for this spirit a spirit of international cooperation and good will . . .

The holder of the Chair, and the editor of the *Survey* as his deputy and successor, was thus enjoined to write his history in a manner devoid of 'nationalistic bias'. In practice this could only be done by attempting to impose as a duty upon the chronicler of the present an objectivity of view and a conscious distancing from historical environment which is neither easy to achieve nor always understandable or pardonable to the chronicler's contemporaries. Professor Barraclough has warned us that the contemporary historian cannot expect and should be wary of easy popular acceptance of his views. He might have added that a conscious adoption of the mantle of Tybalt, while risking Tybalt's fate, does not in itself guarantee genuine objectivity.

Over the years, therefore, the *Survey* has developed from being a twentieth-century analogue in the field of international affairs to the *Anglo-Saxon Chronicle* to something more pretentious—a first attempt not merely to record the events but to write the history of the age. The writers of the *Survey* represent the first

---

[17] Quoted in D. C. Watt, ed., *Contemporary History in Europe* (London, 1958), at p. 55.

professional surveyors of the ever-advancing frontier of history. In playing this role they have to mingle and rub shoulders with as motley a crowd as ever beset the professional geographers who first explored Africa or crossed the American plains. Together with genuine pioneers and refugees from the politics of the past, the writer of the *Survey* has to keep the company of pirates, outlaws, starry-eyed idealists in search of or intent on establishing new utopias, Herodotuses representing hearsay and Munchhausens representing their own fantasies as fact, monopolist exploiters intent on establishing their own version of events as a basis for political propaganda or political power, claim-jumpers with (remarkably similar) ambitions to profit from the spadework of their more honest and scrupulous companions, even the occasional posse of self-appointed vigilantes of left or right intent on establishing their version of law and order and purging from the neighbourhood all those they regard as threatening to undermine it. There are times when the contemporary historian feels more like a character from a TV Western than a Lewis or a Clark first traversing an unknown continent.

It is, of course, the presence of this raggle-taggle crew which caused so many academic historians in the past to recoil so violently from the study of the contemporary world, and to argue that the task of studying it presented problems of such an order that a historian could only tackle them at the cost of his professional integrity. No one, so they felt, could mix with such a crowd of disreputable characters without adopting insensibly their values or lack of them. Indeed, among many academic historians this view would be put much more strongly—in that it would be maintained that only the instincts of a rogue or a crook would lure or compel a respectable historian into the study of the present. To write about the present or the immediate past was to dabble in journalism. No good could come of it —and the motives of those that did so were immediately suspect.

The institutionalization of this view was, it should be noted, a product of the late nineteenth and early twentieth centuries, and spread *pari passu* with the dogma of 'scientific' history, with its belief in the existence of a 'real' world of historical 'facts', the proper advising and discovery of which could be fixed for all time in a 'definitive study'. To do this was the burden laid on the historian. This was, it should be noted, a comparatively new doctrine. It carried the implication that the giants of the historical profession in the past, from Thucydides to Ranke, from Caesar and Tacitus to Marx and Macaulay, from Ibn Khaldun to Frederick Jackson Turner were dead, passé, superseded, exposed as in error and therefore no longer worthy of study. The writing of history ceased to be seen as the imposition of a single vision on the chaos of historical evidence. It became the province of the worker-ant, each busily collecting his single grain of corn and bringing it back to the communal historical storehouse.

The impulse which led to the original formation of Chatham House was very much at odds with this. The galaxy of leading professional historians, who served the Foreign Office's Political Information Department in 1914–18, and wrung their hands behind the scenes at Paris the following year at the abysmal ignorance of international affairs of their professional lords and masters among the politicians and the people of Britain, had already had a devastating lesson as to the consequences of leaving contemporary historiography to the non-professionals. They reacted in general, however, not as historians but as citizens. Chatham House was founded to supply a crying public need. The idea that there was also a professional need for its work was to take much longer to sink in.

The delay was in part imposed by the extreme slowness with which the archival evidence on which the academic historian fed was released by the various governments. The War Guilt question produced one great flood of documentation on the origins of the 1914 war, on which international historians largely nourished themselves in the inter-war period. But in the 1950s the principal British archival material which reached us was still of no later a date than the end of the nineteenth century. The advance of the date, at which the archives were open from 1898 to 1902 was a major event. The report of the Grigg Committee[18] and the Public Records Act of 1958 transformed all this. For the first time the professional academic historian was faced with the problems of a continuously advancing frontier. Each year that frontier advanced a year. True it was still fifty years behind the present. But it moved.

Professional dissatisfaction in the early 1960s eventually pro-

[18] Cmd 9163 (1954), Committee on Departmental Records, *Report*.

duced a revision of the fifty-year period to thirty years.[19] This was of much less importance, however, than that even the most professionally circumscribed of academic historians had to face the fact that the frontiers of what was, even by his own canons, the permissible area of historical study, were now continuously on the move. And as historians both in teaching and in writing and researching moved with them, so the case for not waiting until all the evidence (whatever that meant) was available became obviously stronger.

For as the historian advanced, he constantly encountered versions of events, often of extraordinary pervasiveness and strength, which the evidence available showed not only to be prejudiced and untrue but prejudiced and untrue to a degree which involved the historian in the further mystery of investigating how they had ever come to be generally accepted in the first place. To those few historians who had consistently and deliberately operated beyond the frontiers of the academically respectable, this was nothing new. But the view that they had expressed, that it was a criminal neglect of their professional responsibilities to leave the job of surveying the frontier much closer to the present than the Public Records Act allowed to those whose motives were other than those of the professional historians, was a new one to the bulk of their colleagues. And the truth of their adage that professional abstention does not prevent contemporary history from being written, only from preventing it being written well, now, at last, began to achieve professional recognition.

In this process the *Surveys* of the interwar years, it appeared, had stood the test of time remarkably well. The degree to which teachers of the history of international relations in those years have come to rely on the annual volumes, nay even the appearance of the volumes for the late 1940s and early 1950s in the reading lists of university history courses, paid the editors and authors of those volumes a belated but none the less thoroughly well-earned compliment.

All this, however, bears more on the acceptability of the

---

[19] The reader may find an account of this controversy in (i) Watt, 'Foreign affairs, the public interest and the right to know', *Political Quarterly*, Apr. 1963 and (ii) the same, 'Contemporary history: problems and perspectives', *J. Soc. of Archivists*, Oct. 1969.

Survey as a work of history than on the problems which faced and face its editors and contributors in research into and writing about the contemporary international scene. Foremost among these are inevitably the problems presented by the scope of activities to be surveyed; second only to this come the problems presented by the nature of the evidence available. Conceptually, the two are interlinked in that the scope of the survey must depend upon the nature and the availability of the evidence.

The so-called scientific school of historians, who claim to operate in the tradition of Ranke, assumed that the industrious historian approached each subject of study with his mind a *tabula rasa*, upon which the patterns naturally present in the evidence could impose themselves. It was in the nature of historical evidence, of course, that there has always been a further gap between the picture presented by the evidence available and the underlying reality. This gap the historian filled by deduction, a perfectly legitimate process, provided that what was deduced or inferred from the evidence researched was presented as such, so that the reader, even though he did not share access to the materials on which the individual historian based his publication, could judge for himself whether the historian was presenting a permissible, a legitimate version of the events about which he wrote.

Few would be found today to echo this particular set of assumptions. The historian, it would be generally agreed, approaches his evidence with a set of assumptions about the general nature of the historical process, a set of hypotheses analogous to matrices into which he will attempt to fit the evidence available to him, always being willing to discard or modify these matrices, in part or in whole, if the evidence cannot be made to fit them. For the international historian, these matrices will be in part in the nature of models or sets of assumptions about the processes of current international political and economic relations. In part they will consist of models or sets of assumptions about the nature of the foreign-policy-making processes in the countries whose activities are being studied. In part they will consist of assumptions about the personalities and characters of the principal actors in the events studied, about their perceptiveness of the external world and the nature of their own personal matrices into which their appreciation of external events has to be fitted. The experienced historian learns to develop a feeling for the phenomena he is studying, almost a sense of smell to guide him in the formulation, adaptation, and discarding of the various hypotheses with which he approaches the evidence and with which he attempts to fill in the *lacunae* in that evidence. And it is in this area, part skill, part instinct, that history ceases to be a science and becomes an art.

It is also in this area, the formation of the matrices, the formulation of the hypotheses, that the editor of the *Survey* and all those who aim at the hazardous and unpopular role of 'generalist', run the greatest risks of getting things wrong. The biggest perils arise, firstly, from the assumption that institutions in different countries with similar names in fact play similar roles; secondly, from the almost universal habit of substituting shorthand terms such as 'Britain', 'Washington', the 'Quai d'Orsay', the 'Pentagon' for the differing concentrations of decision-making power and responsibility in the various countries, so that these terms come to assume a spurious identity and existence of their own; thirdly, from the assumption, ridiculed by G. K. Chesterton in the opening chapter of *The Napoleon of Notting Hill*, that existing developments can be extrapolated indefinitely; and fourthly, that institutions should be taken at their own face value and that they are constituted and function in the manner they claim to be and do.

The first of these is among the most seductive, especially in this age of imitation and mimesis among the emergent powers of the third world. A very early example of the disasters that can occur to practical men who fall into this kind of error is that of the great Ashanti rising which a British governor provoked by mistaking the Stool of the Ashanti kings, which they believed quite literally to embody the soul of the Ashanti people, for a regal throne and seat of sovereignty. Among students of the contemporary international scene the present theoretical approach, based as it is on the collection of examples supposedly of the same phenomenon from different political societies and the evolution of a generic theory of explanation, makes this error doubly seductive.

In his recent study of the role of armies in Middle Eastern politics, Professor J. C. Hurewitz[20] has shown only too cogently

[20] *Middle East Politics: the military dimension* (London, 1969).

how the general theory, on which so much American policy has been based, of the modernizing role of the armed forces, and the inevitability of military dictatorship in developing nations, breaks down completely when applied to the various armies of the Middle East. Whatever the radical politics they profess, some armed forces have become the instrument by which minority groups (such as the Alawites in Syria) maintain a privileged status which might otherwise be swamped by majority power.

A rather similar example is presented, again in the Middle East, by the problems presented to contemporary historians in the 1950s by the phenomena of 'Arab nationalism' and 'Arab unity'. The temptation to see parallels between the processes at work in the Middle East and those with which historians of nineteenth-century Europe were familiar was too strong for many to resist. Cultural and linguistic nationalism seemed inevitably to lead to political nationalism and thence to political unity. The movement seemed in Gamal Abd al-Nasir to have found its Cavour, if not its Bismarck. The drawing together of the Arab states of the Levant and the Arabian peninsula into a single union, the establishment of an Arab Common Market, the revival of the glories of the Abbasids or the Umayyads, were regularly predicted. The events of the year 1958, the establishment of the United Arab Republic, the overthrowing of the Hashimite dynasty in Iraq, the civil war in the Lebanon and the temporary replacement of King Saud by the Emir Feisal at the head of Saudi Arabia, all seemed part of the same pattern.

Yet these assumptions were quite clearly wrong. To a colder, cooler eye the Arab world seemed to lack any real, as opposed to rhetorical, bases for unity. No single centre drew or dominated Arab culture, not even Cairo. The Arabic language itself discriminated between the *umma* and the *watan*, that is between universal *Volk* and geographical–political *Staat*, as was pointed out by Sylvia Haim at the time.[21] The patterns and dominant forces in Syria and Iraq, let alone in the Lebanon, proved amenably adaptable to Arabic rhetoric but obstinately persistent otherwise. The relations between Maronite Christians and Sunni Moslems in the Lebanon,[22] between Druzes and Alawites

[21] 'Islam and the Theory of Arab Nationalism', in W. Z. Laqueur, ed., *The Middle East in Transition* (London, 1958).

[22] See K. S., 'The Lebanese crisis in perspective', *The World Today*, Sept. 1958, pp. 369–80.

and Sunnis in Syria, between Sunnis, Shi'ites, and Kurds in Iraq, were what really mattered,[23] as a glance at the composition of the Iraqi government *after* the 1958 revolution should have showed. The only European parallel suggested that perhaps Bismarck's own indictment of the German Liberals of 1848 was correct.

The ideological approach, as developed by twentieth-century writers on totalitarianism, was to prove equally misleading. An erudite and widely recommended study, with a wealth of documentation of such abundance as to arouse suspicions as to its provenance, pointed to the absence of safeguards in the fabric of traditional Arab society against the doctrines of Communism and left the reader with the feeling that Islam, in losing its traditional religious strength, was transmuting itself unrecognized into Soviet communism.[24]

The reality was again very different. Not that much of the traditional apparatus of collective tyranny was not to be found in some, if not most, Arab states. It had, after all, as respectable a pedigree in the practices of the Ottoman Empire as the Soviet secret police derived from the Tsarist *Ochrana*. It was really that the forms of Islamic society, and the weakness of Islamic intellectual education, were such as to prevent the substitution of Marxist–Leninist–Stalinist dogma for the Qu'ran, or to encourage the development of a monolithic disciplined party. In Arab society, the Communist Party itself tended to develop either into the quasi-mystical sect or to the extended patron–client relationship which were the traditional forms of Arab political organization.

The irony of this was that more detailed historical investigation was at the same time casting the gravest of doubts on the monolithic character of even the classic Nazi and Soviet models of the totalitarian state. Germany under Hitler, when studied in detail,[25] took on the appearance of an oriental empire in decay, the intrigue-ridden politics of the tyrant's court being matched only by the freedom often exercised by his more distant satraps. The Soviet countries remained more opaque to historical

---

[23] See Elie Kedourie, 'From Amurath to Amurath: a survey of the Middle East scene', ibid., July 1963, pp. 285–94.

[24] Laqueur, *Communism and Nationalism in the Middle East* (London, 1956).

[25] See e.g. E. N. Peterson, *The Limits of Hitler's Powers* (Princeton, 1969).

scrutiny. But it seemed very difficult to reconcile the Russia of the purges, as depicted by a John Erickson or a Robert Conquest,[26] with the imagined Behemoths of the 1940s;[27] and the phenomenon of the politically religious, the 'dead souls on furlough' of European communism in the 1930s, seemed in the examination to become less the product of a new form of Assassinism, imported from the Soviet Union, and more something that could only be explained in terms of the social psychology of the European milieu from which it sprang. Whatever the case, there was clearly nothing in the dedicated, self-destroying single-mindedness of the European communist underground in the 1930s and 1940s which could in any way be identified with the wordy self-justification, the wounded complexes of the emergent Levantine professional classes among whom Nasserite Arab nationalism found its echo.

The war in Vietnam was to create equal problems. This is no place to embark on any lengthy critique of the massive literature on this contentious subject. It is however instructive to see how little of it attempts to place the fighting in the long perspective of Vietnamese history, to disentangle the continuing civil war between those who gained power in the Red River delta in 1954 and those whom they expelled to the South from the struggle between the three traditional centres of political power, Saigon, Hué, and Hanoi, and to keep both separate from the war by proxy being fought between the superpowers and also from the processes by which since time immemorial the city cultures of South-east Asia have sought to impose their administrative power upon the land. All too often the assumption is that the war concerns simply the attempt by an oriental 'people' to resist foreign non-oriental aggression. Such an assumption clearly begs the whole question. The ethnological and geographical term 'people' cannot be used as though it was automatically the same as the political term the 'people' used by Western political thinkers, to cover the development of the Latin 'populus' and the Greek 'demos' via Rousseau into the nineteenth-century contest between middle class and aristocracy and between

[26] Erickson, *The Soviet High Command* (London, 1962); Conquest, *The Great Terror* (London, 1968).

[27] F. L. Neumann, *Behemoth, the structure and practice of National Socialism* (London, 1942).

competing national middle classes over the diffusion of political power. First, it must be proved that there is, in political terms, any such recognizable entity as the Vietnamese 'people'.[28]

The generalist, or at least the editor of the *Survey*, then has to be the opposite of his popular image. Far from it being his task to reduce all the phenomena he has to study to some fairly general and universal themes, to simplify and to assimilate, he has to keep the alertest of eyes and the most open of ears for the differences beneath the foundations. What he has to describe is in fact an extremely complicated overall system of relationship within which there may exist, much as separate planetary systems exist within a galaxy, whole constellations of powers who relate far more to their own subsystems than they do to the major systems within which they revolve. The links between these different subsystems are themselves something which require constant observation. The African role of the UAR or Algeria may disappear completely from one year to the next as the charismatic leader's attention is diverted by events on Israel's borders or the dangerous progress of the Ba'th party in Syria and Iraq. The fall of a Nkrumah or a Soekarno can alter completely the dynamics not merely of the external relations of their own countries but of the whole African nationalist or neutralist movement as such.

The Middle East, as has been pointed out elsewhere,[29] forms a particularly effective example of such a subsystem. Apart from its so-called Northern Tier of Turkey, Iran, and Afghanistan, to which Iraq is sometimes added, as by the Sa'dabad Entente of 1937 and the Baghdad Treaty of 1954 (and, of course, Israel), all the states are Arab-speaking members of the Arab League. With the exception of the extremities of the Arabian peninsula, they share a common heritage of Ottoman rule. All lay, however briefly, within the British sphere of influence during and after the second world war. All respond, whatever their local circumstances (of which more below), to a single rhetoric, that of 'unity'. This rhetoric, this common membership of a single subsystem has set certain effective limits on their performance in the field of international politics.

[28] Dennis Duncanson, *Government and Revolution in Vietnam* (London, 1968).
[29] Leonard Binder, 'The Middle East as a subordinate international system', *World Politics*, Apr. 1958.

One of these limits has had to do in the past with over-close relations with the former imperial powers. Whether from the peculiar internal logic of the country's internal balance of minorities, as with President Shamun of the Lebanon in 1958, or from the weakness of the central machinery of control, as with Iraq in 1949 and again in 1958, the attempt to establish close relations with an outside power *in order to use that relationship against another member of the subsystem,* has involved the loss of control of the domestic political scene by the government that attempted it. To seek external support to balance external pressure, or to balance the alien factor of Israel, is quite another matter.

Another of these limits has to do with effectiveness on the larger world scene. Of all the Arab leaders since 1945, only Gamal Abd al-Nasir has enjoyed what the world press would call international stature. And apart from his single visit to Bandung in 1954 and his, on the whole, unsuccessful incursions into Pan-Africanism, his role on the world stage was forced on him from outside by the failing efforts of Britain, France, and the United States to control him in 1955–6.[30] Significantly he never came to New York to the UN.

For the third element of limitation which defines the Middle Eastern subsystem is the obsession of its members with the international politics of the subsystem itself. For the statesmen of the Arab World there, politics were circumscribed by a number of interlinked problems, each of which was, to a certain extent, modal to its neighbours. There was the problem of relations between the rival centres of Cairo, Damascus, and Baghdad, each claiming a position of authority within the subsystem by virtue of history and culture, if not as a necessity to balance against even nearer rivals. There is the problem of Islamized as against secular nationalism (the refuge of the non-Sunni sects). There is the problem of the balance between the tribal monarchies and the patterns of military dominance inherited originally from the Ottomans (and the Mamlukes). There was the problem of outside efforts to control an area so geopolitically significant as a bridge between the continents and a barrier across the seaways. And there was the return of the children of Israel, more

---

[30] Watt, 'The High Dam at Aswan; a study in the politics of control', in Neville Rubin & M. Warren, *Dams in Africa* (London, 1968).

single-minded, more monotheistic, more tribal, more martial, and more united, the epitomization of the ideal towards which so much Arab rhetoric reached out, at once the centre of all Arab politics, the yardstick by which the 'Arabism' of the individual countries could be measured, the challenge to Arab aspirations, and the continuing obsession of their waking and their dreaming. For no other subsystem can so many forces be found to work together, not Sub-Saharan Africa with its trans-Zambezian obsession, not Latin America with its gringophobia and pan-Hispanic sentiments, not South-east Asia crouched beneath the shadow of China and the anxieties of Washington.

In this work the generalist is more than usually dependent on access not merely to sources but to opinions and ideas. The source materials on which he has to rely fall into two very general categories, official materials, speeches, press conferences, publications of diplomatic correspondence, presentations to the UN, public relations presentations, etc., and unofficial materials ranging from early memoirs to the investigations of the world press.

The generalist needs therefore a command of languages, English, French, and German being the very least. Spanish is more than useful for Latin America, Russian equally useful for Soviet studies. Such a combination has not in fact been exercised by any of the most recent editors of the *Survey*, even where they have possessed some facility in Russian or Spanish. In practice, English, French, German, and occasionally Italian have been the basic languages of research, except where an area specialist has been subcontracted, as it were, to deal with the problems of his own area. English and French are still the basic languages of diplomacy and therefore of official publications of all these governments which are anxious to reach an international audience. German is still one of the great languages of scholarship, and the generalist who has not access to it is much the poorer for it.

Official publications are very much of two categories, publications of record and publications of persuasion. In the first category are Hansard's *Parliamentary Debates*, the *Congressional Record*, the *Public Papers of the President*, the *Official Records* of the UN, the proceedings of the Bundestag and of the Assemblée Nationale. To these one must add the press releases of texts of speeches, treaties, etc. But with these one moves into a second category: that of publications inspired by official information policy. These can of course themselves be journals of record like the *Department of State Bulletin*, the journals published by the various Soviet embassies (the London journal is called *Soviet News*), the French *Documents Officiels*, the *Bulletin der Bundesregierung*. Other governments rely more on press and radio. The GDR is most likely to print its documentation in *Neues Deutschland*. The Yugoslav government publishes a documentary section in its fortnightly *Review of International Affairs*. For the Arabic governments one relies on the extensive BBC monitoring reports, which also catch a significant percentage of East European official speeches. China has its own agency, the Hsinhua News Agency, as well as the *Peking Review*, an almost unreadable compilation of speeches, leading articles, and loyal and humble addresses to the great Chairman.

The value of these differs greatly. The one element in them which makes it worth the historian's while to persist in trying to disentangle their evidential side from their often depressingly crude and obvious propaganda content is the role the official statement plays, even in the so-called totalitarian states, as an instrument of internal communication. Paradoxically it is much easier for a democratic bureaucracy to conceal its intentions from its electorate than it is for a totalitarian state. Democracies, even of the modern bureaucratic kind, enjoy a level of internal communication, that is of communication verbally and horizontally within their agencies of government, which appears, if only because of the hazards to the individual of too free a manner of expression, to be much less effective in so-called totalitarian states. In these latter, the major public speech, to the Party Congress or other gathering of the faithful, or the editorial in the party newspaper, plays an important role in the whole process by which the energies and loyalties of the faithful are maintained through the various checks and switches of party policy. It can, in essence, be at least as informative as a ministerial statement in a democratic parliament by a government spokesman.

The historian has to recognize, of course, in using these official statements that the narrative he constructs from them is essentially a record of official actions and official justifications. Even where these justifications seem to him to provide the wherewithal with which to reconstruct a concurrent narrative of the intellectual arguments used to rationalize and defend the official actions, the historian has to acknowledge that he has only a part of the story. Given the closed societies of totalitarian councils or democratic bureaucracy, that may well be all the overt evidence he can secure.

It is at this stage that the historian is forced back on deduction and speculation. Such processes can only be justified if they are related to what is known or inferred about the manner in which decisions are reached and policies formulated in the different societies with which he has to deal. In part these inferences may be purely concerned with mechanical matters. For the historian to elucidate the timing of the original Soviet decision to implace MRBMs in Cuba, for example, he has to allow for a certain lapse of time for the release from store, loading in port, shipping to Cuba (presumably from Black Sea ports) of the missiles. The political preparation—the persuading of the Castro regime to give room to the missiles—provides him with a different time scale. But taken together they make it clear that the Soviet decision must have been taken *before* Raúl Castro's visit to Moscow in early July 1962 and that those who put the vital communication with the Cubans at Guevara's visit at the end of August are crediting the Soviet machinery of state with an organizational flexibility which is probably unrealistic. Knowledge of the Soviet system of reserving major moves to the most senior members of the Soviet hierarchy make it very difficult to accept that the Soviet decision to place MRBMs in Cuba was given to the Cubans on any later occasion.[31]

The contemporary historian must pause at this point to note a continuing deterioration in the general level of official documentation on international affairs, a deterioration which is not confined to a single nation or, indeed, group of nations, but which appears so universal as to suggest a sociological rather than a political explanation. This deterioration can be observed in two particular aspects. The first is in the quality of official publications of the variety known to the historian as 'coloured

[31] For a more detailed argument on this point see Watt, *Survey, 1962*, pp. 47–8. This account agrees with that given by Hugh Thomas, *Cuba, the pursuit of freedom* (London, 1971), pp. 1387 ff., who tentatively dates the Soviet decision in April. Thomas suggests, however, that the Soviet decision may have been hinted at to the Cubans *before* Raúl Castro's visit to Moscow.

books', Blue Books, Yellow Books, White Books and white papers, etc. This deterioration has long been marked in the case of British Blue Books, which were originally collections of diplomatic correspondence between the Foreign Office and embassies abroad.[32] Since 1945 they have dwindled to being mere collections of public documents introduced by a historical narrative or essay whose ordinary merits are much reduced by the official style and the anonymity of the author.[33] An exception should still, in the British case, be made for those command papers which cover the reports of the British delegations to the UN and to the disarmament conferences. Even here the current practice of printing the individual speeches separately rather than in sequence neither illuminates the course of the proceedings nor enlightens as to British policy.

But these are very much the exception when compared with those parliamentary papers which are intended to be an annual presentation of British defence policy. Time was when the annual *Statements on Defence* were detailed and intelligible statements of policy.[34] Of recent years they have degenerated into glossy exercises in Dr Panglossery. Even the quinquennial statements are not as illuminating as they used to be.[35]

Britain once led the way with her diplomatic publications. Her example on the extension of open diplomacy is now being echoed as she slides ever further into Madison Avenue. Three examples of this will suffice. In 1969 the West German government produced, for the first time, their own defence white paper.[36] The following year was to see its successor, the product of an unprecedented cooperation between the West German military authorities and civilian advisers called in by the Social

---

[32] For comments on the decline, even in the 19th century, in the quality of British Blue Books, see H. V. Temperley & Lilian Penson, *A Century of Diplomatic Blue Books* (London, 1938). See also A. J. P. Taylor, *The Struggle for Mastery in Europe* (London, 1954), pp. 569 ff., and Watt, *Personalities and Policies, studies in the formulation of British foreign policy in the twentieth century* (London, 1965), pp. 223–5.

[33] For a typical example see Cmnd 1552, Germany No. 2 (1961): *Selected Documents on the Berlin Question 1944–61.*

[34] e.g. Cmd 5107 (1936), *Statement Relating to Defence.*

[35] Compare e.g. Cmnd 124 (1957), *Defence, Outline of Future Policy*, with its successors, Cmnd 1639 (1962), *Statement on Defence 1962, the next five years*, Cmnd 3203 (1967), *Statement on the Defence Estimates 1967*, and Cmnd 3357 (1967), *Supplementary Statement on Defence Policy.*

[36] Bundesministerium für Verteidigung, *White Paper 1969 on the Defence Policy of the Government of the Federal Republic of Germany.*

Democratic Defence Minister, Helmut Schmidt.[37] Nothing could make German intellectuals write as vacuously as the authors of the British defence white papers. But the presentation of what was supposedly an important restatement of German defence policy leant heavily on the often unsubstantiated citation of foreign authorities and the employment of visual aids more usually encountered in sales presentations than in statements of government policy. The Japanese were to be seduced by the same concern for packaging with their white paper on defence published in the fall of 1970.[38] But neither could match the syrup-bland verbosity of President Nixon's report to Congress of 18 February 1970, entitled *United States Foreign Policy for the 1970s: a new strategy for peace*,[39] or, as it is familiarly known to Nixonologists, the 'End of the World Message', which will long stand as a monument to the disasters which have befallen the language of Washington, Jefferson, Adams, and Lincoln.

The second cause of deterioration arises from the inability of government information agencies to leave well alone, and confine themselves to providing the consumers of these products with the raw, unpolished information they need. It is getting more and more difficult for a contemporary historian actually to lay his hands on the actual text of official government statements or communiqués. What one gets instead is an information officer's rewriting of it, all recast into *oratio obliqua*, often rearranged in an order which seems dictated only by the rewriter's sense of the fitting, and generally so transmogrified that the historian has not the faintest idea how much of the actual text he is getting.

Once again the prime offenders in this are the British government. The only official publications which review the actions and manifestations of British foreign policy are the fortnightly *Survey of Commonwealth Affairs*, retitled in 1971 the *Survey of Current Affairs*, published by the Central Office of Information, and the series *British and Foreign State Papers*, published intermittently by the British Foreign Office through the Stationery Office. It is not unknown for the editors of the *Survey of Commonwealth/*

---

[37] The same, *Weisbuch 1970: Zur Sicherheit der Bundesrepublik Deutschland und zur Lage der Bundeswehr.*
[38] Japan Defense Agency, *The Defense of Japan* (Tokyo, 1970).
[39] USIS London text, 1970.

Current Affairs to print actual texts of communiqués, but it is very rare for them to publish the texts of official speeches. In part, one suspects this arises from the convention that only ministerial statements to parliament (faithfully recorded by the shorthand writers of Hansard) have any real validity as statements of British foreign policy. Speeches outside parliament can only be counted if they are laid before parliament in the form of parliamentary papers.[40] In actuality, however, the curiosity of MPs (whether individual or constitutional) is satisfied by the increasingly frequent practice of placing texts of ministerial speeches made to other audiences in the Library of the House of Commons; and there would seem no real excuse for not gathering together such texts into an official publication. At the moment, however, there is no sign of this being done. And the author of this essay is, as a result, editing an unofficial publication designed to fill the gap.[41] (It should be noted that, unlike any other major government, Her Majesty's Stationery Office reserves the right to charge a royalty on all unofficial republication of texts covered by crown copyright—a practice which could face those who attempt to do what HMSO will not do itself with a financial charge sufficient to make their attempt impossible without a subsidy. How this curious practice is reconciled with the duty laid on the government of any democracy of facilitating the spread of knowledge of its own actions is not clear.)

As for the series *British and Foreign State Papers*, its main defects are that it is extremely expensive, superfluous, and very much delayed in appearance. Its contents reduplicate those of the Parliamentary Papers series on the one hand, and the UN Treaty Series on the other.

The practice of rewriting is spreading to the publications of other governments. The West German *Bulletin*, issued weekly by the Press and Information Office of the Federal German government; the *Democratic German Report* published in East Berlin; even the invaluable *Soviet News* issued by the Soviet Embassy in London are coming more and more to be the

[40] As, for example, Anthony Barber's opening statement in Brussels on the third British application to join the Common Market, Cmnd 4401, Miscellaneous No. 12 (1970), *The United Kingdom and the European Communities*.

[41] D. C. Watt & James Mayall, eds., *Current British Foreign Policy; documents, statements, speeches 1970* (London, 1971).

province of the rewrite men. The Italian bimonthly review, *Italy, Documents and Notes*, published by the Presidency of the Council of Ministers almost entirely belies its name by reason of its editorial policy; while the governments of the third world —and, be it said, their Organizations of Unity, etc.—either do not believe in publishing texts at all or allow their own series to fall so far behind as to belie most of the purposes for which they are being published. Only the American government, with its admirable *Department of State Bulletin*, and the various European and inter-American international agencies can really be said to pursue a publications policy which is designed to help the contemporary historian by providing him with accurate and timely copies of their own documentation. An exception, an unhappy exception, is the UN itself whose distribution machinery is so slow, and the publication of whose official proceedings is so far delayed at times as seriously to inconvenience the historian outside New York.[42] The UN *Monthly Chronicle* goes some way to bridge the gap; it also publishes the texts of speeches and press conferences given by the Secretary-General.

The President of the United States is, of course, alone among American elected or appointed officials immune to that curiosity of Congress which makes the investigation of American foreign policy at first sight so comparatively simple a task for the contemporary historian. Such a historian, however, can easily be misled. The evidence of the American official subjected to the processes of Congressional inquiry is liable to two great distortions. In the first place he can plead security to censor and edit the evidence he gives in closed session. In the second, both national pride and diplomatic practice make it impossible for him, save in exceptional circumstances, to depict the decisions of the American government as responses to communications from foreign governments. American foreign policy has come therefore to be discussed (save where as with the court of J. F. Kennedy, evidence in other terms has been provided) as though it was the product of autonomous intellectual processes and judgements of an ethical or conceptual nature. Much is made of 'doctrines' and 'designs', of responsiveness to movements of American public opinion in and out of Congress, factors

---

[42] In Dec. 1970 Chatham House Library's collection of printed records of the Security Council was not complete beyond 1966.

no doubt of considerable importance, yet misleading if they are taken as the only factors bearing on the President and his advisers. The international historian has to resist the picture this evidence provides (and his American colleagues often insist on) of a political institution in the field of international politics for which in some mysterious way the normal range of actions and interactions that make up international relationships have been suspended.

From the official handout the historian is forced to turn to the parliamentary statement. Here again the historian has to consider in each case the circumstances, both national and particular in which each statement is given. In general, however, the convention by which concealment is legitimate but misdirection is not, and the common experience in the administration of foreign affairs shared between minister and opposition (something almost entirely lacking in the Congressional system) makes for fuller and more reliable information. There is still the irritating convention by which governments may refuse to reveal the sense of diplomatic communications. But in general these statements are among the most important official sources the contemporary historian can command.

They are, nevertheless, by no means sufficient. Nor are they the only channel by which a government seeks to inform us and enlist our support by the release of information about its policy. There remains the press, to be employed directly and openly by the medium of press conferences, or indirectly by means of the off-the-record briefing, or the plain or planted 'leak'.

The press conference itself has, of course, become a recognized medium of diplomacy—or at least of international communication—when used by a head of state, head of government, minister of foreign affairs or his deputy. The use made varies with the personality of the particular *Prominenter*. John Foster Dulles was famous for using the press conference as a means of conveying to his allies messages either too unpleasant to be entrusted to the normal channels of diplomacy or intended publicly to pull the rug out from under any stand of theirs of which he disapproved.[43] President Kennedy, calling in the television and radio men, used them as an instrument of com-

---

[43] For extracts from Dulles's famous press conference of 13 Sept. 1956 see *Documents, 1955* (1959), pp. 210–19.

munication with his electorate so immediate as to cause most of his successors to recoil from something so totally beyond the scope of any second thoughts. His press secretary, Pierre Salinger,[44] has revealed that he did this against the advice of his most experienced foreign policy advisers, Dean Rusk, McGeorge Bundy, and Theodore Sorensen. President de Gaulle, following Kennedy's practice, though not perhaps his example, made his press conferences sufficiently occasional as to be events of major international importance. At least one, that of January 1963, combined the methods of both Kennedy and Dulles. His successor has made little use of the device, well knowing that the ability to address a gathering of newsmen as though they represented a world congress of historians of the future is given only to a very few.

With the press as a source of leaks, of assessment and information the contemporary historian faces a much more difficult task. The 'leak' or the off-the-record briefing can usually be recognized for what it is, and has to be submitted to the usual process of speculation as to its accuracy or motivation before it can be embodied in the historian's collection of evidence.[45] But a great deal of the press evidence today comes from analysis and interpretations of such evidence provided by editorial writers or foreign correspondents of the various newspapers—and here the contemporary historian is in a more difficult position since he has to assess the source of the correspondent's information, the motivation of the correspondent and the editorial policy of the newspaper in which the report appears, all items which can only really be assessed on the basis of more evidence than the written sources themselves supply. For that reason the contemporary historian often finds that he has to turn social anthropologist and examine the whole social milieu in and out of which the report may come. There is, it is true, an element of instant historiography in this—but it is in essence unavoidable. And the contemporary historian can only with difficulty dispense with his own or others' first-hand appreciation of the authors of press reports and the *milieux* in which they operate. It is difficult

[44] 'Exposing the President', *NYT*, 24 Sept. 1970.
[45] A very interesting exercise in comparing briefings given by different departments on the same subject is, for example, those given by the Foreign Office and the Ministry of Defence in Aug. and Sept. 1956 on British policy towards Egypt.

for example not to be struck by the way in which *The Times* correspondent in Washington in the first year of the Kennedy presidency became the mouthpiece for a 'doveish' group whose arguments otherwise found no echo in the American press, or how Henry Brandon, the Czech-born Washington correspondent of the *Sunday Times*, managed to achieve a rapport with the administration of President Johnson which made him a far better source than any of the other correspondents in Washington, American or foreign. The historian of the twentieth century will be able to draw parallels with the evidence provided by the *History of The Times* (see especially vols. iii & iv), a recent study of the Soviet ambassador in Britain, Ivan Maisky,[46] or with Admiral Sir John Fisher's use of J. L. Garvin.[47] The most extraordinary example known to the author is that of the late G. E. R. Gedye, correspondent in Vienna of various British newspapers in the 1930s, whose study of Austria's submergence under Hitler, *Fallen Bastions* (1939), though written in 1939, has not been shown by any of the researches of more recent historians, to have missed any significant detail of his story. His accuracy of vision and width of sources of information must have been remarkable in the extreme. It is only too rare to encounter a foreign correspondent in the 1960s, let alone the 1970s, who can command so consistently accurate and well-informed a picture of the policies on which he writes. The contemporary historian finds himself therefore growing ever more chary of the press, save where he can compare the reportage of a number of the world's great newspapers, the *Financial Times*, *Le Monde*, the *Neue Zürcher Zeitung*, the *New York Times* with the more leisurely (and better researched) analyses to be met in the pages of *The Economist*, *Die Zeit*, *Le Monde diplomatique* or in the more specialized publications of the various research institutes,[48] in whose pages the journalist has moved through the intermediate stage of political commentator into that of analyst or historian. For parts of the world where both press and news services operate under strict government control and command only a limited degree of ability as in Indonesia, Latin America, or much of

[46] Sidney Astor, 'Ivan Maisky and Parliamentary anti-Appeasement', in A. J. P. Taylor, ed., *Lloyd George: twelve essays* (London, 1971).

[47] Alfred M. Gollin, *'The Observer' and J. L. Garvin, 1908–14* (London, 1960).

[48] Among which should be mentioned *The World Today*, *Survival*, *Europa-Archiv*, the *China Quarterly*, *Orient* and *Oriente moderno*, *Osteuropa*, and *Orbis*.

Africa and the Middle East, the historian's mistrust of the press must increase.

Clearly underlying all these problems of source materials is the width of evidence the generalist now has to cover. For a chapter on Sino-Soviet relations, for example, he will have to examine not only the pronouncements of the Soviet and Chinese press. He will also have to survey the whole spectrum of the international communist movement, paying particular interest to the position occupied by the Italians, the Rumanians, the Indonesians, and the North Vietnamese. Even to bring together the pronouncements of all these various parties is not easy. To compare them, to spot the varying nuances of position and language, the generalist has to seek guidance. Not all even of an annual *Survey* today can be original research. All that the generalist can contribute is his own feel for the way a large-scale socio-political organization like the world communist movement functions, and his judgement of the degree to which each participating national party has come to look on the world through national rather than ideological glasses.

The *Survey* today has to comprehend six or seven distinct subsystems of international relations, in addition to the larger sets of relationships between each of the leaders of the two blocs with themselves and with China. Western Europe, Eastern Europe, Latin America, the Middle East, Sub-Saharan Africa, the Indian Ocean, South-east Asia, all form individual subsystems the states of which both serve as an arena for great-power relations and comprise a functioning set of interrelationships between themselves, and with other subsystems. For many of them these politics are in part institutionalized in regional schemes for defence or economic collaboration. Over and above them rides the UN and the other major global institutions, the IMF, the World Bank, GATT, the Organization of Petroleum Exporting Companies, the Conference of the Committee on Disarmament. To deal with reports from these subsystems the British Foreign Office maintains forty-one departments. To write reflectively on these is not beyond the task of the historian: but it needs time.

Hence the new approach Chatham House is to adopt in the future to the question of providing a first narrative in the general field of international history. The concept of an annual

Survey is to be abandoned. Instead the general editor of a new series would advise on commissioning and writing volumes dealing with sections of these various systems and subsystems over more extended periods of time. His advice would naturally be given in accordance with his general historical view of the course of international affairs in the contemporary period, and it will follow his general analysis of the structures and substructures of the international system. So far, this approach has been incorporated in the individual volumes of the 1961–3 series, each of which is divided into three main sections: relations between the major powers and power blocs, relations within the subsystems of the third world, and interaction and interventions of powers within the first category with powers and groups of powers within the second. Thus within the *Survey 1961* volume, the Berlin crisis, disarmament negotiations, the Soviet attempt to introduce the Troika principle into the UN, the British decision to apply for membership of the Common Market, the annual conference of the IMF, and the development of the Sino-Soviet split fitted fairly obviously into the first section. The Indian annexation of Goa, the Belgrade conference of 'uncommitted states', and African problems (excluding the Congo) fell fairly naturally into the second category, while the setting up of the Alliance for Progress, the Kuwaiti appeal to Britain, the Bizerta incident between France and Tunis, the developments in the Congo, and the Évian negotiations between France and the Algerian FLN fall into the third category, that of 'Great Power intrusions into the Third World', as it is styled in the list of contents.

Following this model the contemporary historian of the 1960s would find no difficulty in projecting four or five volumes to follow this general pattern. The major element in relations between the great powers in the latter part of the 1960s is clearly the gradual separation of the United States and the Soviet Union from their associates, their abstention from initiatives in Europe in favour of concentration on direct negotiations on aspects of the international limitation of armaments, and their consequent partial loss of control over the actions and initiatives of their European associates. The distance between the abandonment of the proposals of 1963–4 for a NATO multilateral force and the doubts and hesitations expressed in the United

States in 1970 over the conclusion by the West German government of treaties with the Soviet Union and Poland, while, at
the same time, the United States government was moving from
signing the Non-Proliferation Treaty on to bilateral talks with
the Soviet government on the limitation of strategic arms, is
clearly considerable; such a movement must form the subject
of a single study in itself, to which developments inside Western
and Eastern Europe make an obvious appendage.

The growing American involvement in Vietnam is, of course,
the other side of American policy during the same period. What
makes it in a way isolatable from the general development of
East-West relations over the same period is that the course of the
Vietnam war had remarkably little direct effect on the balance
of power in Europe or, for that matter, on the course of direct
American-Soviet relations. The United States authorities were
well aware of—indeed they made great propaganda capital out
of—the Soviet support, both material and moral, for the forces
of North Vietnam. But apart from bewildering their own
soldiery, who seem never to have been quite sure whether they
were engaging in a limited war to maintain the power balance
in South-east Asia or whether they were crusading for Christian
civilization against Asian communism, the American government was unwilling to allow Soviet intervention to influence
American-Soviet relations elsewhere, so long as that intervention took the form of arms supplies only. The Soviet government,
for its part, having its own preoccupations along its Asian frontiers, appeared willing to maintain the status quo in Europe,
save for the terrible year of 1968 when the actions of the Dubček
government in Czechoslovakia, the initial success of West
German overtures to Eastern Europe, and, perhaps also, the
brief appearance of the National Democratic Party in West
Germany brought them to reassert their control in Eastern
Europe and to seem momentarily to threaten a new forward
policy in Central Europe. For this reason, and by reason of the
complexities of American alliance policy in Eastern and South-
east Asia and in the Pacific, it would seem logical to treat the
course of the international aspects of the Vietnamese war at
least from the incident in the Gulf of Tonking in 1964 to the
opening of the Paris Peace talks in a single volume. A third
volume should obviously deal with the course of economic

and financial diplomacy, the Kennedy round negotiations, the development of the IMF special drawing rights, the gradual bonding together of the countries of the third world in UNCTAD, etc. A fourth would cover the development of sub-Saharan Africa as a subsystem and the ebb and flow of the 'confrontation' between the Anglophone and Francophone states and between both and the Portugal–Rhodesia–South Africa 'white African' bloc.

Thus far we could have four separate studies of international affairs in the mid- and later 1960s. One further theme is the development of international politics in the Middle East. Here the historian is, at the time of writing, still unclear as to the period he should favour. The outbreak of the Six-Days' War in 1967 has already been more than generously treated by contemporary historians, though perhaps 'freely' would be a better description than 'generously'. Yet seen in a longer perspective, it was clearly (as the author of this piece argued at the time) a quite inconclusive episode in the general development of international politics in the Middle Eastern subsystem. The co-operation it appeared to have established between the American and Soviet governments was a temporary phenomenon. The strength which the state of Israel demonstrated placed her government in a better bargaining position militarily than before 1967, but her basic problem was political rather than military, and all that can be said of the effects of the Israeli victory over Egypt and the territorial improvement in her overall strategic position was that in political bargaining terms it placed Israel in a different position, rather than a stronger one, than that she occupied in previous years. The contemporary historian must, on balance, decide that the commissioning of a survey of international affairs in the Middle East ought perhaps to be delayed, until a more justifiable *terminus ad quem* can be recognized.

It is, of course, with the twin problems of periods and perspective that the historian who attempts, as the editor of the annual *Survey* and whatever volumes take over the task of historical pioneering laid down some forty-seven years ago by Arnold Toynbee does attempt, to work up to the ever receding historical frontier of the present, must be most continuously concerned. It is very easy to be misled or to fall in too easily for whatever fashion is current. Mistakes are of course inevitable.

The historian cannot afford, however, to be deterred by the fear of making such mistakes. It is his task to stand back from the present, to attempt to view it and the recent past from the perspective of the future, recognizing that it is in the nature of pioneering work both to leave its stamp on and to be overtaken by the work of those who follow after. If all historical work is an expression of the state of mind of an age, if, as R. G. Colling-wood argued, events are fixed and only historical perspective changes, then the historian of the advancing frontier must abandon his fears of supersession and recognize the myth of the definitive study for what it is, the outcome of a historical view of reality as metaphysical in its way as Plato's shadow pictures. The avoidance of fashion, the rejection of febrility, the main-tenance of historical balance, the avoidance of these pitfalls into which the receding telescope effect of the present so often lures the unwary, the maintenance of objectivity so clearly urged by the founder of the Stevenson Chair, and the application of the tested and tried processes of historical research and hypothesis, are tasks laid on him. He could do much worse than follow the example set in 1923–4 by the original initiators and begetters of the annual *Survey of International Affairs*.

7 Commonwealth Studies

J. D. B. MILLER

THE study of the Commonwealth has often been an untidy business, because the Commonwealth has been in a state of continual change. Basically, it consists of a former imperial power and its former dependencies: it is an international association, comparable, though not similar, to the UN or the OAS. The problem of continual change has arisen because the rate of progress towards independence of Britain's dependencies has not been uniform, and so the Commonwealth has been a different thing at different times. In 1920 it was an association of Britain with four or five settler colonies; in 1970 it was an association with thirty former dependencies, only a small minority of which had been settled by the British or any other group of Europeans. At all stages during the fifty intervening years the Commonwealth was either undergoing significant change or was likely to do so. It is not surprising, therefore, that studies of it have not confined themselves to the relations between Britain and those countries which had attained full self-government, but have also dealt with its progenitor, the British Empire, in its various stages of development; with the domestic politics of its various parts; and with the process of self-government as an aspect of British policy.

I

Impressed by the latter point, a Canadian scholar has maintained that Britain's preoccupation with the Commonwealth has been essentially with 'those of its problems which precede rather than postdate the independence of its members'. He goes on:

One may discern this preoccupation alike in politicians and in academicians. Westminster abounds with expertise in problems of colonial administration, but one reads Hansard in vain for significantly specialized knowledge of, say, Anglo-Canadian relations, Anglo-Indian relations (after 1947), or the nuances of Commonwealth constitutional development. In the same way, if one examines the literature of Commonwealth studies, one is struck by the fact that most of the outstanding contributions are the work of hands outside the United Kingdom. Australians, Canadians, Irishmen, and, recently, Indians (working out of the School of International Studies in New Delhi) have illuminated the Commonwealth scene; but few if any Englishmen. This is not to denigrate British scholarship. There are brilliant contributions from Britain, but on colonial affairs, not Commonwealth affairs. Is it wholly coincidental that the interests of such intellects as Margery Perham or Lord Hailey or Kenneth Robinson—to name the first who come to mind—are centred upon problems of pre-independence rather than those of independence and after? Books have of course been written by Englishmen about the Commonwealth. But these are mostly exhortatory, not analytical: they proclaim the Commonwealth to be a good thing, they extol the ideal of a multi-racial community, they urge rich nations to share their wealth with poor nations. This Baden-Powell conception of Commonwealth is admirable in its way, but offers little to people trying to make up their minds about policy.[1]

Professor Eayrs's point about the number of non-English writers on Commonwealth affairs will be amply illustrated below. It is fair to say, however, that much of their work was done in Britain: for example, the Australian Duncan Hall's *The British Commonwealth of Nations* (1920) was commissioned by the Fabian Society; the Australian Hancock's and the Irishman Mansergh's major works were done for Chatham House; and the Australian Wheare's book on the Statute of Westminster was written while he was Beit Lecturer in Colonial History at Oxford. Moreover, all this work received more recognition in Britain than in the countries from which the men in question had come. Nevertheless, it is perhaps understandable that more should have been done by people from countries which had only recently received the accolade of independence and Commonwealth membership, and which might be expected to be curious

[1] James Eayrs, 'The Condition of the Commonwealth' (written Apr. 1964) in his *Minutes of the Sixties* (Toronto, 1968), pp. 181–2. Cf. also the statement of another Canadian that the work of Hancock and Mansergh 'is evidence that creative writing on the Commonwealth as well as its creative statesmanship tends to come from the periphery rather than from the center' (Frank H. Underhill, *The British Commonwealth* (Durham, N.C., 1956), p. 105).

about the institution to which they now belonged, than by Englishmen who were still concerned about how their remaining dependencies might behave. There has not been, at any stage since Canada, India, Ireland, Australia, and New Zealand became self-governing, much interest in those countries in British colonial policy, except when that policy, as in Rhodesia, became an issue of widespread international concern. Certainly, there was little readiness on the part of their governments to take any responsibility for British colonial policy. In Britain, on the other hand, it was a matter of frequent debate in the 1930s and 1940s (in the context of India), the 1950s and the 1960s; there was no escaping it.

We need not be surprised if British scholars have spent more time on imperial than on post-imperial problems, especially since some of the scholars from outside have sympathized with this position. To Sir Keith Hancock, in the 1930s, the Empire was flowing too vigorously to let itself be congealed in two separate seas of 'Empire' and 'Commonwealth' respectively: it was 'best to regard the British Commonwealth, not as part of the British Empire, but as the whole British Empire. . . . In this view, the British Commonwealth is nothing else than the "nature" of the British Empire, defined, in Aristotelian fashion, by its end.'[2] The end was 'the government of men by themselves'. Such a view, while appropriate to the constant state of flux in which both Empire and Commonwealth have been involved, was less attractive in the 1930s to Canadians and South Africans, hungry for status, than to Australians and New Zealanders; and as colonies have become fewer and the balance of Commonwealth relations has tilted away from the familial towards the diplomatic level, it has become less popular in Britain itself.

Now that decolonization is almost complete, and the imperial sea has, as it were, dried up rather than congealed, British scholars may find the post-imperial aspects of the study more congenial—may, indeed, be drawn towards them of necessity, because of the need to understand the complexities of overseas Commonwealth attitudes towards Britain, if the Commonwealth framework of relationships is to be retained. Whether

---

[2] *Survey of British Commonwealth Affairs*, i: *Problems of Nationality 1918–36* (London, 1937), pp. 60–1.

one is concerned with the earlier or later periods, the substance of the Commonwealth is the relations between Britain and certain overseas countries. For people in those countries the crucial questions have been whether Britain would do what they wanted (whether in granting self-government, providing defence, or providing aid, investment, migrants, and markets); for Britain, the questions have been whether these countries would do what Britain wanted (whether in accepting peaceably the instalments of self-government provided, or in taking Britain's side in wars, or supporting British policies at the UN and elsewhere, or favouring British trade and investment). Since the settler colonies achieved self-government, and others began to move towards it, these matters have given significance to official and scholarly discussions of Empire and Commonwealth.

The business of clear definition and of division of the field between imperial and post-imperial aspects has been made more difficult by the absence of a political constitution for the Commonwealth. Even regular procedures, as distinct from a written constitution, have often been hard to define: what, for example, has 'consultation' meant at different times, in spite of its being regarded as an indispensable aspect of Commonwealth relations? The absence of constitutions and definitions has often obscured the fact that the Commonwealth is an international organization. Study of it as such has been much more difficult than, say, study of the UN and the OAS, which have written constitutions, regular procedures, and staffs of long standing. The Commonwealth is, in contrast, a protean affair which, at any stage, can accommodate conceptions of its end and operations appropriate to its past, present, and future. This gives great diversity to the literature about it.

Here we are concerned with writings about the Commonwealth as such, rather than about the individual members, between 1920 and 1970. Discussion in print was intermittent and was often variable in quality. Nevertheless, much work of high significance was done, with Chatham House books playing an active part.[3]

---

[3] Chatham House was also foremost in organizing the occasional unofficial British Commonwealth Relations Conferences, at which Commonwealth problems were discussed by delegations from the member countries. Some of the reports of these conferences are mentioned below.

It is noticeable that the literature undergoes a genuine change with the advent of the Asian members in 1947. Before that date it is one sort of Commonwealth that most books discuss; afterwards it is another. A few books bridge the gap and might be read with profit at any time, because of their insight into the essential character of the Commonwealth association. By and large, however, 1947 forms both a symbolic and an actual divide. In the twenty-seven years between 1920 and 1947, men were writing about the preparation and realization of the 'Statute of Westminster Commonwealth' which was formally defined in 1926 and 1931. In the twenty-three years from 1947 to 1970 they wrote about the achievement and working out of what might be called the 'Afro-Asian Commonwealth'. It could be argued that the association was different after 1947, because of its changed membership and the changed international circumstances in which it had to operate; certainly, the tone of the discussion is very different indeed.

II

In 1920 it was still possible to discuss the Empire in much the same terms as before the first world war, provided one was sufficiently single-minded. Two notable theoreticians of an earlier decade, Lionel Curtis and Richard Jebb, were still writing, and might have carried on their previous argument as 'centralist' and 'autonomist' respectively.[4] Jebb did continue with his previous notions, publishing *The Empire in Eclipse* in 1926, and *His Britannic Majesty*, a book almost totally unnoticed, in 1935. These took up many of the points already made in his more vigorous prewar works, but Jebb could not be satisfied with postwar politicians, even when they seemed to be following a path which he had already charted. Although he had applauded the 'autonomism' of Alfred Deakin and Sir Wilfrid Laurier, he could not stomach the same line expressed in Afrikaner and Irish terms; and he was appalled by 'the heresy of multiple monarchy', in spite of having espoused something very like it in earlier days.

---

4 This argument is discussed in my *Richard Jebb and the Problem of Empire* (London, 1956). Curtis had wanted a federated Commonwealth with a parliament deciding issues of peace and war; Jebb, impressed by colonial nationalism in the settler countries, believed this would not be acceptable and would not work.

Perhaps Curtis sensed better the movement of time. In the 1920s he was absorbed in Indian dyarchy, Irish status, and Atlantic solidarity; his earlier Round Table concerns were less urgent. Although he still held the views expressed before the war in *The Problem of the Commonwealth* (1916) and *The Commonwealth of Nations* (1917)—and although, when the term 'British Commonwealth of Nations' began to be used widely, its origins were often attributed to him—he was moving on to wider horizons, and to that sense of the organic unity of mankind which was to be expressed in *Civitas Dei* (1938) and in a series of later books, now totally forgotten, on world federalism. The Commonwealth which was emerging in the 1920s, impelled by the meetings of Dominion representatives during the war, and pushed towards its 'Statute of Westminster' status by Irish, Canadian, and South African pressure, was not the body he had envisaged in his earlier works. Increasingly, he was concerned with other things, especially Chatham House.

Thus, neither of these two notable men contributed much to discussion of Commonwealth relations in the 1920s. If they had done so, it would have been with a backward look. That in itself would at first have been fashionable, since the experiences of the war, while ultimately responsible for encouraging further autonomy on the part of the overseas Dominions, seemed to demonstrate the essential unity of the Empire under British leadership. The recollection of the Dominions' wholehearted participation was stimulated by two of the men who had taken part in the events of the war, Sir Robert Borden and W. M. Hughes, who both published their reflections in 1929—Borden's *Canada in the Commonwealth* and Hughes's *The Splendid Adventure*. In neither case was much added to existing knowledge. Both men were past their prime and took little significant part in their countries' politics thereafter. To both, the excitements of the war were still real, and the arrangements which had produced the Imperial War Cabinet, the wartime Imperial Conference, and the representation of the Dominions at the Peace Conference seemed the summit of likely achievement for consultation and co-operation between Britain and the Dominions. It was true that these institutions had sufficed to implement the Dominions' participation in the war, which had so signally contradicted the prewar fears of Curtis and others; but were they sufficient to contain the new and less 'loyal' forces of Dominion nationalism that were becoming evident in Ireland, South Africa, and Canada?

As is well known, the 1926 Imperial Conference produced a definition which asserted the equal status of Britain and the Dominions: they were said to be freely associated and in a state of common allegiance to the Crown. It was widely considered that any government which took a 'disloyal' view (i.e. one different from what was common to the conservative and anglophile political parties of the Commonwealth) would be able to interpret 'freely associated' as 'free to dissociate', and common allegiance to the Crown as allegiance only to the Crown in respect of its operations in that government's own territory. It was feared that ideas of neutrality and secession might be encouraged. On the whole, Australians and New Zealanders shared the concern felt by conservative forces in Britain; it was the Afrikaner Nationalists, French-Canadians, and Irish Free Staters who were thought to be loosening the bonds of Empire. As before the war, a centralist and an autonomist view of the Dominions' position confronted each other, though with less precision than in the debate between Curtis and Jebb, since this time they were reflecting more closely the actual relations between Britain and the Dominions.

One highly influential work—though modish rather than deep in its treatment of the issues—was Alfred Zimmern's *The Third British Empire* (1926), written before the 1926 Imperial Conference but prefiguring much of the discussion which succeeded it. Zimmern's particular contribution lay in magnifying the role of the League of Nations (of which the Dominions were members) into that of a kind of super-Commonwealth, which would take from the Commonwealth itself the agonizing decision of peace or war, and would nullify any Dominion desire for neutrality. On the dilemma of peace or war, Zimmern wrote (p. 61), 'the Covenant of the League provides a complete and adequate solution. The pledge which Canada has refused to give to London, she has already given to Geneva.' Such an assertion assumed that the League would be able to command both a single policy and the loyalty of its members; this assumption was more tenable in 1926 than it proved to be ten years later. The apparent cogency of Zimmern's argument was so great, however, that it was still being used at the British Commonwealth Relations Conference at Toronto in 1933.[5] It enabled those who wanted to maintain the 'unity of the Empire' to remit the problem of war and peace to another body altogether. The temptation to do so was very strong.

Much of the writing about the Commonwealth in the 1930s was devoted to explanation of the Statute of Westminster of 1931, which put into legal form the decisions of the 1926 Imperial Conference. Much of the work was heavily legalistic, in particular the many volumes in the name of A. Berriedale Keith. This extraordinary man had been in the Dominions section of the Colonial Office but finished his days as a Professor of Sanskrit. He probably wrote more about the Commonwealth than anyone else before or since. The books are legalistic and repetitive, and the prose is soporific. Whether one takes *Imperial Unity and the Dominions* (1916), or *The Dominions as Sovereign States* (1938), the same droning voice seems to be saying much the same thing. Yet Keith's virtues were many. He knew, from an early date, that the Curtis 'centralist' formula would not work; he had a close knowledge of the Dominions (*War Government of the British Dominions*, published in 1921, is a remarkable piece of synoptic recent history); he provided detailed reasoning for all his conclusions; he edited an invaluable book of documents for the World's Classics; and his three volumes of letters to the newspapers[6] constitute a remarkable commentary on most of the interwar period, bringing back to life a number of long-dead controversies.

A lawyer cannot be blamed for being a lawyer; the trouble in the 1930s was that the slippery phrases of the 1926 Conference and of the Statute of Westminster gave lawyers too much scope for their own style of argument. Moreover, since 'neutrality' and 'secession' were two extreme outcomes which might emerge from the newly defined Dominion status; since South Africa was the Dominion most likely to embrace these outcomes; and since South African experience and finance were

[5] A. J. Toynbee, ed., *British Commonwealth Relations* (London, 1934), pp. 42 ff. & 179–81.

[6] The three (all published in London) are *Letters on Imperial Relations, Indian Reform, Constitutional and International Law 1916–35* (1935); *Letters and Essays on Current Imperial and International Problems 1935–6* (1936); and *The King, the Constitution, the Empire and Foreign Affairs: letters and essays 1936–7* (1938).

still very active in those circles in Britain in which Commonwealth questions were discussed, it is not surprising that there
was often a stress upon formulas to the exclusion of actuality.
Attention was too often concentrated on phrases to the exclusion
of things. Such a criticism can even be made of the brilliant
R. T. E. Latham's *The Law and the Commonwealth*.[7] The British
Commonwealth Relations Conferences of 1933 and 1938 were
very much concerned with 'status', and their reports are over-
loaded with argument about what it might entail.

The definitive work in this sphere, however, was K. C.
Wheare's *The Statute of Westminster and Dominion Status* (1938).
Combining wide legal knowledge with a canny political understanding, this book clearly stated the dilemmas of the situation,
and provided wise guidance about how they might develop;
five editions later, they had developed so much that the author
felt impelled to write a new book with a new title to replace his
former work.

Much of the discussion in the books mentioned had been foreshadowed by a pioneering work published in London in 1920,
H. Duncan Hall's *The British Commonwealth of Nations*. It had a
considerable effect on Smuts, who used it in his attempt to get
a definition of Dominion Status in 1921.[8] The Statute of Westminster is very much anticipated in its pages, together with the
development of Dominion diplomatic resources and the change
in the position of Governors-General, which came about as a
result of the 1926 and 1930 Imperial Conferences. Hall argued
by logical extension of the principle of responsible government,
as enunciated by Lord Durham for Canada. He did not see some
of the difficulties that would arise in the 1930s, especially in the
League, which was little more than a sketch on a drawing-board
when he was writing; but he did accurately foresee the implications for constitutional change which, in due course, were
accepted by Britain.

Alongside this Australian effort of 1920 (which undeservedly
gained little lasting acclaim in the author's own country) we
may place a much larger and more widely recognized achieve-

---

[7] This first appeared as a long 'Supplementary Chapter' to Hancock's first
Survey volume (1937). It was republished as a separate volume for Chatham House
in 1949.

[8] H. Duncan Hall, 'The genesis of the Balfour declaration of 1926', *Commonwealth Polit. Stud.*, Nov. 1962.

ment, that of Hancock in his monumental *Survey of British Commonwealth Affairs*, published for Chatham House in two volumes in 1937, 1940, and 1942.[9]

Hancock's work is the most significant yet done in the field of Commonwealth studies. Almost single-handed, he made it an exciting field for students. His approach was very different from that of the often lifeless courses in Imperial History which had existed for so long. His *Survey* was detailed, eloquent, and readable. They were marked by four characteristics not often found in combination: a clear sense of political ideals; a strong grasp of political reality; a close, exact consideration of actual problems as those existed at the time; and a command of economic questions which had been sadly lacking in previous writers on the Commonwealth, who had usually confined themselves to the advocacy or rebuttal of imperial preference as it had been enunciated in the days of the Tariff Reform movement. Hancock combined a careful study of the past with a projection into the future of current trends in such unfamiliar fields as demography (as in respect of Palestine) and market conditions (as for Canadian wheat and West African cocoa). He has described[10] how, year after year, he visited colonies and Commonwealth member-states to investigate conditions on the ground. This approach, somewhat like Jebb's in prewar days, but much more extensive and exact in its application, was very different from that of the scholars who were splitting hairs about what the Statute of Westminster might mean if it meant anything. In span, scope, and style, the Hancock volumes were an advance on anything previously written.[11] Dealing equally with the Dominions and the colonies, they prepared the way for much later work.

They were not Chatham House's first, or only, efforts in the Commonwealth field during the interwar years. Apart from Lord Hailey's mighty *African Survey*, there had been a previous approach to Commonwealth relations in Arnold Toynbee's *The Conduct of British Empire Foreign Relations since the Peace Settlement*

[9] In what follows, and in later references to Mansergh's *Surveys*, I have drawn upon my contribution to *Essays presented to Sir Keith Hancock*, a special issue of *Historical Studies* (Melbourne), Oct. 1968.

[10] *Country and Calling* (London, 1954), chs. V & VI.

[11] It is very difficult to understand why they are not mentioned in Wilfrid Knapp's article, 'Fifty years of Chatham House books', in the special issue of *International Affairs* (Nov. 1970), marking the fiftieth anniversary of Chatham House.

(1928), a work which, while often shrewd in its political judgements, was vitiated by its anachronistic insistence that the British Empire (including the Commonwealth) was still a single state in relation to foreign countries. Toynbee believed this was 'not only a theorem of international law but an empirical fact of outstanding importance in international affairs' (p. 3), although he saw Dominion Status as 'a new "variation" or even "mutation" in the political life of mankind' (p. 15). The book is useful now for its examples of Dominion diplomacy in the 1920s and its illustration of the legalistic way in which Dominion status was being discussed. Something similar may be said of a Chatham House work published in 1937, *The British Empire*, a report on the structure and problems of the Empire by a Study Group headed by Field-Marshal Sir Philip Chetwode.

Chatham House's one effort in the Commonwealth field during the second world war was *The British Empire: its structure and spirit* (1943), by Eric Walker, who had spent twenty-five years as a professor of history in Cape Town. Apart from its emphasis on federalism as a political form for the Commonwealth (perhaps the final expression in print of the original Curtis doctrine), this is a type of book which appeared at intervals during the war. Lord Elton's *Imperial Commonwealth* (1945) and Ernest Barker's *Ideas and Ideals of the British Empire* (1941) were others; Hancock wrote one (*Argument of Empire*) as a Penguin Special in 1943. The aim seems to have been to refute allegations, whether from British or American sources, about the tyrannical and exploitative nature of the Empire. 'John Bull wakes up one morning to read newspaper headlines which give him the impression that Americans are making the liquidation of the British Empire one of their war aims', wrote Hancock; and this situation, coupled with the arguments at home about post-war colonial policy, produced a number of works of a more or less polemical nature, defending the Empire as something different from what much popular opinion believed it to be. Polemics rarely last. Most of these books, except for Barker's and Hancock's, can be regarded as very much works of their time. Another, rather different in its approach, was Sir Edward Grigg's *The British Commonwealth: its place in the service of the world* (1943), which took up Churchill's and Smuts's notions of a combination of Commonwealth institutions and regionalism.

Chatham House was host to the third British Commonwealth Relations Conference in London early in 1945, the year the war ended. Its report (Richard Frost, ed., *The British Commonwealth and World Society*, 1947), showed the effects of wartime experience in its lack of concern for the former status question and its strong concentration on economic issues and questions of world security. One British data paper foreshadowed the future in a prophetic manner:

Hitherto the Commonwealth has been composed of self-governing nations of the white races, but in the future it will comprise also self-governing nations of coloured peoples. This will have an important bearing on the various outlooks of the existing member nations, who will then have to accustom themselves to new ways of thinking and to a fresh conception of the British family of nations (p. 24).

Such an attitude was, however, unusual. Apart from recognizing that India would soon be independent, the participants—British as well as those from overseas—were much more concerned with social and economic progress in the remaining colonies than with political change.

III

However, once independence was achieved by India, Pakistan, and Ceylon, and particularly after India's assumption of republican status, there was a new tone in writings about the Commonwealth. On the one hand it was recognized that the 'Old Dominions' could no longer regard the Commonwealth as their own affair; on the other, that the independence of these Asian countries might be the forerunner of independence for colonies in Africa and elsewhere. Both attitudes took some time to develop. In H. V. Hodson, *Twentieth Century Empire* (1948) and John Coatman, *The British Family of Nations* (1950), there is something of a comforting feeling that things will be much the same as before the second world war, provided machinery of consultation is improved and there is some change in nomenclature. The fact that India had actually stayed in the Commonwealth was a source of relief and even surprise to many people interested in the Commonwealth. The point is apparent in F. H. Soward's report of the fourth Commonwealth Relations Conference, *The Changing Commonwealth* (1950). Nicholas

Mansergh's first contribution in the field was *The Commonwealth and the Nations* (1948), a series of essays published soon after he became Abe Bailey Professor of British Commonwealth Relations at Chatham House. These, attentive to the problems of the Old Dominions, also gave much attention to the changes that Asian membership of the Commonwealth would bring.

Pleasure at the changed but continuing character of the Commonwealth did not prevent awareness of tensions which might develop with its enlargement. In Mansergh's report of the fifth Commonwealth Relations Conference at Lahore, *The Multi-Racial Commonwealth* (1955), it is clear that by 1954 the implications of the Commonwealth's multiracial structure had begun to be felt, especially in divergence of views about foreign and defence policy and about South Africa; the beginnings of concern about colonial Africa are also apparent. One can see the same thing, from a Canadian standpoint, in the admirable lectures by Frank H. Underhill, *The British Commonwealth*, with which in 1955 the Commonwealth Studies Center at Duke University in the United States began its operations. This was the first of a valuable series of books largely concerned with individual Commonwealth countries. The Duke Center tended at first to concentrate on the Old Dominions; the Institutes of Commonwealth Studies which had been established at Oxford and London gave most of their attention to the colonies, especially in Africa, and to the growing problems of self-government. That at least one British politician had a firm grip on the nature of the Commonwealth and the problems which might arise with African membership was shown by Patrick Gordon Walker's contribution to *Fabian International Essays* (ed. T. E. M. McKitterick and Kenneth Younger, 1957).

From about 1955 onwards, writings on the Commonwealth began to show mainly an African face. This was because of the heavy British concentration upon the advancement of the African colonies. It was still widely felt that the Empire and Commonwealth could not be congealed into two separate seas. The feeling was right enough in its way, but for a time at least the Commonwealth as an association of sovereign states suffered some loss of scholarly attention in the widespread determination to equate the Commonwealth with Africa and Africa with the Commonwealth. One may note as an admirable exception

Dennis Austin's Pelican for Africans, *West Africa and the Common-wealth* (1957), in which were spelt out many of the implications of future African membership.[12] In the main, however, much of the writing of this period was as indicated in the earlier quotation from James Eayrs: it was pre- rather than post-independence. Margery Perham's admirable and perceptive writings, now happily collected in her *Colonial Sequence 1949–69* (1970), may be taken as representative of this kind of preoccupation at its best. Many books were written on Rhodesia, on South Africa, on race relations and on the individual colonies in Africa, and much was made of newly independent countries, beginning with Ghana.[13]

The Commonwealth as such was not, however, entirely neglected during this period. Nicholas Mansergh's two *Survey* volumes appeared, as did his two collections of documents.[14] This was a highly significant contribution to Commonwealth studies. Mansergh, even when writing about prewar events, wrote very much in postwar terms. There was little about colonial policy, but a great deal about how independence had been achieved and was being exercised. Both his *Survey* volumes were very much concerned with the exercise of external policy by the Dominions and the second showed a lively awareness of the new dimension that Asian membership of the Commonwealth had introduced. Much of Mansergh's work, like Hancock's, is concerned with nationalism, but Hancock's is the nationalism striving for status, while Mansergh's is the nationalism of states already established and executing policies that demonstrate their independence and their sense of national interests. Both men's *Surveys* pointed towards the future of the Commonwealth, even when dealing with its past: Hancock anticipated, to a considerable extent, the sort of Commonwealth

[12] Mention should also be made of C. E. Carrington, *The Commonwealth in Africa* (1962), a report of an unofficial study conference arranged by Chatham House at Lagos in January 1962.

[13] The decolonization process still awaits proper attention, which it is expected to get from Professor Dennis Austin in a further volume of the *Survey of Commonwealth Affairs*. Meanwhile, an engaging and helpful journalist's book is W. P. Kirkman, *Unscrambling an Empire* (London, 1966).

[14] The two *Surveys of British Commonwealth Affairs: Problems of External Policy 1931–9* and *Problems of Wartime Co-operation and Postwar Change, 1939–52*, appeared in 1952 and 1958. The two collections of documents, covering the years 1931–62, appeared in 1953 and 1963.

that Mansergh would chronicle; Mansergh looked forward to the kind that his successors would have to deal with. It was to be, essentially, a Commonwealth in which the diplomatic element predominated.[15]

This element has been emphasized by four writers from the outer Commonwealth, the Canadian James Eayrs, the Indian M. S. Rajan, the African Ali Mazrui, and the Australian T. B. Millar. Eayrs's *The Commonwealth and Suez* (1964), subtitled *A documentary survey*, is a collection of documents and commentaries on the reactions of Commonwealth members to the Suez crisis of 1956. Much more than a set of documents, it shows an acute and sophisticated awareness of the diplomatic strains engendered by the event. In *The Postwar Transformation of the Commonwealth* (1963), and in various articles, Rajan has tried to put India into the Commonwealth context, and to estimate the effect of Indian membership upon the Commonwealth. Mazrui's *The Anglo-African Commonwealth* (1967), a collection of varied essays, attempts the same for African membership. Millar, in *The Commonwealth and the United Nations* (1967), has written the only extended study of the Commonwealth in the context of international organization.

Two other notable works of the 1960s remain to be considered: Patrick Gordon Walker's *The Commonwealth* (1962) and Mansergh's *The Commonwealth Experience* (1969). Gordon Walker's is the harder to assess, even at this distance in time. He remains the only British politician to have given close attention in print to the Commonwealth;[16] his knowledge of its past is profound; and he has had ample experience of how the system of Commonwealth relations works. There is, however, a troublesome smoothness about his treatment of it in this book, arising from his conviction that the Commonwealth is a natural growth and that teleology is apparent in its development. Such an approach, as a younger scholar has trenchantly suggested,[17]

[15] Mansergh's work in this sphere had useful forerunners in C. A. W. Manning's *The Policies of the British Dominions in the League of Nations* (London, 1932), and Gwendolen Carter, *The British Commonwealth and International Security: the role of the dominions 1919–39* (Toronto, 1947).

[16] Earl Attlee's *Empire into Commonwealth* (London, 1961), the Chichele Lectures at Oxford in 1960, must be one of the most commonplace and uninformative books ever written by a politician about matters with which he was closely concerned.

[17] Peter Lyon, 'Aristotle and the Commonwealth of Nations', *Australian Outlook*, Apr. 1963.

leads to unconvincing explanations of events which diverge from what is held to be inherent in the Commonwealth's growth, and there is a sense of all being for the best in the best of all possible Commonwealths that detracts from the book's effect, fascinating and provoking though it is.

The Commonwealth Experience, a finely wrought work, is the first satisfactory history of the development of the Commonwealth from Lord Durham to the present. It draws on recently available public records for material not previously used; it is synoptic of the various historical and analytical works previously published, including Mansergh's own; and it provides a perspective which, while it is sufficiently non-English to satisfy Professor Eayrs's demands of 1964, involves close understanding of the British viewpoint on the events of this century, especially of the past forty years. Commonwealth studies come of age with this book. It is perhaps significant that in Mansergh's valedictory chapter he sees the Commonwealth as neither the continuing revelation of inherent capacity nor the continued exemplar of British freedom, but as something which may now be past its zenith, and about which disenchantment has already set in. The probing questions with which the book ends are those which politicians as well as scholars were asking in the late 1960s and will continue to ask in the 1970s.

IV

Certain conclusions may be drawn from what we have seen of the record of Commonwealth studies since 1920.

First, it will be noticed that none of the books listed is by an American, something which could probably not be paralleled in any other branch of international studies. Some Americans have worked in the field,[18] but mostly in its legal and bibliographical aspects. Americans have not found the Commonwealth of Nations an attractive topic, in spite of their investigation of so many other international bodies.[19] It would be intriguing

[18] e.g. R. B. Stewart, *Treaty Relations of the British Commonwealth of Nations* (New York, 1939), and Robin W. Winks, ed., *The Historiography of the British Empire–Commonwealth* (Durham, N.C., 1966).

[19] There is an incisive discussion in Inis L. Claude, Jr., *Swords into Plowshares* (New York, 1959), pp. 116–20, of some of the more naïve ideas about the Commonwealth. M. Margaret Ball, of Duke University, will shortly publish a study of the Commonwealth as an international institution.

to know why. One reason may be that the Commonwealth has traditionally been regarded by the American State Department and the military as a British affair, and money may not have been available to study it to the same extent as to study the organizations of Western Europe and Latin America. Another may be that, in the move away from WASP (White Anglo-Saxon Protestant) preoccupations which has characterized American scholarship since the second world war, an obviously British affair has seemed less interesting than in the days of Nicholas Murray Butler. I am inclined to think, however, that the main reason may lie in the nature of the Commonwealth itself. It is very changeable and pragmatic in its behaviour: such a body demands not only an empirical approach but also frequent changes of judgement if one is to make an effective study of its character. The looseness of arrangements and the lack of a formal constitution and formal voting records preclude both a quick understanding and an approach through legalism.[20] The Commonwealth makes theorizing hard. American scholars, imbued with systems theory, have trouble with such a loose system, especially when it is so difficult to accommodate in terms of categories of power.

It is not only Americans, of course, who have eschewed theorizing when writing about the Commonwealth: our second conclusion may be that the literature reviewed here contains very little that could be called theoretical, and is mostly historical, descriptive, and at times analytical. Hancock and Gordon Walker, of all the writers noted, come closest to theoretical constructs, with Gordon Walker as the more ambitious. His effort can hardly be regarded as successful. Yet, stripped of its teleological overtones, it amounts to little more than an analogy: the growth of the Commonwealth is like organic growth. This sort of analogical reasoning has been common to writing about the Commonwealth: it is like a club, it is like a family, it is growing up, it is breaking down. Perhaps theory can go no

[20] It is significant that Sir Kenneth Wheare's *The Constitutional Structure of the Commonwealth* (Oxford, 1960), his replacement of *The Statute of Westminster and Dominion Status*, is a much sparer and less obviously legal book than its predecessor. Two other more recent books which have effectively blended legal and political analysis are S. A. de Smith, *The New Commonwealth and its Constitutions* (London, 1964), and J. E. S. Fawcett, *The British Commonwealth in International Law* (London, 1963).

further with confidence than along analogical lines, if one is dealing with something that is not organized but has slowly developed out of a previous situation—in this case the existence of the British Empire. Some help can be gained from comparisons with other post-imperial situations, such as the Spanish, the Dutch, and the French. But each of these has such special features that the comparison can be only broad and suggestive, not exact. There is room for much study of the post-imperial relationships of the European powers, but it will need to take account of as many differences as similarities.

If it is true that little theorizing has been done, it is also true that little work has been done on the most practical side, the actual machinery of Commonwealth relations. One Chatham House book of the early 1950s (Heather J. Harvey, *Consultation and Co-operation in the Commonwealth*, 1952) stands out for its lucidity and its careful marshalling of the evidence available at the time. Hancock's and Mansergh's *Surveys* contain something, but not much. While many books have listed the variety of institutions with 'Commonwealth' in their names, little has been written about two vital aspects of the Commonwealth system, the meetings of heads of government and the activities of High Commissioners; and there is nothing which describes with any accuracy the varying degrees of access to the British government available to different Commonwealth members in the 1950s and 1960s. Similarly, we have nothing, from the standpoint of the capital of an overseas Commonwealth country, describing the impact of the Commonwealth in that particular place. Much of what has been written about machinery is derived from British official handouts, not from actual inquiry.

A fourth conclusion must be that the works listed here are disproportionately political and legal, and that hardly any of them are economic. Hancock is the one shining exception. Even the Sterling Area, the aspect of Commonwealth relations which seemed most obviously significant to many people in the 1950s, and which, while declining in the 1960s, is still significant, has had hardly any study, apart from the technical study of sterling as a currency. A. R. Conan's *The Sterling Area* (1952) was an admirable start which was not properly followed up. It is typical of the British approach to sterling that Christopher McMahon's lively Chatham House essay, *Sterling in the Sixties*

(1964), should have said almost nothing about the Commonwealth. The situation has been repaired by the publication for Chatham House of Susan Strange's *Sterling and British Policy* (1971). But, even so, it will still be the case that most books purporting to deal with Commonwealth economics have been barely concealed demands for imperial preference or for more British economic aid. The actual complications of Britain's economic relations with Commonwealth countries, in trade, aid, and investment, still await extended study.

A further conclusion may be that, in recent years, the great concentration upon Africa by people writing on the Commonwealth has been to the exclusion of other parts of the Commonwealth which could provide fascinating and enlightening study. The Caribbean countries, for example, should not have been left to a novelist like V. S. Naipaul, in spite of his perceptive touch. As Professor Eayrs has suggested, British writers seem not to have been interested in their own country's relations with India and Canada. At the same time, it is fair to say that the Indians and Canadians, while sometimes writing about the Commonwealth, have not written about relations with Britain. In 1964–5, when trying to write a book on Britain's relations with the Old Dominions, I could not find any good study of British relations with Canada, Australia, New Zealand, or South Africa, whether written in Britain or in these countries themselves; and although this has been remedied in respect of South Africa,[21] it remains true in other cases. There is still a great lack of studies of the web of bilateral relations which has so far sustained the Commonwealth. The task is difficult in each case, since it involves not only political relationships but also those of a social, economic, and legal character; but it is a challenge which should be taken up.

The basic problem for the future will not be the lack of things to study about the Commonwealth, but the lack of will to do so. The Commonwealth has suffered from over-selling by politicians in the past; it is now being under-sold in Britain and in most of the countries which belong to it. The under-selling is largely a result of the unsatisfied expectations aroused by the over-selling. In any case, study of the institution has been hampered (though in some ways encouraged) by its constant rele-

[21] By Dennis Austin's Chatham House book, *Britain and South Africa* (1966).

vance to politics in Britain: the Conservative Party has had its own Commonwealth, as it were, in the Old Dominions, while the Labour Party has had its rival Commonwealth in Asia and Africa. Such a division is grotesque in terms of governmental policy, but not in terms of attitudes and opinions. 'Progressive' people have found the old Commonwealth stuffy; their opposites have found the new Commonwealth unfamiliar and unwelcome. Academic attitudes have often developed out of these popular stereotypes. The Commonwealth itself, so obviously feeble in comparison with organizations of alleged power such as NATO and the EEC, has not rated highly as something to study. Whether the increasingly bilateral nature of Britain's relations with Commonwealth members will lead either to closer studies of those bilateral relations, or to analysis and theorizing about the Commonwealth as it was before this state of affairs set in, remains to be seen.

8   Ex Africa Semper Eadem ?

DENNIS AUSTIN

WITHIN the general province of international relations, Africa
has not been given much attention for reasons which are per-
fectly plain. Relations between states are determined by their
past, and may be studied as diplomatic history; or by their power
(to alter the balance between opposed interests) as the central
fact in international politics. The African states have tended to
be excluded from both kinds of study since most of them have no
recorded history other than that of a colonial dependency and
because, with few exceptions, they lack the power to play a
major part in world affairs. Underlying this disregard in earlier
years was perhaps an old established view also of Africa as a half-
savage continent set apart from the main centres of civilization. There is little account of tropical Africa (south of Ibn
Khaldun and the Mahgreb) in Toynbee's ten volumes.[1] Some
exceptions had to be made. The Near East spilled over into
North Africa. South Africa, the country of Smuts, was of interest as a member of the British Commonwealth. And from
time to time Africa was acted upon, dragged into the world by
external powers as in Abyssinia in 1935 or during the military
campaigns of two world wars. But the great heart of Africa was
imperial territory, for which the proper study was Commonwealth or colonial policy, and within that special field in the
1930s and 1940s there appeared a work of monumental splen-
dour (Greek not Roman in its artistry) by Sir Keith Hancock.

[1] There is a strange reference to African nationalism in vol. ix, p. 455. 'The
example of an insurgent Asia might be followed by an effervescent Africa whose
soldiers had seen the World and taken stock of it in the South-east Asian and West
European war zones of a Second World War; and, as the spark ignited by Russian
Communism travelled along a train of gun-powder long since laid by Western
Imperialism, it was not inconceivable that it might fire the native peasantry in a
chain of Latin American republics, from Mexico to Paraguay inclusive, that had
been planted on the volcanic soil of buried Andean and Central American worlds.'

How firmly it stands still! And how interesting is the strong affection—respect, too, and concern—which the Commonwealth once inspired in scholars. But in the great *Surveys* there was no examination of 'black Africa' in world affairs. How could there be? In Hancock's volumes it was palm oil and cocoa on the west coast, the conflict of imperial interests in East and Central Africa. Nor was there much awareness that the spread of nationalism through Africa was to be as characteristic a feature of the mid-twentieth century as it had been of Europe and Asia in earlier decades. 'Not much awareness': but there was some, and perhaps understandably it found expression in the large *African Survey* by Lord Hailey who brought his Indian experience to bear on Africa: an often undervalued and now neglected book which, like its four successor volumes on *Native Administration*, is full of a concealed wisdom and doubt about the ability of the colonial regimes to contain the pressures for change which they themselves had encouraged.

And today? The floodgates are opened and we have almost drowned. 1960 was designated by the UN 'Africa's Year', a dismal label in view of the troubles which have since befallen the continent from the problems of the Congo to the most recent coup[2] in Uganda in 1971. But the publishing world seems to have taken the designation seriously. Books on Africa—tragedy, comedy, history, pastoral—filled the shops and libraries and post-graduate seminar rooms, a profitable flood for those carried along with the tide, although there still remained the problem of describing Africa's place in 'world affairs'. Many of the early studies were of nationalist politics and the achievement of independence, the leading scholars being Americans, with whom political science had been closely related to sociology and the taxonomy of terms. As part of an attempt to 'place' the new states, the African regimes were arranged and frequently re-arranged under classificatory systems which must certainly have mystified the African leaders themselves, assuming they came across them: pragmatic-pluralist systems, revolutionary-centralizing, mobilizational, reconciliational, modernizing-transitional, even 'prismatic' societies and regimes.[3] Alas, poor

---

[2] At the time of writing.

[3] The prototype being G. Almond & J. Coleman, *Politics of the Developing Areas* (Princeton, 1960).

readers, and unhappy students, beset by terms which now mean too much to mean anything at all. There were of course books about African politics of a simpler kind, some by British and African authors, others by American scholars, which tried to describe what was taking place—Chatham House published two straightforward studies, first of the politics of Ghana and then of post-independent politics in the Congo—until by the end of the 1960s the continent had been well mapped, more than adequately for the former British colonies, rather less so for the French-speaking territories.[4] Most scholars were also concerned not simply with the transfer of control from imperial to nationalist hands, but with the movement of power between local institutions in the former colony: from parties and parliaments to armies and police, and sometimes back again. Some of the accounts of these local struggles depicted an extraordinary world, as if the African states were more akin to fifteenth-century Europe than to known parallels in this century. Kenneth Younger once confided to the writer that he had not really understood what was happening in the Congo, despite Catherine Hoskyns's book, until he re-read Shakespeare's *Henry VI*, and it seemed, at the time, an apt comment.

Tragically interesting as many of these accounts were, what bearing did they have on the larger world of international affairs? In recent years, much of the research into the politics of many of the newly independent states has actually narrowed and sharpened its focus: there is a whole new world of 'micro-studies' in which political scientists have turned for help to social anthropology. There is little point here in trying to argue for and against the models of political behaviour, and of the inter-relationship between central and local politics, now being constructed. They are very interesting, very erudite: but they are also as remote from the general interests of Chatham House as are the politics of Acholi from the general concerns of the OAU.[5] And it was often a source of wonder to the writer (as great as his content) that the Institute should have sponsored a study of the domestic politics of a small African country. It is true that

---

[4] See the bibliography by Austin & Tordoff in *The Reader's Guide to Contemporary History*, ed. at the Inst. of Contemporary History by W. Z. Laqueur & Bernard Crikler, to be published by Weidenfeld.

[5] See Colin Leys's interesting little study *Politicians and Policies, an essay on politics in Acholi, Uganda 1962–5* (Nairobi, 1967).

a serious student of international relations might wish to know something of a particular country before looking at its external policies towards other states. Still: 'Politics in Ghana'! Can one argue that, since the primary concern of the African states is with their domestic and not their external affairs, then that should continue to be the prime focus of study? It raises the question once again, now as in earlier decades, of the scale of importance of Africa in the study of international relations. And of an Africa parcelled out, not between three or four European empires, but among over forty independent states.

Over the past decade, there have been three stages of argument about 'Africa and the World' often overlapping each other: first, an advocacy of the need to look closely at Africa as a likely area of international concern; then the counter-argument that there was a 'stability of powerlessness' about Africa and its fragmented states which removed it and them from the centre of the world's problems; thirdly—and still to be assessed fully—that the world of great-power rivalry was drawing closer to Africa, where local crises of varying scale might merge into conflict between outside powers. It may be useful to say something about each of these stages, if only to sharpen argument over present controversies.

The first wave of books offered a simple proposition: that the momentum of African nationalism had brought not only the withdrawal of British, French, and Belgian rule from almost the whole of tropical Africa, but the revival of a pan-African sentiment which (it was argued) would soon complete the task of liberation begun in the 1950s. Already, by 1963, an Organization of African Unity was in being. The independent African states had begun to crowd into the UN General Assembly and to raise demands for an enlargement of the Security Council; they were regularly engaged in the ritual slaughter of the colonial scapegoat (against the darkening sky of their own domestic difficulties); and they did what they could to mobilize the international world against the dangers of apartheid. The 'illegal declaration of independence' by Ian Smith and the Rhodesia Front in November 1965 added an extra dimension to a conflict which (it was said) would soon engulf the world. It seemed that we were back in the 1930s and to 'economic sanctions' as a weapon of international action. Angola and

Mozambique were under attack from guerrillas, aided by a Committee of Liberation of the OAU. The world was in crisis. And the African states were part of a 'third world' of new states which might inflame the crisis to the point of international conflict: *racial* conflict between the rich and the poor, a picture calculated to make the flesh of western man creep. Books began to appear on the third world, including the essay of that title by Professor J. B. D. Miller for Chatham House; on the UN, including the closely argued inquiry by Dr Rosalyn Higgins into the international legal implications of UN resolutions concerning apartheid;[6] and on the OAU itself.

The OAU was something of a puzzle. No writer has yet quite got to grips with it, although Catherine Hoskyns may succeed in doing so.[7] Should it be seen as a subsystem of the international world, perhaps as an example of Professor Ernst Haas's belief in the 'continued drift towards supranationality'.[8] It was pleasant to praise the OAU for its ideals. Certainly Colin Legum and others found it easy to do so.[9] A colder eye was more likely to note the drift towards a status quo position as the heads of state and of governments proclaimed their belief in the need to preserve what existed—including the frontiers of the newly independent states and the safety of the newly independent leaders. As the decade drew on, it was noted also that the Organization was of very limited use in the settlement of the misfortunes which befell the African states. It was the UN which helped to restore order in the Congo. It was Britain and the Soviet Union which helped the Nigerian federal government to end the civil war. The southern 'battle line' was still there: but it was not clear what help the OAU was actually able or prepared to give to those in the field. Moreover, the 'Unity' of the organization itself was seen to be very frail either because (as Zdenek Čer-

---

[6] *The Development of International Law through the Political Organs of the UN* (London, 1963).

[7] In her forthcoming study for Chatham House.

[8] As an example too of 'metapolitics' despite its 'heterosymmetry'? Ah! such phrases! (see his *Beyond the Nation-State* (Stanford, 1964)).

[9] Legum actually held the belief that 'Africa alone has produced a highly developed "pan-continental movement"', and that 'economically and politically the continent has everything to gain from Pan-African planning; more even than Europe, and much more than Asia'. But that was in 1962, in his *Pan-Africanism, a short political guide*, the useful collection of documents and commentary published by Pall Mall Press.

venka observed)[10] its structure was rudimentary, or because its
member states were often divided among themselves—radical
versus conservative (Tanzania/Malawi), former French against
ex-British (Ghana/Ivory Coast), Islamic peoples against non-
Islamic peoples within a particular state (the Sudan, Chad,
Ethiopia). So the excitement faded; the enthusiasm ebbed: and
the notion that 'pan-Africanism' might become a populist,
revolutionary doctrine soon disappeared. Military rule cast its
shadow over the nationalist fervour of earlier scenes. Yet it was
often the case that the soldiers were received with much the
same enthusiasm formerly given to the nationalist politicians.
A great deal of literature, therefore, was used to explain (*ex post
facto*) the growing number of coups d'état. Some of the hopes
once put upon the single party were transferred to the army as
an 'instrument of modernization': but that too was not very
convincing. And most critics confined themselves to trying to
explain why the coups had taken place—by describing the weakness of the civilian institutions bequeathed to the new states at
independence, of which the best analysis perhaps was in Professor S. E. Finer's *Man on Horseback* (1962), or by the tensions
which existed in the very small armies which had intervened,
as in the studies by Morris Janowitz[11] and J. J. Johnson.[12]
There was room for a study which combined both approaches
to the problem, and eventually it was supplied through Dr
Robin Luckham's detailed examination of the two Nigerian
coups.[13]

Gradually, therefore, the second stage of the argument was
reached, and it stressed the double fortune, or misfortune, of the
African states. No one was very interested in them, and they
were powerless to have any influence on the rest of the world.
Certainly, the writer felt that to be so in the mid-1960s, and
several studies began reluctantly to admit the fact. There were
three characteristics in particular worth noting. First, that the
danger centres of the world were still in Eastern Europe, South-
east Asia, the Middle East, and, perhaps, Latin America: that
is to say, areas within the immediate concern and protection of

[10] *The Organisation of African Unity and its Charter* (London, 1969).

[11] See W. E. Daucherty & M. Janowitz, *A Psychological Warfare Casebook* (Baltimore, 1958).

[12] *The Role of the Military in Underdeveloped Countries* (Princeton, 1962).

[13] *The Nigerian Military* (London, 1971).

the Soviet Union or China or the United States. Africa was lucky in this respect not to have a great power on its frontiers. Chou En-lai might announce on a state visit to Tanzania in 1965 that 'Africa was ripe for revolution'; the Soviet leaders made similar calls on a number of African capitals; and both the Chinese and the Russians dabbled locally in the murky politics of Guinea, Zanzibar, Burundi, and Gabon. But in the mid-1960s these were surely marginal interests, a little outlay for an unknown dividend: and both powers ran into difficulties when the local politics turned sour. The Russians were later to gain a measure of goodwill and influence through arms sales to Nigeria and Somalia, but it was not until their interests were involved directly in the Middle East that arguments began to be heard about Soviet involvement 'south of Suez'. Secondly, there was almost a universal paralysis—the safety of impotence—about the continent in respect of its own inter-state relations. The picture was not only that of a lack of armed power, particularly of air transport, and the Adelphi Papers by William Gutteridge and others showed that very clearly, but of a troubled absorption with the problems of domestic control. Nigeria was divided by a cruel civil war. One by one the radical leaders were overthrown—Nkrumah, Modibo Keita, Milton Obote—or, like Sekou Touré and Kaunda, were concerned primarily with their own survival. And there was a spreading disenchantment, not only with the UN but with earlier beliefs in a collective Afro-Asian world of peaceful 'non-aligned' nations. Thirdly, 'white power' was seemingly impregnable in the southern half of the continent. Smith held on in Rhodesia; Portugal resisted; South Africa moved from anxiety over Sharpeville to a confident expansion in Southern Africa as the British withdrew from the High Commission Territories and trade treaties were concluded with Malawi and the Malagasy Republic.

A few years ago therefore this essay might have stopped at this point, with the conclusion that although studies in the local politics of the African states might be of continuing interest, their external relations were unlikely to be of concern to serious students of the international scene. Then other ideas were started. It was not that the diagnosis was wrong: but perhaps there were future dangers to attend to? In a short article, the writer tried to sketch a number of possibilities for which close inquiries, of a continuing kind, might be useful.[14] They would not be focused on Africa directly, or, at least, not on the newly independent states which had hitherto borne the main weight of interest. If the continent was to become of international importance, some breaking of the deadlock—an end to the paralysis—was necessary. How might it come about? The answer was reasonably clear. If the African states were self-absorbed, what about their opponents in Pretoria and Lisbon? Despite all the fury and anguish very little was really known about white South Africa except that it was wicked. It seemed at one time as if the whole of the Penguin African Library was concerned to prove the fact. But the wicked were also powerful, and it was surely sensible to look at the basis of their financial and economic strength on which the police, the barbed wire, the tear gas, the informers, and the whole apparatus of apartheid depended. Since there was no Prospero to change the South African Caliban, perhaps one ought to look more closely at Caliban himself. Yet so little was known about the kind of political animal meant by 'Afrikanerdom'. The last detailed book on South African politics and parties was by Gwendolen Carter in 1958.[15] The only study which tried tentatively to look at the restraints and temptations which might affect Pretoria in its external relations was by J. E. Spence.[16] Surely there was need for a dispassionate assessment not only of the political forces at work in South Africa, but of the decisions which might be made about what the leaders considered their 'external interests' to be? The Republic was 'under pressure': but suppose it reacted strongly to the demands made on it. And suppose the counter-attack was surprisingly successful? What then?

[14] 'White Power', *J. Commonwealth Polit. Stud.*, July 1968. See too the author's *Britain and South Africa* (London, 1966).

[15] *The Politics of Inequality* (London, 1958). A related field of inquiry might be into the effect on the Republic of economic *growth*, including its external trade and financial relations. There used to be a 'hormone weed-killer theory' about South Africa which argued that apartheid might be destroyed by 'over-growth'. Let it die by excess, by the poison of prosperity: or, more simply, 'feed the brute until it die':

> Our natures do pursue,
> Like rats that ravin down their proper bane,
> A thirsty evil, and when we drink we die.

But perhaps it ought not to be taken as seriously as those who trade with South Africa would have us believe. The relationship between politics and economics in the Republic is part of a current Chatham House study.

[16] *Republic under Pressure* (London, 1965).

Add, too, another dimension, namely the possibility of change in Lisbon. Was it really possible for the Portuguese to continue spending over 50 per cent of their budget on 'defence', the prime purpose being to keep 125,000 troops in Angola, Mozambique, and Guinea—nearly a third of the total number of soldiers in tropical Africa?[17] Every month there were, and are still, some Portuguese soldiers and local levies killed in the field, every year the likelihood either of 'pacification' or 'liberation' grows less. When will Portugal tire of the effort? The answer must surely be when the war is no longer worth the oil and timber and minerals which Portugal extracts from its 'overseas provinces', or when after a further period of conflict the calculation is made in Lisbon that to transfer power might be less damaging than to retain control. Then perhaps a future government may repeat in Africa the peaceful surrender of its rule which took place in Brazil in the 1820s; it may turn again to Europe, and discard its imperial role if only to retain, as the reward of magnanimity, its dominant position in the economic life of its former territories. The Belgians did so in 1960. The Portuguese may reach the same conclusion: that of all the legacies bequeathed by history the colonial burden is the most onerous. The effect of such a decision would certainly be very interesting, particularly on South Africa and its present 'outward policy' towards black Africa.

There is of course another possibility, that the Portuguese will refuse to withdraw. The war in Angola and Mozambique may then continue for many years, as simply one more example of the miseries which mankind inflicts on itself. That is certainly possible, and in such a situation Lisbon may turn more and more to Pretoria, arguing the need for a common defence policy and a joint forward battle line in southern Africa. At this extreme of policy, as the writer once tried to argue,[18]

the South African government might reach the point when it was under-pinning militarily and financially, not only client African governments in Malawi, Botswana, Lesotho and Swaziland, but Portugal and Rhodesia across the whole of central Africa: garrisoning in immense area of nearly two million square miles. . . . Drawn

---

[17] See the Adelphi Paper, *The Armed Forces of the African States 1970* (London, 1970).
[18] *J. Commonwealth Polit. Stud.*, July 1968.

into Mozambique because of the need to defend South Africa's own boundaries, drawn northwards as far as Angola because of the fear of subversion across the huge empty area of South West Africa, the Nationalist government might find itself in the unlooked for role of an expansionist power, struggling with uneasy allies and an evasive enemy. Given the present weakness of the African states and the limited ability of the local guerrilla forces, it might hold such a position for some years to come, but the long-term dangers of such an attempt—including divisions within the main body of Afrikanerdom over the degree to which South Africa ought to be involved—might do more to weaken the structure of white rule in southern Africa than any direct challenge to its authority has so far been able to accomplish.

Then it is that a closer understanding of the strains and lesions within Afrikanerdom would repay study.

Notice that such arguments are concerned either with Pretoria or more distant capitals: Lisbon and (perhaps) Brussels. That is to say, the 'second-stage argument' has not yet been abandoned, Africa being important only so far as external interests make it so. But in recent years an interesting question of 'convergence' has arisen. International crises, it can be argued, do not arise simply when the interests of the great powers clash directly but when they are drawn into disputes over 'third parties', as in the Middle East or South-east Asia or Cuba. The Chinese are already in Zanzibar, although with what effect no one knows. They are responsible for constructing the new railway from Lusaka to Dar es Salaam, the largest single programme overseas supported by Peking and comparable (it may be argued) with the Soviet construction of the Aswan Dam in Egypt.[19] This can be explained possibly as part of the search for

[19] Ian Adie has painted an elaborate scenario of a militant kind, postulating that when the railway is completed in about 1975, China's possession of ICBMs will have 'made the world safer for the people's wars' whereby it hopes to resist global encirclement by the USSR, the US and their allies. He believes that by that date South Africa is likely to have undertaken reprisals against the guerrillas which will have aroused pan-African sentiment and a world-wide supporting movement, and that simple economics will tend not only 'to bring Zambia into the orbit of Black Africa' but to make Dar es Salaam 'the metropolis of all East Africa', at the expense of Nairobi, 'thus swinging the centre of gravity to the place where Peking's influence is strongest and the liberation movements centred' (Africa Research Ltd., *Africa Contemporary Record* (1970), pp. A 50–2). If that really is the view from Peking, then it looks as if the Chinese expect more from their investment than they are likely to receive, since it is not easy to see either Dar es Salaam as a metropolis or any Zambian government as a militant crusader.

a supply of copper, for ideological advantage over the Americans and Russians, and for whatever economic benefits can be secured from taking up a request which was rejected by London and Washington. But from such a position of advantage in Central Africa, it is conceivable that the Chinese might give aid and comfort to guerrilla forces in Mozambique. The spill-over of Soviet power from the Suez Canal into the Red Sea and Indian Ocean is also the kind of blind thrusting forward that might give rise to a great deal of uncertainty as it encounters not only local quarrels but a degree of Chinese and American involvement. There are minor wars along the African coast and inland in which rival leaders might turn for help to external powers. The United States is the main supplier of arms to Ethiopia, the Soviet Union to Somalia. The Soviet Union is directly interested in Aden and the Horn of Africa, the United States is beginning to be drawn into the Indian Ocean. Arab states look sympathetically on the Eritrean Liberation Front, Israel has a minor interest in keeping the dissident southern Sudan as an area of concern to the government in Khartoum. If it is really true that the Soviet Union is interested in getting the Suez Canal open, in order to operate more effectively to the south, then at the very least the East African states—from Ethiopia and the Sudan on the Red Sea to Kenya and Tanzania (including Zanzibar) on the eastern seaboard—may no longer be so distant from the primary areas of conflict in the international world. And if one puts these still relatively minor grounds for uneasiness alongside the earlier argument about a widening area of conflict northwards from South Africa to Mozambique and Tanzania, then there may be much more to interest the student of international affairs in Africa than there has been in the past decade.

Uncertainties are bound to cloud an argument which sees the immense length of the eastern seaboard of a vast continent as being brought within a single theatre (or related areas) of conflict. Both Moscow and Washington—and, so far as one can see, Peking—have a cautious look about them at the present time. It would be interesting none the less to learn from Sovietologists about the present degree of Soviet interest in Africa; similar information is, of course, picked up about Peking from the China watchers who, like learned astrologers, look for changing fortunes in the eastern sky. One might ask too about the influence (if any) on the US State Department of the large minority black population in the United States. Earlier studies tried to read these signs[20] but prematurely, when rhetoric was confused with policy, and when it was often assumed, quite wrongly, that many of the African leaders were predisposed, as militant nationalists, towards Moscow or Peking. But it may now be a sensible time to look at the competing interests of outside powers in Africa in the light of the very obvious weakness of the African states.

Whether it is also useful in this connection to look at the 'foreign policies' of the African states themselves is more doubtful, since it is not at all clear what is implied by such studies. The difficulty lies in the shifting nature of the evidence. The foreign policy of, say, Tanzania can hardly be interpreted in terms of national interests shaped over a long period of time, since the state was only born yesterday; nor can its external policy be said to reflect a large body of shared opinion in the country, since that too hardly exists. Certainly one should be careful not to confuse the particular international stance of a contemporary leader with permanent interests. In 1969 there appeared the carefully prepared book on Ghana's foreign policy by Dr Scott Thompson: a good, detailed, scholarly account.[21] But it is a poor guide to the external policy of Dr Busia's Ghana. More worthwhile perhaps would be some consideration of local ratios of power and wealth. Admittedly, the bitterest disputes have been within rather than between states: hence their essential weakness. But that may change, as differences of size begin to tell. Nigeria, for example, is clearly a country whose growing wealth, numbers of people, and renewed sense of nationalism are likely to have a growing effect on her smaller neighbours. The writer is not positing an aggressive Nigeria; nor is he forgetful of the protection given those smaller neighbours at present by France and by their UN membership: but large states *do* influence smaller states at different levels, even below that of deliberate policy. And it may be sensible to look at the disparities

---

[20] e.g. Vernon McKay, ed., *African Diplomacy* (New York, 1966), a basic assumption being that 'Radicalism is inherent in the new Africa'. See too I. W. Zartman, *International Relations in the New Africa* (New York, 1966), and Z. Brzezinski, ed., *Africa and the Communist World* (Stanford, 1963).

[21] Princeton, 1969.

of power within the continent, north as well as south of the Zambesi.

What one is arguing needs little justification: that in the present state of uncertainty about particular African regimes, academic study is likely to be worthwhile only if what is examined has some lasting element to it. Given this simple proposition, what other areas of interest are there? One answer diffidently put forward by the writer, who is well aware of the idiosyncratic nature of his own interests, might be that area of international relations which marks the end of a colonial and the beginning of a post-colonial relationship. Constantly one is astonished to see how long the European empires have taken to die. Even such old fashioned concepts as 'Eurafrique' are still occasionally discussed in Brussels (of all capitals!) where the Commission and its servants are jealous guardians of a residual imperial heritage in the Associated States. And perhaps something should be said about this area of research.

It may be asked why Africa should be singled out for scrutiny since the end of the European empires was of global proportions: why not India and Indo-China, Malaya and Indonesia, as well as Africa? One may also note in passing, looking back over the period of colonial government, that European imperial rule was really a single phenomenon with several very different strands. The end of British, Dutch, French, and Belgian rule also had a profound effect not only on the former colonial territories but on the metropolitan powers themselves, and part of any inquiry into the end of empire ought to be to discover

> Who clipped the lion's wings
> And flea'd his rump and pared his claws?

But, within the modest limits of current research, Africa has a special place in the story; or, to reverse the proposition, the ending of colonial rule has had a precise and distinct effect on the external relations of many of the now independent African states. An interesting feature of the withdrawal of European rule from Africa (north of the Zambesi) was that it took place at roughly the same time: almost in a single year.[22] *Annus*

---

[22] 1960, when Mauritania, Senegal, Mali, Upper Volta, Ivory Coast, Niger, Dahomey, Chad, Central African Republic, Gabon, Congo (Brazzaville), Madagascar, Congo (Kinshasha), Ruanda, Burundi, Cameroun Republic, Somalia, and Nigeria became independent. Between 1960 and 1970 both the French and British

mirabilis! But although independence was an international fact
—all the African states joined the UN and were accorded inter-
national recognition—the relationship between Africa and
Europe remained close. The former French colonies (except
Guinea), the former Belgian territories, and the Italian Trust
Territory of Somalia, agreed to remain associated with the
EEC under the Rome Treaty.[23] Apart from the former Anglo-
Egyptian Sudan, the British territories remained within the
Commonwealth, comforted in 1961 by South Africa's withdrawal. If the European Community is enlarged by Britain,
and Association is widened by some kind of linkage between a
number of Commonwealth African countries—varying from
full association to a form of the Arusha Treaty[24] or the 'Morocco
Protocol'[25]—Europe will continue to have a formal relationship
with a large part of the continent. It would be wrong to exaggerate the tie, since the major preoccupation of the European
countries is certain to be turned in other directions, and most
African governments are still concerned to maintain their new
links with the rest of the world. Yet as a persistent element in
the national life of the African states, the post-colonial relationship is worth looking at, not simply as an exercise in trade flows
or technical assistance or aid, but as part of the history and,
therefore, of the international interests of a large number of
African governments. It is most evident between France and
her former colonies because of the peculiarly closed nature of
the French-speaking world—London can hardly be the centre
of an English-speaking world as is Paris of *La France d'outre-mer*—
but there is life too in the Commonwealth connection in Africa.
And the legacy of France and Britain, to which one should add
Belgium and its former dependencies, is to be seen in a wide
array of domestic and external interests.

empires all but vanished from the continent except for the French in the territory
of the Afars and Issas (former French Somaliland) and the British (nominally) in
Rhodesia.

[23] By the Yaoundé Convention of 1963 between the Community and 18 African
states including Madagascar, renewed by the second Yaoundé Convention, 29 July
1969.

[24] Agreement between the EEC and Tanzania, Uganda, and Kenya, 24 Sept.
1969.

[25] A protocol attached to the Rome Treaty providing for the continuation of
preferential treatment for imports from dependent territories (see the pamphlet by
W. Gorrell Barnes cited in n. 26).

One writes of the post-colonial relationship as being a matter of much more than 'trade flows or technical assistance or aid', but the African governments are far from indifferent to economic interests. The facts are perfectly clear. The Commonwealth plus the European Community—or an enlarged European Community of Ten—is far and away the major economic grouping for nearly all the African countries. The American market, of course, is important; the sub-Saharan, Soviet and Eastern European market small, the Chinese insignificant; the EEC plus Britain dominant. A similar picture can be put together of aid and technical assistance, whether bilaterally or through joint agencies; and both Britain and the Six are not only major donor countries for the African states but for their most important source of private capital. It really is very odd that the consequence of this striking African-European relationship has not been thought worth a major study.[26] It may be that the notion of looking at Africa from a joint British-EEC standpoint, or at 'Europe-plus-Britain' from Africa, is still a novel idea, despite the blurring of the old division between Anglophone and Francophone Africa. It is interesting, for example, that it was a Commonwealth African country—Nigeria (followed later by the three East African countries)—which first 'crossed the Commonwealth-Community boundary' by her application for association with the EEC, drawn in the same direction as the United Kingdom.[27]

There may be a less simple explanation of the lack of academic interest in Africa's relations with Europe, namely, the once widely held belief that African governments were eager to draw away from their former colonial rulers, the assumption being that they were part of the 'third world'—that imprecise area of the globe for which no adequate definition exists since it is doubtful whether a collective entity can be given to so disparate an area. The notion had a certain plausibility perhaps at the time of the Belgrade Conference of Non-Aligned Nations in 1961; but it was then retained as a description not simply of

[26] Early studies included the Chatham House PEP pamphlet by W. Gorrell-Barnes, *Europe and the Developing World: Association under Part IV of the Treaty of Rome* (1967); and Pierre Uri, ed., *From Commonwealth to Common Market* (Penguin, 1968). A specialist study of Association is being undertaken by Carol Cosgrove, to be pubished by Praeger in 1972–3.

[27] The Association Agreement was concluded in 1966 but never implemented.

those who were detached from both the Western and communist alliances but as a general label for the Afro-Asian, non-white world. And on this basis there was a great deal of loose talk about the dangers of a 'global race war' widening out from Southern Africa. In practice, the more numerous and bloody conflicts have been between people of the same 'nation' in civil wars (e.g. Nigeria), or between rival states whose national interests are opposed—the Soviet Union against Germany (the same race), China and India (the same race?), China and the Soviet Union, China and the United States (different races), India and Pakistan, Ethiopia and Somalia, and so on. Moreover, Africa has much less in common with other areas of the 'third world' than is sometimes supposed. It is true that most of its states are poor, and some are very poor: they have that in common with all the UNCTAD countries. But they are also very different from other UNCTAD members. South of the Islamic frontier, Africa belongs predominantly to the Christian world, unlike the greater part of Asia. Their political culture— armies, bureaucracies, parliaments—is derived largely from northern Europe, unlike that of Latin America.[28] There is (to be sure) some emphasis still on an ideological commitment to a unique form of African Socialism; but in practice the very small modern sector of the economy in almost every African country consists of a mixture of private (including expatriate and local) capital and state-controlled enterprises. Of greater significance is the fact that, throughout tropical Africa, the peasant owns his land or the use of it, the towns are small, and the élites are absorbed in the party-state (or army-state) machinery of control. The new regimes have been subjected to a good deal of analytical abuse by critics as different as Frantz Fanon, René Dumont, and Stanislav Andrewski; but social revolutions are not made by words alone, and power may simply shift from politician to politician, or from party leader to military ruler, and back again. One cannot easily see a Castro-communist or even

[28] Except for Angola, Mozambique, and Portuguese Guinea which might perhaps grow to resemble parts of Brazil? Critics of the African states might argue that the new leaders have abandoned much of their 'received political culture'. But the framework of the state and its principal instruments of authority are Western in origin. A study of Spanish colonial rule and its partial withdrawal (from 'Spanish Morocco' in 1956, Equatorial Guinea in 1968, and Ifni in 1969) would also be interesting, particularly in relation to Gibraltar, Ceuta, and Melilla.

an Allende-Marxist regime of any weight and power in such a context. The African states and their rulers seem likely to remain for a considerable time what the European colonial powers fashioned them to be—fashioned them not wilfully or even consciously but as the result of a period of colonial history which, though short, was decisive.

If that is so, then relations between Africa and Europe will probably remain close, despite South Africa, despite Portuguese rule, despite (and perhaps because of) Soviet and Chinese interests in East and Central Africa. At a certain level of public debate at the UN or the OAU or the Commonwealth, some African governments will of course continue to oppose Britain (and even France?) over Southern Africa. But it does not seem likely, on past evidence, that the great majority of OAU members will want to do more than that. Neither the OAU's call to its members to break off diplomatic relations with Britain over Rhodesia in November 1965, nor the differences which threatened to disrupt the Commonwealth meeting in Singapore in January 1971, were as fierce in the outcome as they were in the promise. Commonwealth African quarrels with Britain are still well short of open rupture despite a profound irritation, of varying degree, with current British policies. The restraint is not (in the writer's view) because of a neutral assessment of financial interests, though that may play some part; nor because of a growing indifference towards Rhodesia and South Africa, though some African governments may have reached that stage; but because of an underlying knowledge, trust, and even an exasperated affection among African leaders for the former imperial power. How else can one explain the persistence of Commonwealth and Community ties? There must surely be something of value in these extraordinary outgrowths of empire beyond a rational weighing of the advantages and disadvantages of membership in the cold scales of national interest. Just as empire was built on something stronger than force and profit, so the ties which link the Commonwealth countries with Britain, or the Associated States with Europe and France, have their origin in an attachment which cannot be explained simply in terms of material advantage. There remains, it would seem, in most African countries a genuine interest in the former metropolitan countries. And it is hardly surprising. European society

played a profound part in the shaping of their national histories: frontiers, language, law, religion, politics, trade, family
customs, social values—all were touched or transformed by
European ways. How can they fail to be interested still in the
European scene? The pity is, alas, that European society was
largely unaffected by the traditions and culture of pre-colonial
Africa. The imperial traffic of ideas, habits, and beliefs seems
to have been in one direction only, a curious phenomenon of
European colonial rule which might also be worth investigating
(by African sociologists?) as a revealing characteristic of Western
society.

A closing note of caution. In January 1964 the British government responded to an appeal for help from Tanzania, Kenya,
and Uganda to put down the army mutinies in East Africa. In
1964 France intervened on behalf of President M'Ba of Gabon,
and she has troops fighting still in Chad on behalf of President Tombalbaye.[29] Should one see these decisions as proof of
paternal care in both countries for their former dependencies,
foreshadowing perhaps a claim by a 'resurgent Europe' that
Africa lies within its regional sphere of influence—the vast
southern shore of the Mediterranean? The writer is unimpressed
by such arguments. There is little supporting evidence that
Britain or any other power in Europe will want to retrace their
steps towards a masked imperialism of control. Admittedly,
France is a protective figure of authority still for a number of
African countries; but that, too, may be a slowly fading legacy
of Gaullist sympathies, and a reflection of her once dominant
economic position which is also changing.[30] No. One should see
the relationship between Africa and Europe as close but not
exclusive; as being of considerable interest to the African governments concerned but not as crippling their freedom of action
in other directions. Association under Part IV of the Rome

[29] France had about 12,500 troops stationed in Africa on 1 April 1970, the largest
number (4,400) being in the Afars and Issas Territory. The government also has
bilateral defence agreements with twelve African countries (Ivory Coast, Senegal,
Chad, Gabon, Madagascar, Cameroun, Dahomey, Niger, Mauritania, Togo,
Congo (B), Central African Republic).

[30] 'Among the member states, France is still by far the best customer of the
Yaoundé countries, taking over two-fifths of their exports to the Community. In
value, however, the level of France's imports has remained virtually stationary
($610 m. in 1967 and $614 m. in 1968) and the role of the French market as the
leading outlet continues to diminish' (AAMS Division, *EEC Report*, Feb. 1970).

Treaty began, in a sense, as the continuation of a colonial system, but it is probably fair to say that none of the African governments (save that perhaps of Sekou Touré in Conakry?) now sees it as a post-colonial bid for control. On the contrary. If there is evidence of uneasiness today among the Associates under the second Yaoundé Convention, it is over the danger of a falling away of interest and help. Similarly, it was the East African countries which beat a path to Brussels to ask for an association agreement: there was no fierce desire among the Six (or among the Eighteen Associates) to enlarge the area of their co-operation. A more cogent fear, therefore, than that of economic control might easily become that of indifference—a neglect by the rich of the poor—an indifference and neglect which the continuance of Community and Commonwealth ties may actually help to avert.

Such is the position in 1971, and there is little point in trying to extend it into the next decade. One can only indicate what appear to be enduring features of a past relationship between the two continents: but nothing can be said with assurance. And certainly we ought not to try and predict into the 1970s or 1980s the outcome of the scenarios sketched earlier. They are simply a number of possibilities which exist at present—not guides to an unknown future, when conflicting policies of very many interests will interact in ways impossible to foresee.[31] So we reach a conclusion which is hardly a conclusion at all, and the writer is very much aware of the fact that to end this short essay on such a note is a little unheroic. But that may not necessarily be out of key with the times. And if over the next decade the picture set out here is seen as a fair reflection of Africa and its 'external relations' in 1971–2, well, it will be something to be honoured even with yesterday's wreaths!

[31] Indeed, we have Herman Kahn's warning about 'scenario writing': that 'the scenario ought not to be used as a predictive device' since 'the analyst is dealing with the unknown and to some degree unknowable future'. *Ipse dixit*, in Morton A. Kaplan, ed., *New Approaches to International Relations* (New York, 1968).

9 The Politics of Co-operation and Integration in Western Europe

ROY PRYCE

FOR most of its history Western Europe has been a battleground. Today this is no longer the case. On the contrary, it has given birth to an ambitious—and remarkably successful—experiment in economic and political union. A group of its states has not only abandoned the armed rivalries of the past, but has voluntarily decided to pursue a common destiny.

This experiment has now been going on for over twenty years. The original six members of the European Community have already achieved a significant degree of economic integration, and some measure of political integration. It is now likely that they will be joined by other neighbouring states, and that the enlarged Community will enter into a wider network of association and other agreements covering most of the remaining states of Western Europe. Already the repercussions of what the Six have achieved have spread far afield. In addition to the Community's association with eighteen African states, it has also concluded a series of trade agreements with countries in many other parts of the world. At the same time, as the world's largest trading group, it has also had important repercussions on international organizations dealing with economic, monetary, and developmental problems. An enlarged Community including Britain will clearly assume even greater importance in this context, with a substantial influence—for good or ill—on the future development of the world at large.

This extraordinary and radical transformation could hardly have been anticipated twenty-five years ago, when Europe had only just emerged from yet another disastrous conflict. This time Europe's internal rivalries had sown death and destruction into the far corners of the world. And this time the world took its revenge.

The end of the war brought to a close the long period of European dominance over the world scene. The colonial empires of Germany and Italy had already been liquidated: those of France, Britain, the Netherlands, and Belgium were destined soon for a similar fate. But it was not only that the end of hostilities signalled a retreat from empire: it also ushered in a new era in which European states, far from being the leading protagonists on the world stage, now found themselves overshadowed by the two new superpowers. Europe was no longer master even of its own destiny. It became a pawn in the postwar competition between the United States and the Soviet Union.

The line where the victorious armies met was soon transformed into frontiers sown with minefields. Germany was not only occupied, but also divided. To the east the Soviet Union either imposed or supported the birth of a series of new regimes, modelled in its own image. In the west the United States gave equally strong support to regimes friendly to herself. Britain and France had inherited, through their wartime exertions, seats at the top table, but the disparity in the power and influence they could now wield compared with that of their powerful protector only underlined how much the world had changed.

In the immediate postwar years it was not at all certain what sort of response the states of Western Europe would make to this new situation. Much of their initial effort had in any case to be directed to the heavy tasks of economic and political reconstruction within each of their frontiers. There were no lack of calls for a new Europe: for a framework within which the internecine strife of the past would be put aside and a new economic and political unity created. But there had been many such calls in the past, and though they were now reiterated by a statesman of the stature of Churchill, there was no certainty that action would follow.

In the event, Western Europe did respond—though not in the manner that was envisaged by the British who initially assumed (and it was not an unreasonable assumption in the late 1940s) that they would be able to control the pace and shape of developments, and participate on terms most convenient to themselves. Nor was progress so smooth, or so rapid, as the early protagonists of unity had hoped. In fact, the path towards unity has proved to be extremely tortuous and complex, with peaks and troughs of achievement; moments of triumph and periods of despair; and constant shifts of tempo and leadership. Nevertheless, a great deal has been achieved. And if the process has presented a succession of tests of will and determination to the statesmen and politicians of our part of the world—and is likely in the future to continue to do so—it presents an equal challenge to those, and particularly academics who, following in the wake of events, seek to explain and understand them.

Patterns of co-operation and integration

One of the major problems which has confronted scholars studying the developments of postwar Western Europe is the plethora of organizations which have been created, apparently without any coherent strategy, and sometimes even without any clear consensus with regard to their goals. For although the desire to achieve a greater degree of unity has provided one common strand, not all states have been equally strongly motivated in their search for it, and there has been little agreement on what the form or content of unity should be.

Some co-operative ventures have been undertaken on a bilateral basis; others by subregional groups such as the three Benelux countries or the Scandinavians. At the same time the notion of a wider framework embracing most of the countries of Western Europe has also persisted, while in defence matters the ultimate dependence of the region on the nuclear power of the United States for its defence needs has imposed an Atlantic framework for co-operation—a framework which some have sought to develop into a partnership covering other major policy areas. In many cases these different views of how Western Europe should be organized have offered competing rather than complementary solutions; and the organizational pattern which has emerged has been further complicated by the fact that individual states have quite frequently changed their own strategies with regard to co-operation.

In the immediate postwar period developments were largely dominated on the one hand by Western Europe's heavy dependence on the United States both for its economic recovery and defence needs, and on the other by the United Kingdom preference for a geographically wide, but loosely-organized framework for co-operation within Western Europe itself. The OEEC and NATO were the main embodiment of the first set of pressures: the Council of Europe—which was set up in 1949 with ten member states—of the second. But these were by no means the only organizations operating at this time. As a result of decisions taken by their wartime governments in exile, Belgium, the Netherlands, and Luxembourg had already embarked on the formation of a Benelux customs union; the Scandinavian group of states were also evolving a distinctive pattern of co-operation between themselves, destined in 1952 to lead to the creation of the Nordic Council; while the fears in Western Europe of Soviet military intentions led to the extension of the 1947 Franco-British treaty of Dunkirk and the formation of the Brussels Treaty Organization in 1948, which combined these two countries together with the Benelux trio in a group which had as its explicit objective not only common defence, but closer political and cultural co-operation.

After 1950, however, developments in Western Europe were increasingly dominated by the response given to the French initiative in proposing a partial economic union—the ECSC— as a first step towards an eventual United States of Europe organized on federal lines. It was at this point that the six Continental countries first came together without Britain, creating in the process a nucleus of economic and political power which rivalled the looser, wider pattern of organization favoured by successive governments—both Labour and Conservative—in London. Although the new group's bid to hasten towards military and political integration failed in 1954 when the European Defence Community treaty was rejected by the French Assembly, and was replaced by the British-sponsored Western European Union which provided an alternative means for the rearming of Western Germany, this new organization did not prove capable of providing an effective framework within which Britain and the Six could take further steps together.

When the Community countries decided in 1955 to undertake further steps towards the integration of their economies, and to do this by the formation of two new Communities (Euratom and the EEC), the British once again decided that they could not join. The risks attendant on such a decision were thought, however, to be too great for the United Kingdom not to seek an alternative means of access to the Continental common market. It was this which led to the proposal for a European Free Trade Area, negotiations for which were undertaken within the framework of the OEEC in 1956–8. When it was found impossible to reconcile the interests of the British and the Community by such a device, the United Kingdom resorted to the formation of a smaller, rival group—the European Free Trade Association—in company with the Scandinavians, Austria, Switzerland, and Portugal.

A central strand in the development of co-operation in Western Europe in the 1950s and early 1960s was therefore provided by successive British attempts to come to terms with the Communities. It was only when all available alternatives had been exhausted that the Macmillan government gingerly began to explore the option of membership. As part of the Conservative government's more pronounced European policy, Britain also embarked at the same time on a number of new ventures in scientific and technological co-operation with her West European neighbours. One of these, the European Launcher Development Organization (ELDO), had its origins in the British desire to find some continuing use for the Blue Streak rocket; another was the European Space Research Organization (ESRO). At the same time—and again partly as a token of her new European policy and partly in the face of the extremely high costs had Britain attempted the venture on her own, she joined with France in the Concorde project. Together with the European Centre for Nuclear Research (CERN), a successful joint venture in high-energy physics among eleven countries dating from 1951, these new organizations added a new dimension to the range of co-operation being undertaken among the countries of Western Europe.

In the 1960s the central focus of attention was nevertheless the bid by Britain and several other countries to gain admission to the Communities. This was twice frustrated by a French veto imposed by de Gaulle. Although he himself had originally been opposed to the creation of the Communities, he had now come round to the view that, suitably controlled, they could serve French interests, both economic and political. The fact that successive British governments shared his views on the need to preserve a maximum degree of national autonomy within the Communities was less important in deciding his attitude to Britain's entry than the threat it implied to his hopes of continuing French leadership within them. The British, however, persisted. Although the Labour government under Harold Wilson was divided on the desirability of membership, it formally maintained the British application even after the second veto of December 1967. This proved to be of crucial importance. It rallied the support of the other five members of the Community, as well as the Commission, and led to a virtual stalemate within the Community itself.

The departure of de Gaulle from power in the spring of 1969, followed just over a year later by the election of a Conservative government in Britain under Edward Heath, at last provided a conjunction of forces favourable to an enlargement of the Community. If this is achieved, it will open up the prospect of a much more coherent framework for the future pursuit of closer unity in Western Europe, at least in the long run.

At all events, the experience of the past twenty-five years offers to students of international affairs a fascinating and complex body of data bearing on the processes and problems arising out of the search by a group of independent states for closer forms of joint action. It is hardly surprising that these developments have generated a very extensive literature,[1] as well as attracting a substantial body of academic activity. A recent survey covering 30 countries designed to find out the current extent of research activity relating to the various aspects of European integration identified over 41 centres and institutions specializing in this type of work, and no less than 1,373 doctoral theses in preparation.[2]

As far as Britain herself is concerned, courses on various aspects of co-operation and integration are now offered at the undergraduate level in a large number of universities, and also at an increasing number of polytechnics, several of which have

---

[1] For a useful survey of the literature, see Carol Anne Cosgrove, *A Reader's Guide to Britain and the European Communities* (London, 1970). For an extensive annotated bibliography see *Bibliographie zur europäischen Integration*, 3rd ed. (Cologne, 1970).

[2] *University studies on European integration*, no. 6, 1970 (European Community Inst. for Univ. Stud., Brussels). See also the supplementary bulletin from the same source, *Completed Published Theses, 1959–69*.

introduced new patterns of European Studies involving a close integration of linguistic work with the analytical techniques of the social sciences, leading to Council of National Academic Awards degrees. A number of universities also offer postgraduate courses in the same field, and an increasing volume of research is being undertaken. Several specialized centres have made their appearance, including the Centre for European Industrial Studies at the Bath University of Technology, the Centre for European Governmental Studies at Edinburgh, the Graduate School of Contemporary European Studies at Reading, and the Centre for Contemporary European Studies at Sussex.

In these developments a significant role has been played by Chatham House. Talks and discussions on current issues relating to developments in Western Europe have been a regular feature of both its general and private discussion meetings throughout the postwar period, and it has maintained a steady output of publications relating to co-operation and integration.[3] Another important service which Chatham House has performed with regard to the academic community is the series of meetings it has organized, which have brought a number of members of the Commission of the European Communities and their senior staff to join in discussions with those engaged in teaching and research at universities. It has also organized, in co-operation with the London School of Economics, several series of seminars.

These activities led in 1969 to the setting up of the University Association for Contemporary European Studies, which now groups academics in a number of disciplines concerned with the study of co-operation and integration. This is indeed a field where a number of disciplines have an important contribution

[3] These include J. E. Meade & others, *Case Studies in European Economic Union* (London, 1962), and (in the Chatham House Essays series), Miriam Camps, *What Kind of Europe?* (1965). This was later revised and enlarged to appear as a full-length study under the title of *European Unification in the Sixties: from the veto to the crisis* (London, 1967). In that same year the Institute joined forces with PEP (which had been developing in parallel a substantial body of work on various aspects of integration, published in its series of *Broadsheets* and *Planning*) to launch a new European Series of pamphlet-length studies on current issues relating to the Communities and Britain's relations with them. These provide an invaluable source of information for those working in the field. So, too, do the articles published from time to time in both *The World Today* and *International Affairs*; the latter has also performed an invaluable service by its wide coverage of current literature in its book reviews.

to make, and much to learn from one another. Each, however, has its own particular focus of interest, and has tended to develop its own specialized vocabulary and range of concepts. Up to now the interchange between them has tended to be rather limited, and there are relatively few scholars who would claim to be equally at home in the economic, political, and legal literature which all has a bearing on this field of study. To find effective means to increase this interchange over disciplinary frontiers remains a major task for the future.

Themes and methods

The specifically political aspects of co-operation and integration cover a very wide range of subject-matter. For if the study of politics is essentially concerned with power, rule, and authority, and with the factors that influence the organization and exercise of power in society, there is a great deal arising out of co-operation and integration in Western Europe that provides data for political analysis. It is not only that a plethora of new government-sponsored organizations have made their appearance in Western Europe, creating a new dimension of governmental activity and decision-making. Their creation has been accompanied by significant changes in other types of political structures, including parties and interest groups; the development of new patterns of political attitudes and behaviour within the area; and shifts in relations both between the states in area, and between them and other parts of the world. In general terms, those who have devoted their attention to these political aspects have sought to describe the nature of the changes that have been taking place in these various spheres; to construct theories about them—both in terms of the goals being sought and the nature of the processes themselves; to provide explanations for the empirical data relating to these processes; and—in the case of the more ambitious—to seek theories or models with predictive capacity. And while some have laboured away at relatively modest endeavours designed to record with care and precision what has happened—for instance, with regard to the evolution of the European policy of an individual political party—others have set themselves much more ambitious targets, such as constructing theories designed to provide a comprehensive explanation for the dynamics of European political integration, or testing hypotheses seeking to relate the European experience to other forms of co-operation and integration elsewhere in the world.

Just as the issues that have been studied range widely over many subjects, the methodologies employed also vary considerably. Until recently, most European scholars have employed traditional approaches—often mainly historical or legal in nature—while the majority of American scholars who have made a prominent contribution to the literature, have applied a range of newer techniques associated with the behavioural school of political science. It is mainly due to their work that an extensive new terminology has been developed as scholars have sought to give greater precision to their analytical tools. Terms such as 'spillover' and 'spillback' have acquired new connotations; concepts such as 'the autonomy of functional contexts' and 'the index of relative acceptance' have made their appearance; and the vocabulary of systems analysis has been put to work in an attempt to provide a more precise language with which to discuss the subject.

To the layman much of this may seem to be an unnecessary proliferation of obscure jargon. What is certainly true is that there is continuing argument about the exact meaning that should be attached to certain words. Scholars continue, for instance, to use the word 'integration' in a variety of senses. Although in most cases this is now used to refer to a process, there are others who prefer the word 'unification' to indicate this, and use 'integration' to refer to an actual state of political organization. There is also disagreement about the distinction to be made between 'co-operation' and 'integration'. The majority of those who have worked on the European Communities use the latter term to mean the process by which a group of states moves towards economic and political union. They— like the majority of those who are personally involved in the work of the Communities—usually therefore make a sharp distinction between this process and intergovernmental co-operation. It is not always clear, however, what the exact nature of the distinction is. Some would argue that it consists essentially of a difference in objectives: co-operation does not involve the notion of an eventual union. Others would add that it does not involve either a merging of sovereignty or the creation of supranational institutions. But, again, few writers are agreed on a definition of 'supranational', and some would argue that the existing Community institutions are essentially inter-governmental in character, with only minimal elements of supranationality. So although conventional usage continues to assume a substantial distinction between 'co-operation' and 'integration', the exact nature of this distinction remains in dispute.

Behind these disagreements about the use of particular words, there lie more important disagreements about theories relating to co-operation and integration.[4] Those, for instance, who consider that functional co-operation is a more desirable method of achieving a new relationship between states than the creation of a regional grouping based on economic and political union tend to attach far less significance than supporters of the latter to the role of institutions, and emphasize the dangers attendant upon developments which, in their view, could pro-duce a European super-state exhibiting many of the undesirable characteristics of the nation-state, and on a larger scale.[5] Those who have focused on the Communities, on the other hand, usually stress the limitations of what can be achieved through co-operation between states, and the need for a substantial modification of the powers exercised by the nation-state. Much of their writing has therefore focused on the growth of central institutions, and the contribution made to this by the 'neo-functional' strategy adopted by the founders of the European Communities—that is, the gradual widening of the scope of joint action from the base originally established by the ECSC, and the 'spillover' effects set in train by the growing circle of those involved in the process, and the need perceived by the states involved to strengthen the machinery for joint decision-making.

[4] For a recent important review of the state of theories on integration see L. N. Lindberg & S. A. Scheingold, eds., *Regional Integration: theory and research*, issued as the Autumn 1970 number of *International Organization*. In particular the contribu-tion by Ernst B. Haas: 'The study of regional integration: reflections on the joy and anguish of pretheorizing'.

[5] See e.g. F. A. M. Alting von Geusau, *Beyond the European Community* (Leyden, 1969). For a discussion of functionalist and neo-functionalist theories, see Paul Taylor, 'The concept of Community and the European integration process', *J. Common Market Stud.*, Dec. 1968.

Although the neo-functionalists have had to modify their theories about the ways in which spillover occurs, there remains a substantial difference between their views on integration and those held by federalists. Although few would now argue—as some federalists did in the immediate postwar years—that the way to integration should lie through the convocation of a constituent assembly and the establishment of a new political constitution for Western Europe, federalist writers remain sceptical about the 'incremental' approach of the neo-functionalists. They underline the need for a deliberate act of political will if progress towards effective union is to be made, leading to an explicit transfer of authority from national governments to Community institutions.[6] At the same time, however, federalists also emphasize that the creation of effective common institutions is only part of the process of integration, and that it should be accompanied by a corresponding devolution of power by national governments to regional and local authorities, and more effective forms of participation in decision-making in all organizations which impinge on the life of the individual.[7]

The main thrust of the academic study of co-operation and integration has, however, been less concerned with the development of prescriptive theories about goals than in empirical work concerned with the analysis of observed behaviour. Much of the work in recent years has been centred on integration rather than co-operation: so, too, has the attention of the more sophisticated analysts. The literature on the intergovernmental organizations is, however, far from negligible and there have been some signs recently that some of the newer techniques of analysis are also beginning to be employed in this field of study.

General studies

Before examining the literature specifically relating to Western Europe's postwar experience of co-operation, mention should first be made of a number of studies of a more general nature. There is in the first place a substantial number of books which seek to give an overall account of the developments relating to

[6] See e.g. Altiero Spinelli, *Rapporto sull'Europa* (Milan, 1965).
[7] John Pinder & Roy Pryce, *Europe after de Gaulle* (London, 1969), rev. & trans. as *L'Europa oltre il Mercato Comune* (Bologna, 1970) and *Europa: Supermacht oder Entwicklungskontinent?* (Zürich, 1970).

the search for closer unity in Western Europe: these include works by Henri Brugmans, Jacques Freymond, and Achille Albonetti.[8] Others give general historical and institutional accounts of the activities of the various institutions: in this category one of the most useful is the symposium *European Unity: a survey of the European organisations* published in 1968 by Allen & Unwin for PEP.[9] Several extensive collections of documents have also been published: one of the most recent, and most comprehensive—a volume of almost 700 pages—is *L'Europa incompiuta* (1970), edited by Roberto Ducci and Bino Olivi.[10]

Literature on co-operation

It is hardly surprising that the great bulk of the literature on Western Europe's recent experience of co-operation is concerned with studies of individual organizations. What is surprising, however, in view of its importance in the early postwar period, is that the literature on the OEEC is not particularly extensive. Studies on the Economic Commission for Europe (ECE), the UN agency set up in 1947 when the postwar hopes of a pan-European form of organization were still alive, are also rather scanty.[11] This is perhaps to be explained largely by the fact that the onset of the cold war compelled that organization to operate at a low level of saliency, its activities being largely confined to factual studies and the compilation of statistics.

Most of the standard literature on the other individual inter-governmental organizations consists of straightforward historical accounts of their activities.[12] The study by Ernst B. Haas (*Consensus Formation in the Council of Europe*) of voting patterns

[8] For details of these and other similar works, see Cosgrove, and *Bibliographie*.

[9] See also Roger Pinto, *Les Organisations européennes*, 2nd ed. (Paris, 1964); Paul Reuter, *Institutions internationales* (Paris, 1969); and A. H. Robertson, *European Institutions* (London, 1966).

[10] See also Howard Bliss, ed., *The Political Development of the European Community, a documentary collection* (Waltham, Mass., 1970).

[11] For the literature on the OEEC and ECE, see PEP, *European Unity*.

[12] In addition to the works cited ibid., the following recent studies should be noted:

Council of Europe: *Manual of the Council of Europe: its structure, functions and achievements* (1970); Oliver Crawford, *Done This Day* (1970); Anthony Haigh, *A Ministry of Education for Europe* (1970), all published in London.

WEU: Armand Imbert, *L'Union de l'Europe occidentale*, (Paris, 1968); V. B. Conin the Consultative Assembly of the Council of Europe remained for a long time an isolated example of the use of quantitative techniques of analysis, the rather meagre results of which may well have dissuaded others from this type of approach.[13] Today, however, these techniques are much more in vogue, most notably in the case of work on the Scandinavian experience of co-operation,[14] and studies currently being carried out on the various organizations concerned with scientific and technological co-operation.[15]

It is still the case, nevertheless, that relatively little attention has been paid to a number of general issues which arise out of the creation and subsequent activity of the various individual intergovernmental organizations. In the first place, little work has been done in the field of the systematic comparison of the experience of these various bodies with a view to establishing why some have been more successful in achieving their goals than others, and the relative importance of various factors— for instance, the number and size of the states involved, the scope and saliency of the issue area or project, the size of resources allocated to the institution (either in absolute or

falonière & others, *Qu'est-ce que l'UEO?* (Paris, Dec. 1968; spec. issue of the review *Synthèses*).

EFTA: Hugh Corbet & David Robertson, eds., *Europe's Free Trade Area Experiment: EFTA and economic integration* (London, 1970); Eric Roethlisberger, *La Suisse dans l'AELE* and *Mot d'ordre Intégration? La Suisse et l'AELE 1967–69* (Neuchâtel, 1969 & 1970).

Scientific and technological co-operation: Christopher Layton, *European Advanced Technology: a programme for integration* (London, 1969); J. Grosclaude, *L'organisation européenne pour la mise au point et la construction de lanceurs d'engins spatiaux* (Paris, 1969); J. Tassin, *Vers l'Europe spatiale* (Paris, 1970).

[13] London, 1960. The author himself concluded (p. 62) that 'the best that can be said for the statistical material adduced earlier is that it verifies and lends some precision to conclusions which could have been stated merely on the basis of observations of the activities of the Assembly'.

[14] See S. V. Anderson, *The Nordic Council: a study of Scandinavian regionalism* (London, 1967; includes extensive select bibliography). For current work on Scandinavian co-operation and the relations of Scandinavian countries with the European Communities see the journal *Cooperation and Conflict* (Oslo), in particular vol. 1, 1969, devoted to a series of articles on 'Scandinavia and Western European economic integration'.

[15] In Britain these currently include work being undertaken at the University of Manchester on CERN and at the University of Sussex a Council of Europe-sponsored project undertaking an analysis of the experience of other intergovernmental organizations in Western Europe concerned with scientific and technological co-operation.

relative terms), and so on. The policies pursued by individual member states towards and within these institutions, and the methods of their policy-making with regard to them, are also very little explored—not least as far as the United Kingdom's own policy is concerned, most of the literature on this theme being of a polemical rather than an analytical nature. The impact of these various institutions is also only imperfectly understood. Often it is not clear what practical importance specific legislative measures have had, or what secondary effects have been generated in economic, political, or social terms. In other words, there is still much to be learned about Western Europe's recent experience of intergovernmental co-operation.

The politics of integration

The same is also true of the process of integration, even if on this theme the existing literature is far more copious. The more intensive study which has been given to this topic can be explained by the fact that for several reasons it is seen as a more exciting and challenging field than that of co-operation. In the first place, the goals of the process are much more far-reaching: although they are a source of conflict within the member states, they clearly point in the direction of a substantial modification of the role of the nation-state in Western Europe. A new type of political system is being created, here and now: it offers a fascinating opportunity to observe a particularly complex process of change actually taking place. The fascination is all the greater because of its complexity. The understanding of the process not only requires the refinement of existing tools of political analysis, but also offers the opportunity—and indeed makes almost mandatory—a dialogue with colleagues in related disciplines. So the study of integration is a mind-stretching exercise, with the added bonus—or temptation—that as the policy-makers themselves are confronted by a range of new problems as a result of being caught up in the process, the political scientist may himself have a role to play in shaping its future course. The subject can, of course, be approached from many different points of view and can be studied in many different ways. The literature on it is already enormous, and it continues to grow at an alarming rate. This applies as much to scholarly works as it does to the official publications of the various Community organs themselves, and the vast output of polemical works which is by no means confined to the Community countries themselves.

At the same time the ramifications of the process itself are constantly widening: this, perhaps, is one reason why there is no single historical study which successfully covers the whole development of the Communities. In his recent study, *The Recovery of Europe* (1970), Richard Mayne has, however, written a lively account of their creation and early years, focused in particular on the work of Jean Monnet. This provides a useful introductory framework to other historical works which concentrate in more detail on particular periods or aspects of the Communities' development. These include, for instance, the pioneer work by Haas, *The Uniting of Europe* (2nd ed., 1968), which deals with the early years of the ECSC and the formation of the new Communities; the study by Roy F. Willis on *France, Germany and the New Europe, 1945–67* (2nd ed., 1968); the excellent account by Miriam Camps on *Britain and the European Community, 1955–63* (1964); and the detailed study by John Newhouse of the 1965–6 crisis in the Communities, *Collision in Brussels* (1968).

There are, nevertheless, some important gaps in the work of historians on the Communities. After the early years of the ECSC, which produced a number of good studies on its origins and initial experience, an almost total silence has shrouded its subsequent work; little, too, has been written about the political aspects of Euratom.[16]

The literature on the various major actors who have taken part in the development of the Communities is also rather uneven, though the volume of memoirs of those concerned has been growing steadily and the contribution of some of them— particularly de Gaulle—has been intensively studied.[17]

[16] For the literature on the ECSC and Euratom, see Cosgrove, and PEP, *European Unity.*

[17] See e.g. Konrad Adenauer, *Erinnerungen, 1945–63* (Stuttgart, 1965–8), 4 vols.; Arnulf Baring, *Aussenpolitik in Adenauers Kanzlerdemokratie: Bonns Beitrag zur europäischen Verteidigungsgemeinschaft* (Munich, 1969); Edmond Jouve, *Le Général de Gaulle et la construction de l'Europe, 1940–66* (Paris, 1967), 2 vols.; M. & S. Bromberger, *Jean Monnet and the United States of Europe* (London, 1969); René Hostiou, *Robert Schuman et l'Europe* (Paris, 1970); P.-H. Spaak, *Combats inachevés* (Paris, 1969), 2 vols.; P.-H. Laurent, 'Paul-Henri Spaak and the diplomatic origins of the Common Market,

Political scientists, for their part, have been mainly concerned with two aspects of integration: the dynamics of the process and decision-making processes. With regard to the first of these the creation of the Communities has stimulated a new consideration of a set of problems which has long been familiar to those concerned with federalism: in the first place, the explanation of why a group of states should decide to seek to unite, and the conditions under which such a decision may or may not lead to a successful outcome. Following on the pioneer works by Karl Deutsch and Amitai Etzioni, a substantial new literature has been evolved—notably by Haas, Philippe C. Schmitter, and Joseph Nye[18]—which has been mainly concerned with the identification of the relevant variables.

In recent years the frontiers of the subject have moved into the area of seeking to interrelate these variables and so arrive at a comprehensive model for the understanding of the on-going dynamics of the process. Here the work of Leon Lindberg of the University of Wisconsin has been outstanding. By applying the techniques of systems analysis developed by David Easton, and by marrying them with neo-functionalist theories of integration, he has produced two seminal studies on the Communities—the second in co-operation with Stuart Scheingold—which have a central place in the literature on the subject. In the first of these works, *The Political Dynamics of European Economic Integration* (1963), Lindberg pointed to the central role of the Community institutions in their development. In this he wrote:

What is striking about the Treaty of Rome and the first years of the EEC is the *scope* of the tasks assigned to the central institutions and the extent to which these tasks appear to be inherently expan-

1955–6', *Polit. Science Q.*, Sept. 1970. On Britain's relations with the Communities, recent memoirs include H. Macmillan, *Riding the Storm* (1971); H. Wilson, *The Labour Government 1964–70; a personal record* (1971); Lord George-Brown, *In My Way* (1971), all published in London.

    [18] K. W. Deutsch, ed., *Political Community and the North Atlantic Area* (Princeton, 1957); Amitai Etzioni, *Political Unification* (New York, 1965); E. B. Haas & P. C. Schmitter, 'Economics and differential patterns of political integration: projections about unity in Latin America', *Int. Org.*, no. 4, 1964; M. Barrera & E. B. Haas, 'The operationalization of some variables related to regional integration . . .', ibid., no. 1, 1969; P. C. Schmitter, 'Three neo-functional hypotheses about international integration', ibid., no. 4, 1958 and his 'A revised theory of regional integration', ibid., no. 4, 1970; J. S. Nye, 'Patterns and catalysts in regional integration', ibid., no. 4, 1965 and 'Comparing Common Markets: a revised neo-functionalist model', ibid., no. 4, 1970.

sive: that is, the extent to which integrative steps in one functional context spill over into another. An ever-widening circle of actors finds this system to be an effective, logical, and appropriate framework in which to pursue its goals, and this is one essential feature of the Community (p. 293).

Although Lindberg entered some caveats about the possible impact of de Gaulle on the process, he assumed that while it might be slowed down 'it would not be completely arrested . . . because so much is now automatic'. The dominant assumption at this time—Lindberg was writing in late 1962—was that 'incremental politics' was now the order of the day, and that the Six would be carried forward on what at the time seemed to be an almost irresistible logic from economic to political union.

It was not long before these rather optimistic views had to be corrected to take account of the actual impact on the Communities of the policies pursued by de Gaulle which first brought an abrupt halt to the first British bid to join, and then two years later brought the Communities to a complete halt for six months. It was at this point that an area of 'high politics' was discovered, which was immune from the laws of expansive logic. It was now admitted that 'political-dramatic' élites (e.g. the General) as well as 'economic-incremental' élites had a part to play in the process; that this might be subject to discontinuities; and that 'spillover depends as much on political choices as on economic dynamics'.[19]

This view, which was one which had always been held by federalist writers on the Community, was also sustained in a study of the role of the Commission undertaken by David Coombes. He argued in *Politics and Bureaucracy in the European Community* (1970) that 'power in all essentials still rests in the national capitals of Europe' and that the Commission was a prisoner of this situation (p. 308). Moreover, by acquiring an increasing volume of administrative functions, with the bureaucratic implications they brought in their train, the Commission was finding it more and more difficult to exercise its other role of political leadership, which in any case was tending towards a mediatory rather than an initiating function. While it was possible to envisage a gradual evolution of its role—perhaps via

[19] Leon N. Lindberg, 'Integration as a source of stress on the European Community system', ibid., no. 2, 1966, p. 262.

a directly elected parliament—which could eventually give it the basis for a leadership function independent of national governments, Coombes expressed doubts about the willingness of the governments concerned to move in this direction.

The most recent re-statement of the neo-functionalist view does not directly deal with this problem. In *Europe's Would-be Polity* (1970), Leon Lindberg and Stuart A. Scheingold have been more concerned to provide a 'theoretical and conceptual framework [for integration] capable of providing an overall perspective on the often conflicting theories, descriptions, predictions, and evaluations'. This work, which includes a set of case studies in which the authors illustrate their analytical approach, is the most ambitious attempt of its kind that has yet been made. Its main strength lies in its identification of certain patterns of bargaining which have occurred in the Communities, and an analysis of the way in which different outcomes have impinged on their development. It also identifies the major variables which have conditioned the ability of the system successfully to convert the demands made on it into policy outputs. It is far less successful, however, in fulfilling some of the wider ambitions of the authors, and in particular their hopes of arriving at theories and models with predictive capacity. As the authors themselves admit (p. 284), they have not 'probed into basic causes or determinants'. They have chosen to concentrate on the visible tip of the integration iceberg: that is, that element of the process which takes part within the institutions of the Communities. They do not, as a consequence, deal in any detail with the interrelationships between economic, social, and political phenomena; and even in their treatment of the institutional life of the Communities they concentrate on relatively limited bargaining sequences within individual policy sectors, omitting any detailed treatment of the feedback impact of policy outputs, and failing to provide any effective method of re-aggregating the different sectors comprising the system.[20]

Their study is nevertheless an important contribution to the literature, and in its final sections where the authors discuss

[20] For a further development of Lindberg's work, see his article 'Political integration as a multidimensional phenomenon requiring multivariate measurement', *Int. Org.*, no. 4, 1970.

possible future scenarios for the development of the Communities they themselves clearly point to the importance of developments in the socio-political environment of the system as conditioning elements for its future. Here they raise issues akin to those posed by David Coombes, which are essentially problems of sovereignty and the willingness or otherwise of the member states to transfer increased authority to common institutions.

In this context the attitudes and behaviour of élite groups in the various member countries are clearly of critical importance. In recent years a substantial body of data has been amassed both on these and also on the attitudes of the general public. Again it is American scholars who have been the most active in these areas of investigation, both in terms of the elaboration of theoretical concepts and the collection of data. It is they also who have taken the lead in investigating levels of social transactions between the members of the Community, and in charting the growth of social integration at various levels of society.[21] One of the findings of the pioneer work by Karl Deutsch and his colleagues—that 'European integration has slowed since the mid-1950s and it has stopped or reached a plateau since 1957–58'—not surprisingly attracted much attention, and not a little criticism.[22] Some of the mathematical concepts and techniques used for the analysis of the data have also come under fire, and the search continues for more refined tools for assessing this aspect of the progress of the Communities.

Increasingly scholars on the Continent—particularly those of a younger generation—are beginning to familiarize themselves with techniques used by American academics, and to make their own independent contribution to the literature. In this process they have received much encouragement from J. R. Rabier, Director-General of the Communities' Press and Information Directorate-General, who has himself also taken a leading part

[21] For a review of these approaches, see D. J. Puchala, 'International transactions and regional integration', ibid., no. 4, 1970. See also Dusan Sidjanski, ed., *Méthodes quantitatives et intégration européene* (Geneva, 1970).

[22] Deutsch & others, *France, Germany and the Western Alliance, a study of elite attitudes on European integration and world politics* (New York, 1967), p. 218. For a critique of the conclusions of this study, see Ronald Ingelhart, 'An end to European integration?', *Am. Pol. Sci. R.*, Mar. 1967. See also R. L. Merritt & D. J. Puchala, eds., *Western European Perspectives on International Affairs: public opinion studies and evaluations* (New York, 1968), and Daniel Lerner & M. Gorden, *Changing Perspectives of the European Elites* (Cambridge, Mass., 1969).

in the working group on European integration set up by the International Political Science Association.[23] In this context mention should also be made of the body of work now being developed at the Institut Universitaire d'Études Européennes of the University of Geneva, under the impulsion of Dusan Sidjanski who, with Jean Meynaud, has been an important pioneer in several areas of political studies on integration.[24]

In contrast to the relatively advanced work that has been taking place with regard to these various aspects of the dynamics of the process, most of the studies on decision-making have been of a more conventional and traditional sort. This work has tended to be concentrated on studies of individual Community institutions, though there is now an increasing volume of studies of individual political parties, of the role of interest groups, and of policy-making towards the Communities at the national level.[25]

Until recently, relatively little attention has been paid to the political aspects of the Community's external relations, though an honourable exception should be made of several studies sponsored by the College of Europe at Bruges, which has also been responsible for a steady output of works on other aspects of the Communities.[26] This is undoubtedly one area of studies which is likely to attract increasing attention in the future, especially if the Community is enlarged by the accession of new members, and it then moves towards a more effective co-ordination of policies—or the construction of common policies—with regard to the 'third world'.

[23] The papers presented at the 1970 Munich conference of IPSA on European integration are obtainable from the Secretariat General of the Association at rue des Champs Élysées 43, B 1050 Brussels.

[24] Jean Meynaud & D. Sidjanski, *Science politique et intégration européenne* (Geneva, 1965); and by the same authors, *Strutture e compiti dei gruppi di promozione* (Milan, 1968); *L'Europe des affaires* (Paris, 1967); *Groupes de pression et coopération européenne* (Paris, 1968); *Les Groupes de pression dans la Communauté européenne* (Montreal, 1969, roneo., 2 vols., to be published by the Inst. d'Études européennes, Brussels).

[25] For brief guides to this range of literature see Cosgrove, Palmer, and Sidjanski, 'Recherches sur l'intégration européenne', in his *Méthodes quantitatives*. . . . Recent studies include *La Décision dans les Communautés européennes* (Brussels, 1969) and R. Perissich, *Gli eurocrati tra realtà e mitologia* (Bologna, 1970).

[26] See e.g. Gordon Weil, *A Foreign Policy for Europe: the external relations of the European Community* (Bruges, 1970); G. M. Taber, *John F. Kennedy and a Uniting Europe: politics of partnership* (Bruges, 1969); W. C. Cromwell, ed., *Political Problems of Atlantic Partnership* (Bruges, 1969). Also Werner Feld, *The European Common Market and the World* (Englewood Cliffs, 1967). On specific aspects of the Com-

Whether or not enlargement takes place it is clear that the member states will be confronted in the future not merely by the problems of 'building Europe' but by a series of difficult policy decisions with regard to the type of Europe they wish to see built. As the work of 'positive integration' proceeds, particularly in the fields of economic and monetary union, and common action in the fields of foreign policy and defence, decisions will not only impinge more and more on the heartland of national sovereignty, but also have wide-ranging implications for the type of European society that emerges in the future, and the role which Western Europe plays in the world at large. In other words, the policy-content of the process, as well as the purely dynamic aspects of the process itself, are likely to attract increasing attention.[27] In recent years a substantial body of literature has already made its appearance devoted to discussing these problems, and—particularly among younger writers—a distinctly more critical note has been sounded.[28] And while some of a new generation of European scholars have been primarily concerned to master the quantitative techniques imported from across the Atlantic as tools for their work on integration, others have shown themselves to be less interested in analysing data on behaviour and attitudes than in identifying the policy choices that will have to be made, and prescribing solutions.

As the Communities move forward through the 1970s, and into the difficult problems that lie ahead, both types of approaches will no doubt continue to have their devotees. For

munities' external relations, recent studies include: Hans Mayrzedt & H. C. Bins wanger, eds., *Die Neutralen in der europäischen Integration: Kontroversen — Konfrontationen — Alternativen* (Vienna, 1970); Mayrzedt & Helmut Rome, *Die Westeuropäischen Integration aus osteuropäischer Sicht: Bibliographie, Dokumentation, Kommentar* (Vienna, 1968); *La Communauté et le problème du développement: la Communauté et le tiers monde* (Brussels, 1970); and I. W. Zartman, *The Politics of Trade Negotiations between Africa and the EEC: the weak confront the strong* (Princeton, 1971). For a more theoretical approach, Karl Kaiser, 'The interaction of regional subsystems; some preliminary notes on recurrent patterns and the role of the superpowers', *World Politics*, Oct. 1968.

[27] See e.g. Scheingold, 'Domestic and international consequences of regional integration', *Int. Org.*, no. 4, 1970.

[28] See e.g. David Calleo, *Europe's Future: the grand alternatives* (New York, 1965); Alastair Buchan, ed., *Europe's futures, Europe's choices* (London, 1969); and Louis Armand & Michel Drancourt, *The European Challenge* (London, 1970). For critical views on the Communities see the journal *Agenor*, published in Brussels and—from the same group—A. Zeller, *L'Imbroglio agricole du Marché commun* (Paris, 1970).

if the Communities have their critics, no one is now inclined to underestimate their importance. While their future course may be uncertain, there is no doubt that they will continue to provide material for study by scholars in many different disciplines and many different countries.

10 The Soviet Union and Eastern Europe

MICHAEL KASER

THE October Revolution divided the social and economic experience of Russia from that of the West as well as from its own past so clearly as to suggest to many social scientists that the mainstreams of their subjects would gain little from an analysis of Soviet measures and activities. The Soviet government and Communist Party reinforced this view by their marxist belief that economic, legal and administrative practice, and, in the longer term, the social structure, were inseparable from the political process; all would develop untrammelled by previous concepts of the state, of economics or of law. The economy, Lenin believed, could be operated 'as a single office or a factory'; 'in a socialist economy', wrote Stalin, 'the law of value is no longer the determinant of social production, for social production follows the plan'. 'Law', stated Vyshinsky (who, before and after his appointment as Foreign Minister, was Stalin's senior jurist), 'is the form in which the will of the ruling class is expressed'.

Although such theses began to be eroded during the lifetime of Stalin, the risk of his personal intervention—the *causes célèbres* were in economics, linguistics, and biology—inhibited the publication of ideas which commanded the respect of Western colleagues. His government, fearing 'capitalist encirclement' before the second world war, and thereafter preoccupied with 'Anglo-American imperialism', restricted the factual content of what little was published on contemporary themes: the flow of official statistics rapidly began to shrink in 1935 and postwar legislation imposed severe penalties on Soviet authors who cited data not specifically included in authorized releases.[1] Thus it was that Soviet writings were scanned more for clues about trends in Soviet political, economic, and social life and about recent history than for any contribution they may have offered to the social sciences; in the extreme form 'Sovietology' engendered 'Kremlinology'.

Much of the detailed research of the detective kind was carried out by governmental agencies of the United Kingdom and the United States; the latter, especially during the 1950s, sponsored research on contract at universities and other institutions. Official assistance, again more in the United States than in Western Europe, promoted the establishment of courses to train specialists in Russian and East European studies, and some of the major scholarly works of that decade were doctoral theses written within the new 'area programmes' or symposia of study in progress at university departments with such programmes. There were rare occasions on which either government sponsorship or an author's commitment to Soviet marxism imparted some bias to reported findings. In the United Kingdom official fostering of external research was delayed until the implementation of the Hayter Report[2] which recommended the establishment of a substantial number of university posts for teaching and advanced research in areas including the Soviet Union and Eastern Europe; this, like the earlier, more modest sponsorship of language studies, pursuant to the Report of the Scarborough Commission,[3] was financed through the normal channels of the University Grants Committee, initially as 'earmarked', and later within the 'block' grant to the university concerned.

The emphasis of the Scarborough Commission on linguistic tuition was not inappropriate at the time (1947), for the contemporary expansion of Soviet influence to eight countries of Eastern Europe introduced a disparity of language among the documents for original research and in the provision of teaching materials. By adaptation to the political and economic processes of the Soviet Union, the East European countries rapidly be-

[1] See the present writer's 'The Publication of Soviet Statistics', in V. G. Treml & J. P. Hardt, *Soviet Economic Statistics* (Durham, NC, 1972).

[2] University Grants Committee, *Report of the Sub-committee on Oriental, Slavonic, East European and African Studies* (1961).

[3] *Interdepartmental Commission of Enquiry on Oriental, Slavonic, East European and African Studies* (1947).

came an entity fit for coherent study by the social sciences, but, whereas Russian was an adequate medium for the analysis of the Soviet Union (because writers in its minority languages rarely put more than a local gloss on the corresponding formulation made in Moscow), the other Slavonic languages are not easily understood from a basis solely of any one of them; German, Hungarian, Rumanian, and Albanian would, moreover, be needed for a properly comparative approach. For the same reasons of language, but differentiated still more by their history and environment, the other socialist states which have to some extent emulated Soviet policies (China, Mongolia, Korea, Vietnam, and Cuba) are not usually examined by a single author, university department, or lecture course; the two notable exceptions are the study of international communism, now a significant specialization within politics, and that of international relations, towards which the Sino-Soviet dispute has drawn many analysts. The ability to take a comparative view without the acquisition of all nine national languages has recently been facilitated by the services of the National Association for Soviet and East European Studies.[4]

In sum, the coherence of the study of the Soviet Union and Eastern Europe in the social sciences and recent history is based only partially on adjacent geographical location (as is the case with, say, African and Latin American studies); the more important relationship is an official common ideology which legitimizes a political monopoly to control economic and social activities within their frontiers in a historically determined pattern.

Although the spice of political polemics still gives its savour to Soviet and East European studies, university work in the

[4] The Association, which had its origin in national 'conferences of teachers and research workers on the USSR' starting in 1954, became in 1967 under the aegis of the RIIA an organization, in the terms of its constitution, for 'promoting study and research in the UK and Republic of Ireland on the social sciences as they relate to the Soviet Union and the countries of eastern Europe and of furthering cooperation between scholars working in that field'. Its Abstracting Service, administered and edited at the Institute for Soviet and East European Studies of the University of Glasgow, circulates in a convenient indexed form notes drawn from Soviet and East European newspapers, periodicals, and books in the course of their normal research by those working on the area within the various social disciplines. It supplements the translations and extracts provided since 1949 in the US *Current Digest of the Soviet Press* and enables the specialist in any one field or country to be aware of the significant contributions in other national languages of the region.

field has, since the early 1960s, evolved into recognized constituents of the respective academic disciplines, and an increasing volume of government research has been declassified. In the United States official sponsors became more willing to authorize the publication of the results of contract studies: papers of the RAND Corporation and of the Research Analysis Corporation have been widely circulated and deposited in university libraries, and texts written in government departments have systematically appeared in a series of symposia launched by the Joint Economic Committee of Congress in 1959.[5] In the United Kingdom government officers' work appeared as books under *noms de plume*, or anonymously with an introduction by an established academic authority. Research developed rapidly both in the English-speaking universities (including notably those in Australia and Canada) and in Western Europe (particularly in France, the Federal Republic of Germany, Scandinavia, and the Netherlands); one initiative outside the university framework took place in Italy where CESES (Centro Studi e Ricerche su Problemi Economico-Sociali) of Milan began in 1964 to convene international conferences including Italian scholars (who previously had been little concerned with Soviet and East European studies) and stimulated interest through its published proceedings and periodicals.

Finally, in the countries studied, social scientists and contemporary historians took advantage of the relative academic liberalization which followed the death of Stalin and of the much greater release of appropriate documentation. The prewar statistical flow was resumed in 1956 (although, with a few exceptions, hardly bettered) and the results began to be published of individual and household surveys on social and economic (but not political) topics; the analytical work of the economist was facilitated and that of the sociologist was introduced. The latter still labours in the Soviet Union under more restrictions as to material than does the economist, because the statistical abstracts contain virtually no social statistics and the surveys made public tend to be either partial or selective. In

---

[5] *Comparisons of the United States and Soviet Economies* (1959); the latest in a biennial series is *Economic Performance and the Military Burden in the Soviet Union* (1970). It is a matter of regret that publication may cease as a result of the death of its co-ordinator, Leon Herman (Lib. of Congress), who established the practice that official secrecy would not cloak primary references and analytical methodologies.

Hungary and Poland (as for a time in Czechoslovakia) the distinction has been less marked and the sociologist has a richer
fund of primary data on which to draw. Those in the other
disciplines in Eastern Europe and the Soviet Union which touch
on the socio-economic structure of their country—law, literary
criticism, historiography, human and economic geography,
the history of art or the study of religion, etc.—everywhere
deepened their analysis of their subject, constantly under the
aegis of the Communist Party's conception of government and
society. The student of politics has obtained little benefit from
the liberalization of information and of academic expression,
though the same three countries which have provided more for
the professional sociologist show a correspondingly better record
than the others in publications about political science.

Cumulating and drawing upon the expanded social study of
the area in North America and in both Western and Eastern
Europe, the research units and survey departments of international organizations have undertaken some valuable comparative work. The agencies most concerned in this field are
UN Headquarters, the Economic Commission for Europe, and
UNESCO (with its linked agency, the International Institute
for Educational Planning); the ILO has made a particular
contribution on the study of worker participation (centred
on Yugoslav 'self-management'), trade unionism, and social
security; and WHO every four years assesses the health and
demographic trends of its member-states in *The World Health
Situation*. The other major organizations which publish authoritative commentaries on national economic topics, the FAO, the
IMF, the World Bank, and the OECD, have few East European
members (though Yugoslavia participates in all), and only
occasional studies consequently appear in their publications.

An international periodical, the *Economic Bulletin for Europe*,
linked to the annual *Economic Survey of Europe*, has long been
respected for putting Eastern and Western economic performance and policies under the same scrutiny, and five national
quarterlies and two annuals attract the greatest share of economic, political, and sociological articles from European and
American universities. *Soviet Studies* (University of Glasgow) is
in its twenty-third year, the Italian *L'Est* has been published
by CESES since 1965, and the French *Revue de l'Est*, sponsored

by the Centre National de la Recherche Scientifique, is a relative newcomer (having appeared in 1970), but the *Annuaire de l'URSS*, published by the University of Strasbourg, under the same sponsorship, has been the main non-monograph outlet since 1962;[6] by the reverse process in Western Germany, an annual compendium, *Jahrbuch der Wirtschaft Osteuropas*, has just been started (from the University of Munich), whereas the journal *Osteuropa* has been published for 21 (and *Osteuropawirtschaft*, its more specialist variant, for 16) years by the Deutsches Institut für Osteuropakunden. No less than 47 specialists— mostly from the UK—contributed short 'position papers' to George Schöpflin, *The Soviet Union and Eastern Europe: a handbook* (1970); the bibliographies which each appended to his survey can supplement the selection which comprises the remainder of this essay.

Political and social studies

Western monographs on East European politics may perhaps be classed in three groups: first, those that concentrate on the interplay between a monolithic state and a pluralistic society; secondly, those which primarily describe the 'Apparat', viz. the institutions and ideology of the national Communist Party and the interest-groups or other forces within it; and, thirdly, studies of dissent and of its control. Scholarly interest has shaded into the journalistic in the first and third groups (though no work seems to have drawn together the various strands of dissent), while the second has been the almost exclusive province of the professional political scientist. No more than a cursory survey can be attempted here, and confined at that to books in English and to domestic problems.[7]

---

[6] *Cahiers du monde russe et soviétique* (published since 1959) contains papers on social studies devoted to the USSR but is chiefly concerned with pre-revolutionary history and literature.

[7] Among leading works on Soviet international relations may be cited William Zimmerman, ed., *Soviet Perspectives on International Relations 1956–67* (Princeton, 1969); A. J. Toynbee & others, *The Influence of Bolshevism on the World Outside Russia* (London, 1967); D. J. Dallin, *Soviet Foreign Policy after Stalin* (London, 1962); J. Malcolm Mackintosh, *Strategy and Tactics of Soviet Foreign Policy* (London, 1962); A. L. Horelick & M. Rush, *Strategic Power and Soviet Foreign Policy* (Chicago, 1966); A. B. Ulam, *Expansion and Coexistence: the history of Soviet foreign policy 1917–67* (New York, 1968); P. E. Mosely, *The Kremlin and World Politics* (New York, 1960); W. Hayter, *Russia and the World* (London, 1970), I. Deutscher, *Russia, China, and*

'In our generation', Ghiţa Ionescu points out, in *The Politics of the European Communist States* (1967), 'the study of politics has been transformed by the new methods of political sociology and comparative politics. The stress is laid on political systems and societies as a whole, and modern studies endeavour to see how contemporary states do, or do not, correspond to their respective societies.' The Soviet Union and the East European states are not 'pluralistic-constitutional', to use Aron's formula, but some Western social and political writers suggest that they embrace societies which are as inherently pluralistic as any of their degree of socio-economic development. They go on to affirm that the state machinery must both suppress that implicit opposition and elevate the 'Apparat' as the monolithic instrument not only for the static purpose of running the state but also for the dynamic mobilization of resources for some social or economic transformation. Ionescu finds keynotes of this argument in such watchwords of Lenin as 'We want no more opposition' and 'We would all have perished long ago but for the Apparat', but sees a change of policy in the 1961 declaration of the Soviet Communist Party Congress terminating 'the dictatorship of the proletariat' in favour of a 'state of all the people'. Khrushchev at that time looked forward to the day when 'the masses will administer society without any special apparats', seemingly accepting the possibility of other power groups than that of the Communist Party. Epitomizing a Trotskyist view, T. Cliff, *Russia: a Marxist analysis* (3rd ed., 1970) disbelieves such intentions because 'ensconced and consolidated, the ruling class of the state capitalist regime behaves like every other ruling class: it defends its filched privileges from those it has robbed, the workers', but his class interpretation of the USSR today is dualistic, such that the future is reserved for the 'self-mobilised masses . . . led by a revolutionary Marxist Party'. At the other extreme, J. P. Nettl, *The Soviet Achievement* (1967), proffers a convergence theory based on popular participation in pluralistic expression 'through membership of the all-pervading Party or the local Soviets or other collective bodies instead of choosing between contenders to represent them in office. The guarantee of a vote; or membership of a collectivity

the West 1953–66 (London, 1970). E. P. Hoffmann & F. J. Fleron, eds, *Conduct of Soviet Foreign Policy* (London, 1971).

of action: who can say which offers the more promising or effective means for the masses to make their influence felt?'

Exponents of the conflict between a monopolistic political authority and pluralistic society have frequently placed their discussion in a general context of 'totalitarianism': H. J. Spiro's entry under that title in the *International Encyclopedia of the Social Sciences* (2nd ed., 1968) is the reference statement of the criteria which identify such a confrontation. In this and cognate aspects of comparative politics, the classics on the USSR might be singled out as Z. Brzezinski and S. P. Huntingdon, *Political Power USA–USSR* (1964), Merle Fainsod, *How Russia is Ruled* (1953), and L. B. Schapiro, *The Government and Politics of the Soviet Union* (1965), but it remains an area which demands almost continuous updating as new foci of pluralism emerge in the Soviet Union and as novel situations arise in Eastern Europe; inadequate attention has yet been paid to Hungary, the GDR or Rumania but the Poland of 1956 and Czechoslovakia of 1968 are the subject of numerous books, ranging from ephemera to fundamental political analyses.[8]

The channels of public expression which led to a disruption of political monopoly in Eastern Europe were essentially of the same type that unrepresentative government had engendered for at least a century: the historian of 1848 would find the environment not unfamiliar. But when Soviet cohesion is at issue, there is little to examine in a collective dimension and the observer must trace threads of manifestations which are explicitly personal, in literature, nationality, and religion.

Contrasting with the official fostering of a socialist vision of man absorbed by and morally integrated with the mass of his fellow citizens, the dissenting Russian novel of today is centred on the fundamentally isolated individual, in conflict as always with the managers of society, but withdrawn from, almost fearful of, cognition of the like-minded. The frontier between literary

[8] On Budapest P. E. Zinner, *Revolution in Hungary* (New York, 1962) carefully isolates the several trends within the Party, among intellectuals and of public opinion, while Richard Hiscocks, *Poland: bridge for the abyss?* (London, 1963) is the corresponding basic study of the more peaceable changes in Warsaw. By no means all the evaluations of Prague in 1968 have yet appeared but the professional political scientist is already to the fore, notably Z. A. B. Zeman, *Prague Spring* (Harmondsworth 1969), R. Rhodes James, ed., *The Czechoslovak Crisis* (London, 1969), and V. V. Kusin, *Intellectual Origins of the Prague Spring* (Cambridge, 1971).

criticism and the political analysis of writing has perhaps never been clearer, for the very poverty of the pen can exhibit an author's search for self-expression unsatisfiable in public life. Although few reach the quality of a Pasternak or Solzhenitsyn, recognition of this literature by the award of a Nobel Prize has enabled publishers to convert by translation much *samizdat* (informal circulation by the author himself) into *tamizdat* ('publication over there') and to open this documentation to the political scientist without a specialized linguistic talent. It may be that the opportunity has as yet been inadequately seized, for the authors who have undertaken the deeper assessments are those as fluent in Russian as in English.[9]

A few signs of social pluralism may be found in the literature of the linguistic minorities of the Soviet Union, but the crucial material for a study of Soviet 'nationalities policy', as laid down in 1918 by Lenin and Stalin, is almost totally unavailable, viz. minutes of local government and party authorities, the career structures and selection procedures of officials and records of litigation and social surveys in the non-Russian regions. A beginning has been made through linguistics and social anthropology —for the Institute of Ethnography in Moscow is particularly co-operative with Western, above all French, writers; works, on the other hand, which make their theme political pluralism have perhaps been too passionately concerned with its repression.[10]

Economic and cultural change in the non-Russian republics has readily been examined by the international organizations

[9] M. Hayward & Leo Labedz, eds., *Literature and Revolution in Soviet Russia 1917–62* (Oxford, 1963), P. Blake & M. Hayward, *Dissonant Voices in Soviet Literature* (New York, 1962), and the paper by A. Nove, *Was Stalin Really Necessary?* (London, 1964) on 'The Peasants in Soviet Literature'.

[10] In the first group are A. Benningsen & C. Quelquejay, *The Evolution of the Muslim Nationalities of the USSR and Their Linguistic Problems* (London, 1961) and H. N. Michael, ed., *Studies in Siberian Ethnogenesis* (Toronto, 1962), and in the second, two by W. Kolarz, *Russia and Her Colonies* (New York, 1952) and *The Peoples of the Soviet Far East* (London, 1954), O. Caroe, *Soviet Empire* (2nd ed., London, 1967) and R. Conquest, *The Nation Killers* (London, 1970). The more populous republics have been well examined by historians: A. G. Park, *Bolshevism in Turkestan 1917–27* (New York, 1957), two by R. E. Pipes, *Moslems of Soviet Central Asia: trends and prospects* (Cambridge, Mass., 1954) and *The Formation of the Soviet Union* (2nd ed., Cambridge, Mass., 1964), G. Wheeler, *The Modern History of Soviet Central Asia* (London, 1964) and D. M. Lang, *A Modern History of Georgia* (London, 1962), while many of the smaller ethnic groups have the key feature of their histories described in T. E. Armstrong, *Russian Settlement in the North* (Cambridge, 1965).

(the UN Social Affairs Bureau, the ECE, and UNESCO) as a measure of East–West comparison in what must generally be a North–South confrontation; they and the books in English, Geoffrey Wheeler, *Racial Problems in Soviet Muslim Asia* (1960) and A. Nove and J. A. Newth, *The Soviet Middle East* (1967), demonstrate—though not entirely to the satisfaction of the development economist—the net benefit which the Muslim republics have received from integration in the Union, partly because of greater national coherence and of gains from central investment (both in education and health facilities, and in economic growth). Violet Conolly's *Beyond the Urals* (1967), valuable in any case as a collation of the record of economic developments throughout Soviet Asia, is perhaps the most perceptive, helped by her insight into the Irish Question. She distinguishes from the resident population 'a group in those republics (similar to what were known in Ireland as Castle Catholics) who have linked their fortunes with the Russian ascendancy', and the 'skilled Russians . . . an essential element in the labour force [who] have to be tolerated'. As a comparison of the 1959 and 1970 censuses has just shown, the demographic divergence between Slavic and non-Slavic peoples of the Soviet Union has made the country's cohesion depend ever more strongly on the degree of national identification or toleration.

The social anthropologist has again been to the fore in considering the present state of ethnicity in Eastern Europe, especially of the Slavic nations of Yugoslavia whose political fissiparity has also had its share of academic attention. The groups which have so far escaped detailed political or economic study are those which are too small or scattered for significant autonomies (Turks in Bulgaria, Wends in the GDR, and gypsies everywhere), or those whose institutionalized place in local government has been subject to such sharp changes as to call for updating indefinitely (Magyars in Rumania, Albanians in Yugoslavia).

Apart from the Soviet Union's Jewish Autonomous Oblast (where, significantly, the 1970 circulation of the Yiddish newspaper was only 12,000) no territorial institutions are related to the most dispersed of minorities: whether by perceived identity or by religion, the Jews form a group to which more significant social analysis has been devoted than to any other founded on religious distinction.[11] The influence of Islam is adequately covered by the studies of Central Asia just noted and by S. A. Zenkovsky, *Pan-Turkism and Islam in Russia* (1960); it is perhaps more benignly viewed by the Soviet government because nearly all foreign Muslims live in underdeveloped countries, where Soviet co-religionists can on occasion serve the foreign policy of the Soviet Union.

The Christian religions on the other hand have their strong-holds among imperialist or formerly colonial powers and may operate under disabilities in newly independent states. For the Soviet authorities, one may hence suggest, the group expression of such faiths is unmitigatedly pluralistic and, for ideological reasons, external to government institutions (though the sepa-ration of church and state is by no means absolute).[12] Apart therefore from a few decrees or party denunciations, documenta-tion on the Christian denominations in the Soviet Union must come from non-official sources ready enough to communicate with foreign co-religionists. More information is available from Eastern Europe because the churches have retained not only a much larger proportion of their following than in Russia but also close links with the West, above all in the case of the Catholic Church and the Vatican. This not inconsiderable volume of information has gained proper attention from students of religious affairs but awaits its social analyst.

By contrast, the historian awaits access to the information on which proper political analysis must be founded. Explaining his decision to take his history to 1929 and no further, Carr observed:

Down to that date, debates were conducted in the leading Party organs on major issues of policy; and, though the free expression of opinions hostile to the Party was increasingly restricted, the historian has no great difficulty in unravelling the issues at stake, in appreciating

[11] In an extensive literature early and very recent surveys are respectively S. M. Schwarz, *The Jews in the Soviet Union* (New York, 1951) and L. Kochan, ed., *The Jews in Soviet Russia since 1917* (London, 1970).

[12] Work has rightly been directed towards the Orthodox Church—J. S. Curtiss, *The Russian Church and the Soviet State 1917–50* (Boston, 1953), M. Spinka, *The Church in Soviet Russia* (London, 1956), W. Kolarz, *Religion in the Soviet Union* (London, 1961), T. Ware, *The Orthodox Church* (London, 1969), N. Zernov, *The Russian Reli-gious Renaissance of the 20th Century* (New York, 1963) and W. Fletcher, *The Russian Orthodox Church Underground* (London, 1971); M. Bourdeaux, *Religious Ferment in Russia* (London, 1968) is one of the few on Protestant sects.

the arguments advanced on either side or in knowing, by and
large, who advanced them. This—almost suddenly—ceases to be
true after the spring of 1929. . . . Later the fog becomes thicker still
and, in spite of a few piece-meal revelations, envelops all Soviet
policy in the nineteen-thirties.[13]

The one political history which embraces the entire Soviet
period is of the Communist Party by Schapiro,[14] who is somewhat better served than the historian of the state because the
party continued to report on itself to its congresses, to publish
congress and conference proceedings, and to have pronouncements—albeit Stalin's—made in its name.

Although it is almost exactly a millennium from Prince
Oleg's treaty with Byzantium (912) and the Revolution of 1917,
most general histories of Russia obscure the paucity of recent
documentation by devoting, appropriately enough, space
roughly proportionately between the thousand years before
the Revolution and the post-revolutionary half-century. They
hence fall outside the scope of this paper, though others which
are devoted to the events and ideas which generated the 1917
revolutions could justifiably be considered as studies of Soviet
affairs.[15] Such post-revolutionary history as has been written
has concentrated on the life and work of the key personalities—
Lenin, Trotsky, Stalin, and Khrushchev.[16] No one has yet

[13] E. H. Carr & R. W. Davies, *Foundations of a Planned Economy 1926–9* (London,
1969), the first of Carr's final trilogy, the preceding volumes of which were *The
Bolshevik Revolution 1917–23* (3 vols. 1950–3), *The Interregnum 1923–4* (1954), and
Socialism in One Country 1924–6 (3 vols., 1958–64).

[14] *The Communist Party of the Soviet Union* (2nd ed., London, 1970); J. H. Billington,
The Icon and the Axe (London, 1966) is a social and cultural history of the same
period.

[15] Among those which are devoted to the events and ideas immediately before
1917, J. L. H. Keep, *The Rise of Social Democracy in Russia* (London, 1963), S. V.
Utechin, *Russian Political Thought* (New York, 1964), H. Shukman, *Lenin and the
Russian Revolution* (London, 1966), G. Katkov, *Russia 1917: the February revolution*
(London, 1967), R. Kindersley, *The First Russian Revisionists* (London, 1962), and
D. Lane, *The Roots of Russian Communism* (London, 1969) analyse the political
environment from which the Bolsheviks sprang.

[16] A symposium, L. Schapiro and P. Reddaway, eds., *Lenin, the man, the theorist,
the leader* (London, 1967), I. Deutscher, *Lenin's Childhood* (London, 1970), D. Shub,
Lenin (Penguin, 1966), and L. Fischer, *The Life of Lenin* (London, 1965) are central
to the study of the primary figure, while B. Wolfe, *Three Who Made a Revolution*
(New York, 1948) takes him in a comparative context with Trotsky and Stalin.
The principal works on other Soviet leaders are Deutscher's trilogy on Trotsky,
The Prophet Armed (1954), *The Prophet Unarmed* (1959), 'and *The Prophet Outcast* (1963),
and his *Stalin: a political biography* (1949, all published in London). R. Conquest,

undertaken a general history of the corresponding quarter-century in Eastern Europe, where, again, the biographical approach has been preferred.[17]

Turning from biographical studies to the history of the institutions their subjects created is to discover that the main works are textbooks,[18] but of considerable value and more general appeal are the commentaries of expert journalists, whose chief contribution has been in the analysis of political decision-making.[19] By contrast, there is little in either category on the political institutions of Eastern Europe, though three of the Communist Parties have found historians.[20]

The standing of the party and of its leaders in the socialist countries may compensate the dearth of national histories around other themes, and in similar fashion the study of Soviet society has crystallized on two facets—the party and education.

The interaction of the two is epitomized in Lenin's prescription of 'polytechnical education'. 'The study of Soviet education confirms Durkheim's view that education is a "methodological socialisation of the young" [with] . . . emphasis on technological training and political socialisation',[21] yet it clearly emerges from sociological studies that the family has remained the basic unit

Power and Policy in the USSR (London, 1961) and R. Pethybridge, *A Key to Soviet Politics* (London, 1962) illuminate the most important period in Khrushchev's career, but of the fuller biographies, L. Pistrak, *The Grand Tactician* (New York, 1961), unconvincingly partial, has to be complemented by the more straightforward M. Frankland, *Khrushchev* (Penguin, 1966). The alleged memoirs of Khrushchev, *Khrushchev Remembers* (London, 1971) are useless—as Schapiro has pointed out—as historical or political documentation until their authorship is clarified. S. Fitzpatrick, *The Commissariat of Enlightenment* (London, 1971), which studies Lunarcharsky, and Katkov, *The Trial of Bukharin* (London, 1969) also make biography the key to policy disputes.

[17] P. Auty, *Tito* (London, 1970), N. Bethell, *Gomulka: his Poland and his communism* (London, 1969), L. Blit, *The Eastern Pretender; Boleslaw Piasecki, his life and times* (London, 1965), and W. Shawcross, *Dubcek* (London, 1970).

[18] J. N. Hazard, *The Soviet System of Government* (3rd ed., Chicago, 1964), L. G. Churchward, *Contemporary Soviet Government* (London, 1968), D. J. R. Scott, *Russian Political Institutions* (4th ed., London, 1961), and Schapiro, *Government and Politics of the Soviet Union* (already cited).

[19] Outstandingly B. I. Nicolaevsky, *Power and the Soviet Elite* (London, 1966) and M. Tatu, *Power in the Kremlin* (London, 1968).

[20] M. K. Dziewanowski, *The Communist Party of Poland* (Cambridge, Mass., 1959), G. Ionescu, *Communism in Rumania 1944–62* (London, 1964), and I. Avakumović, *History of the Communist Party of Yugoslavia* (Aberdeen, 1964); N. C. Pano, *The People's Republic of Albania* (Baltimore, 1968) is largely a history of the Albanian Party.

[21] From Lane, *Politics and Society in the USSR* (London, 1970).

of society, not ousted by the workplace to which an earlier generation of communists looked. The failure to effect such an ideological socialization may be of negative rather than of positive interest for inter-society comparison, but the Soviet sociologist, by making scant examination of his fellow citizen as a worker, has offered little evidence for the outsider to analyse. Two studies on labour relations[22] have nevertheless shown the value of evidence derived from interviews, court cases, and local press reports.

Nor is the sociology of education much better served, though there are enough detailed surveys of national educational systems.[23] One particularly fruitful subject, the place and frequently changing role of the university in intellectual life and research, has yet to find an author. Some studies have described the control of scientific life under Stalin,[24] but the role of any intellectual élite today merits detailed examination.

Cadres which have attracted analysis are of course the senior staffs of party and administrative organs.[25] The crucial problem awaiting analysis is the interaction of territorial political jurisdictions and of central economic agencies, briefly resolved under Khrushchev through the replacement (1957–65) of industrial ministries by regional economic councils (*sovnarkhozy*). This examination, and the broader one of the role and tolerance of interest-groups,[26] would raise the question of the applicability to the Soviet Union of structural approaches adopted for pluralis-

---

[22] M. McAuley, *Labour Disputes in Soviet Russia 1957–65* (Oxford, 1969) and E. C. Brown, *Soviet Trade Unions and Labour Relations* (London, 1966).

[23] N. Grant, *Soviet Education* (London, 1964) and N. de Witt, *Education and Professional Employment in the USSR* (Washington, 1961) have described the Soviet system; a monograph on its application to the smallest country of the group, Albania, documented in J. I. Thomas, *Education for Communism* (Stanford, 1969) is one of the very few studies in this field on Eastern Europe.

[24] E. Ashby, *Scientist in Russia* (Harmondsworth, 1947) and D. Joravsky, *Soviet Marxism and Natural Science 1917–32* (New York, 1961) and *The Lysenko Affair* (Cambridge, Mass., 1970).

[25] J. A. Armstrong, *The Soviet Bureaucratic Elite; a case study of the Ukrainian apparatus* (New York, 1959), T. H. Rigby, *Communist Party Membership in the USSR 1917–67* (Princeton, 1968), and J. F. Hough, *The Soviet Prefects* (Cambridge, Mass., 1969) examine the former and J. R. Azrael, *Managerial Power and Soviet Politics* (Cambridge, Mass., 1966), J. S. Berliner, *Factory and Manager in the USSR* (Cambridge, Mass., 1957), and D. Granick, *The Red Executive* (New York, 1960) investigate the latter.

[26] Each of the main functional groups is considered in H. G. Skilling & F. Griffiths, eds., *Interest Groups in the Soviet Union* (Princeton, 1971).

tic constitutional societies. Both group theory and organization analysis have their proponents, but it remains to be shown how to treat those coercive elements in the social structure which pluralism by definition excludes. The police and security forces combine a local with a ministerial administration and were endowed by Stalin with a power that was as fundamental to the theory of state operation as it was arbitrary in execution. Its executive role has been the principal focus of Western writers[27] and, by virtue of the prejudice it brought to the rule of law, has limited the interest of professional comparative lawyers in Soviet juridical practice.[28]

Economics

If political studies have congregated around the theme of how the Soviet state works and how society is managed, economists were for long primarily concerned with what the Soviet state had done, and have only more recently put its mechanism under examination. As in the political and social field, less work has been undertaken on the East European states than on the Soviet Union, but the emphasis has been on economic organization and virtually nothing has been published (the work of the UN Secretariat apart) on the record of economic development.

The attraction of research into the comparative growth record of the Soviet Union (and the asymmetric neglect of that in Eastern Europe) is superficially explicable by the need to measure super-power rivalry. Stalin in the 1930s and Khrushchev in the 1950s publicly aimed at 'overtaking the most developed capitalist state, the United States', and the Soviet maintenance of an economy which withstood the German invasion encouraged comparative evaluation especially when the cold war fanned defence preparations on either side. The work is perhaps better seen as the application to economies with a derelict price system of three of the techniques, invented

[27] S. Wolin & R. M. Slessor, eds., *The Soviet Secret Police* (London, 1957), R. Conquest, *The Great Terror* (London, 1968), and R. Hingley, *The Russian Secret Police* (London, 1970).

[28] H. J. Berman, *Justice in the USSR* (Cambridge, Mass., 1963) reflects on the concept of Soviet law as well as describing its organization; Hazard, *Settling Disputes in Soviet Society* (New York, 1960) traces the system to its origins and I. Lapenna, *State and Law: Soviet and Yugoslav theory* (London, 1964) makes the sole international comparison in opposing centralism and federalism.

for price-sensitive mechanisms, which distinguish postwar economics. Though each has a prewar antecedent, the three concerned—namely social accounting, development theory, and the production function—rank with games theory and structural analysis as the new tools for the student of productive efficiency and decision-taking; the two others by their nature require an access to primary data far beyond what is yet available from the Soviet Union to the foreign investigator. Postwar developments in welfare economics—consumer behaviour, the demand function, merit goods—were unrelatable to the Soviet Union while its government invariably planned from the supply rather than from the demand side; the promulgation of a five-year plan (that for 1971–5) incorporating for the first time a greater proportionate increment in consumers' goods than in producers' goods may foreshadow some change.

Articulated national accounts formed the first framework for the quantitative appraisal of the Soviet economy as a whole,[29] and were followed in the 1960s by the comparison of the Soviet development record with those of earlier-industrialized states.[30] Within the group of studies concentrating on statistical analysis is one on the record and interpretation of macro-economic stability,[31] many on the evolution of industry, transport, construction, and agriculture in production terms,[32] and two presenting a time series for personal consumption.[33]

But the books which contribute most to an understanding of the development process are at the extremes of detail and of generalization, namely a study in depth of the industry which was at the heart of Stalin's industrialization[34] and A. Gerschenkron's

[29] A. Bergson, *The Real National Income of Soviet Russia since 1928* (Cambridge, Mass., 1961) which deflated to comparable values his earlier current-priced accounts (in studies with Hoeffding and Heymann); A. S. Becker, *Soviet National Income (1958–64)* (Berkeley, 1969).

[30] Bergson & S. Kuznets, eds., *Economic Trends in the Soviet Union* (Cambridge, Mass., 1963), A. Maddison, *Economic Growth in Japan and the USSR* (London, 1969).

[31] R. Hutchings, *Seasonal Influences in Soviet Industry* (London, 1971).

[32] A series of volumes on sectoral trends sponsored by the National Bureau of Economic Research, New York, never reached completion, but the weightiest of those published, G. W. Nutter, *The Growth of Industrial Production in the Soviet Union* (Princeton, 1962) aroused controversy and was considered by some to exaggerate the gap between the USSR and the United States.

[33] J. G. Chapman, *Real Wages in Soviet Russia since 1928* (Cambridge, Mass., 1963) and P. Hanson, *The Consumer in the Soviet Economy* (London, 1968).

[34] D. Granick, *Soviet Metal-Fabricating and Economic Development* (Wisconsin, 1967).

broad-ranging examinations of the role of history, institutions, and attitudes before and after the Revolution.[35] Their insights have done much to interpret the Soviet economic experience, but it is fair to stress that economic historians were analysing the Soviet Union as a development model long before the economics of growth were applied to the third world. The opening chapter of M. Dobb, *Soviet Economic Development since 1917* was widely seen, on its publication in 1948, as a perceptive marxian defence of growth by priority sectors to the exclusion of other options by planners or consumers. It represented, moreover, the counterpart in economics to the objective historical determinism which Carr brought to Soviet political development and, as such, was the implicit target of Gerschenkron's stress on subjective factors in economic history.

The wealth of economic histories[36] contrasts not only with the paucity, already noted, of straight political histories of the Soviet Union but also with that of economic histories of Eastern Europe.[37]

The production function—third in the postwar economist's new armoury as earlier described—may become the technique compelling uniform statistical examination of all the planned economies. One book has applied the method to the Soviet Union and a simplified form of it is appended to another,[38] but most work as yet is in articles in periodicals (which for reasons of space could not be surveyed in the present paper). The technique seeks to separate the contributions of the factors of production to growth under such substitution as may be feasible and—though explaining trends at a macroeconomic or sectoral level—requires cross-section data from individual

---

[35] *Economic Backwardness in Historical Perspective* (New York, 1962) and *Europe in the Russian Mirror* (London, 1970).

[36] The date of publication ranks books in ascending order of ability to draw on an ever-increasing volume of documentation, A. Baykov, *The Development of the Soviet Economic System* (London, 1950), N. Jasny, *Soviet Industrialization 1928–52* (Chicago, 1961), A. Nove, *An Economic History of the USSR* (London, 1969), and R. Hutchings, *Soviet Economic Development* (Oxford, 1971).

[37] A. Zauberman, *Industrial Progress in Poland, Czechoslovakia and East Germany 1937–62* (London, 1964); J. M. Montias, *Economic Development in Communist Rumania* (Cambridge, Mass., 1967); J. Goldman & K. Kouba, *Economic Growth in Czechoslovakia* (Prague, 1969): reconstruction of national accounts by a group under the direction of Alton has been published in part, though is not yet complete.

[38] S. H. Cohn, *Economic Development in the Soviet Union* (Boston, 1970) and App. B of Bergson, *The Economics of Soviet Planning* (New Haven, 1964).

firms if the general relationships are to be substantiated. The statistical showing of one country can be used to verify likely ratios in another, but the instances must be taken from countries with similar socialist planning procedures, for microeconomic decisions are influenced by different considerations within a capitalist market.

Some of the comparative and explanatory analysis of Eastern Europe and the Soviet Union together, as of Western Europe, has already been undertaken by the ECE; its *Structural Trends in the European Economy* (1970) projected from the trends it distinguished relative levels of activity, consumption, and investment in 1980. In this sense, it answered Wiles's call that 'Sovietological economics' should 'from the stage of craftsmanship and chronicling . . . become a science, i.e. to predict'. The short-term projections which he collected for nine economies— China being added to the eight in Europe—were each by a different hand, two utilizing an econometric approach. The interest of the operation—the authors contributing afterthoughts on the accuracy of their projections—lay partly in the exercise itself (which, in general, underestimated the actual sectoral growth-rates) and partly in the outsiders' assessment of plan consistency in so far as a government's intentions could be derived from published objectives.[39]

Consistency is perhaps the prime inquiry that economists have made of the Soviet planning system: how has it achieved, if indeed it has, an orderly attainment of society's goals? The question of efficiency follows: have those objectives been gained with the least use of resources, or could a higher return in welfare have been derived from given land, labour, and capital? Finally, the economist, like the political sociologist, desires to know how the aims of a plan were put together and what consensus they represented.

The view was long dominant that economic activities corresponded to the preferences of the planning authorities by the exercise of a series of strict, hierarchical controls. M. H. Dobb and A. Baykov were its historical exponents and the many works of about a decade ago on individual sectors of the Soviet economy in effect concluded that, while different aims could have been adopted, the controls were by and large appropriate

[39] P. J. D. Wiles, ed., *The Prediction of Communist Economic Performance* (Oxford, 1971).

to the task,[40] though Nutter, already cited, showed how widely dispersed around the prewar targets were the fulfilments of individual branches.

The rejoinder of a second group of economists was that the Soviet plan was overdetermined—that is, that the authorities defeated their own ends by issuing too many, sometimes conflicting, commands. The problem was initially considered in a study of Hungarian industry,[41] and contributors on the Soviet Union to a Berkeley symposium of 1958[42] from which a theory emerged of 'trade-offs' between too numerous targets sent down to the firm. All the general surveys of Soviet planning point to discrepancies between goals in physical units and in financial terms[43] but they do not necessarily culminate in accepting that too much planning precludes the optimal use of resources.

A third line of thought—posed by Polanyi in an article and developed by P. C. Roberts, *Alienation and the Soviet Economy* (1971)—was that targets were so irrationally imposed that transactions between firms resembled a market economy. Without that conclusion, something of what Polanyi termed a 'theory of conspicuous production' was used by the present writer in *Soviet Economics* (1970), namely that the all-round expansion of outputs was necessary for Soviet-type planning to assure stability in the flow of inputs, some of the production increment absorbing the errors of plan forecasting. Others have laid stress on minimizing the effects of planners' inconsistencies and mistakes on 'taut planning', that is the assessment of a firm's targets

[40] On industry as a whole, Granick, *Management of the Industrial Firm in the USSR* (London, 1954), H. Hirsch, *Quantity Planning and Price Planning in the Soviet Union* (Philadelphia, 1961), and B. M. Richman, *Soviet Management* (New York, 1965); on controls over specific economic activities, R. W. Davies, *The Development of the Soviet Budgetary System* (London, 1958), F. D. Holzman, *Soviet Taxation* (Cambridge, Mass., 1955), H. Hunter, *Soviet Transportation Policy* (Cambridge, Mass., 1957), E. W. Williams, *Freight Transportation in the Soviet Union* (Princeton, 1962), and M. Goldman, *Soviet Marketing* (New York, 1963).

[41] J. Kornai, *Overcentralisation in Economic Administration* (London, 1959).

[42] G. Grossman, *Value and Plan* (Berkeley, 1960); Grossman's own paper in a further symposium which he edited, *Money and Plan* (Berkeley, 1968), made the point more fully; there are other references in his *Soviet Statistics of Physical Output of Industrial Commodities* (Princeton, 1960) and in Nove, *The Soviet Economy* (3rd ed., London, 1969).

[43] e.g. G. Garvy, *Money, Banking and Credit in Eastern Europe* (New York, 1966); G. R. Feiwel, *The Economics of a Socialist Enterprise* (New York, 1965); H. Kohler, *Welfare and Planning* (New York, 1966); N. Spulber, *The Soviet Economy* (2nd ed., New York, 1969); and H. J. Sherman, *The Soviet Economy* (Boston, 1969).

with supplies inadequate or at most barely adequate to meet them; the contributions on this of Hunter and of Portes have not been embodied in book form.

Part of plan inconsistency has been traced to inadequate knowledge among planners—a central point of 'planning under uncertainty'—and some[44] analyse the system 'as a flow of information passing through a framework of external rules to act upon enterprise dispositions', defining the rules—as operated at different times and places—as non-parametric, state-parametric, or market-parametric according to the arbitrariness or constancy under which the rules are formed. An alternative classification is by degree of centralization both of control and of information,[45] or by 'planning rules' which Zauberman[46] nevertheless claims cannot be consistent (let alone optimal) in Soviet practice, the sole solution being to evolve efficiency prices.

Even though plan consistency may have been assumed, the discussion on efficiency or plan optimality has long received elegant contributions. By its nature the question can only be answered quantitatively: in brief, how well has the Soviet Union (other countries not yet being considered) utilized her resources? Bergson has put this as the core of his latest works: 'Proponents and critics alike agree that economic merit turns largely on efficiency.'[47] He concludes that it is empirically certain that the Soviet use of resources has been less productive than both that exhibited in the United States and that measured by transformation of resources into the Soviet government's own 'intense pursuit of growth'. He looks, like Zauberman in the work just cited, to mathematical programming techniques to rationalize the centralized economic decisions, supporting thereby the significant—and perhaps, since the XXIV Party Congress of April 1971, dominant—Soviet school.[48] The other options are 'praxeology'—or 'improved science of admini-

---

[44] J. G. Zieliński, *Lectures on the Theory of Socialist Planning* (Ibadan, O.U.P., 1968); M. C. Kaser & J. G. Zieliński, in *Planning in East Europe* (London, 1970).

[45] Wiles, *The Political Economy of Communism* (Oxford, 1962) and *Communist International Economics* (Oxford, 1968).   [46] *Aspects of Planometrics* (London, 1967).

[47] *Economics of Soviet Planning* (New Haven, 1964); he devoted *Planning and Productivity under Soviet Socialism* (New York, 1968) to this aspect, which is also central to G. Grossman, *Economic Systems* (Englewood Cliffs, 1967) and Kohler's *Welfare and Planning*.

[48] Whose text is L. V. Kantorovich, *The Best Use of Economic Resources* (trans. from Russian, Cambridge, Mass., 1965).

stration'[49] and enterprise autonomy, a distinctively East European approach.[50] The three contending schools of reform concur in the need for change in a system which has imposed output maximization on the firm, regardless of any consequential waste or of other objectives (opportunity costs). Obsolescent as that directive practice may be, its reformulation into the constructs developed for market economics has held a ready interest for theorists.[51]

The admission of dysfunction in the directive system has opened the question of how the errors showed themselves to the authorities, whose reaction was to introduce, in the mid-1960s, some degree of reform. The theme of many writers has been the deceleration of growth, that is, a failure to meet goals which have, it is suggested, a strong ideological content.[52] Others suggest that change is impelled by convergence towards the practices of other industrialized economies (as the latter themselves converge upon the socialist).[53] A third suggestion is that the shortcomings of non-parametric planning were demonstrated when the governments concerned tried to co-ordinate their plans, though lacking the criteria for rational allocation of resources and apportionment of the gains from international trade.[54]

[49] Launched by O. R. Lange, *Political Economy*, i: *General problems* (trans. from Polish, New York, 1963).

[50] See B. Horvat, *Towards a Theory of Planned Economy* (trans. from Serbo-Croat, Belgrade, 1964); B. N. Ward, *The Socialist Economy* (New York, 1967); O. Šik, *Plan and Market under Socialism* (trans. from Czech, New York, 1967); I. Friss, *Reform of the Economic Mechanism in Hungary* (trans. from Hungarian, Budapest, 1969); and B. Csikós-Nagy, *Pricing in Hungary* (London, 1967).

[51] E. Ames, *Soviet Economic Processes* (Homewood, Ill., 1965), B. Balassa, *The Hungarian Experience in Economic Planning* (New Haven, 1959), Montias, *Central Planning in Poland* (New Haven, 1962), and A. A. Brown & E. Neuberger, eds., *International Trade and Central Planning* (Berkeley, 1968) have centred on microeconomics; M. Kalecki, *Introduction to the Theory of Growth in a Socialist Economy* (Oxford, 1969) and Spulber, *Soviet Strategy for Economic Growth* (Bloomington, 1964) have chosen macroeconomics; and M. H. Dobb, *Welfare Economics and the Economics of Socialism* (London, 1969) and contributors to C. H. Feinstein, ed., *Socialism, Capitalism and Economic Growth* (London, 1967) have examined the gains implicit in growth goals.

[52] Contributors to G. R. Feiwel, ed., *New Currents in Soviet-type Economies* (Scranton, Penn., 1968); L. Sirc, *Economic Devolution in Eastern Europe* (London, 1969); and M. Gamarnikow, *Economic Reforms in Eastern Europe* (Detroit, 1968).

[53] As most of the argument on 'the convergence theory' has taken place in journals, a useful summary is to be found in J. Wilcynski, *The Economics of Socialism* (London, 1970).

[54] Advanced by the present writer in *Comecon: integration problems of the planned economies* (2nd ed., London, 1967), it has been developed by A. Boltho, *Foreign Trade Criteria in Socialist Economies* (London, 1971), both studies drawing on the pioneering

The movement for economic reform has attracted students from other disciplines, some seeking explanations in their own areas, others linking economic devolution with political liberalization; similarly, economists have explored the political tensions which manifested themselves in economic symptoms.[55] But in one economic revolution at least, political science and economics must inevitably converge—on Stalin's decision to industrialize through forced collectivization and thereafter to discriminate heavily against the farmer both in political standing and in material rewards. The pioneering account, from the aspect of the pace of industrial investment by A. Erlich,[56] is more often viewed as discrimination against the peasantry[57] for only after three decades did Soviet agriculture achieve a settled priority in planned allocations. The chronicle of the Soviet farmer's vicissitudes since the Revolution forms a group of studies on its own, demanding of the economic historian an understanding of the social institutions, ideologies, and politics over at least one, and perhaps three, centuries.[58]

A full rehabilitation of the peasant would be as important as the incipient consumer orientation implied in the present five-year plan. These are the economic touchstones to the political prophecy that the Soviet system is emerging into 'benevolent authoritarianism of great vitality and long-range durability'.[59] The more the economist examines farm and house-

analysis of shortcomings in planning intergovernmental economic relations by F. L. Pryor, *The Communist Foreign Trade System* (Cambridge, Mass., 1963).

[55] J. L. Felker, *Soviet Economic Controversies* (Cambridge, Mass., 1966) on the origins of the 1965 Soviet reform, and R. Selucký, *Czechoslovakia: the plan that failed* (London, 1970) on the Czechoslovak attempts of 1968.

[56] *The Soviet Industrialization Debate 1924–8* (Cambridge, Mass., 1960) and his paper in M. F. Millikan, ed., *National Economic Planning* (New York, 1967).

[57] See notably M. Lewin, *Russian Peasants and Soviet Power* (London, 1968).

[58] Jasny, *The Socialized Agriculture of the USSR* (Stanford, 1949) perceived the contemporary situation earlier and more accurately than most and in stark contrast to idealized images of the kolkhoz in S. & B. Webb, *Soviet Communism*, 2nd ed. (London, 1970); S. Swianiewicz, *Forced Labour and Economic Development* (London, 1965) rationalized the link between the deportations of the kulaks and the decision to industrialize; D. J. Male, *Russian Peasant Organisation before Collectivisation* (London, 1971) and R. G. Wesson, *Soviet Communes* (New Brunswick, 1963) have identified the units which the *kolkhozy* had to supersede; the recent betterment of the farmer's lot is observed in R. D. Laird, ed., *Soviet Agricultural and Peasant Affairs* (Lawrence, Kan., 1963); E. Strauss, *Soviet Agriculture in Perspective* (London, 1969); and L. Volin, *A Century of Russian Agriculture from Alexander II to Khrushchev* (Cambridge, Mass., 1970).

[59] A. Kassof, ed., *Prospects for Soviet Society* (London, 1968).

hold behaviour—in Eastern Europe as much as in the Soviet Union—the better will be our understanding not only of the substantial fields of activity in which individual decisions operate within controlled systems, but also of the social and political pressures to which the controllers are coming to be as subject as in pluralistic societies.

11 Touching the Tiger's Buttocks— Western Scholarship and the Cold War in Asia

JOHN GITTINGS

To most Europeans, I guess, America now looks like the most dangerous country in the world. Since America is unquestionably the most powerful country, the transformation of America's image within the last 30 years is very frightening for Europeans. It is probably still more frightening for the great majority of the human race who are neither Europeans nor North Americans, but are Latin Americans, Asians and Africans. They, I imagine, feel even more insecure than we feel. They feel that, at any moment, America may intervene in their internal affairs with the same appalling consequences as have followed from American intervention in Southeast Asia.[1]

THESE words of Chatham House's most distinguished scholar, Professor Arnold Toynbee, are unlikely to surprise many people among the younger generation of Asian scholars, whose historical experience of international affairs has been bounded by the war in Vietnam. Yet even if they do not agree with Professor Toynbee's conclusion that 'America has become the world's nightmare', they will experience some considerable difficulty in disentangling the record of the cold war in postwar Asia, although it is against the Asian backcloth that so many of our worst dreams have been enacted.

Three features stand out strikingly for any serious student of international affairs in postwar Asia. First, the replacement of the colonial powers by the much greater might of the United States; second, the rebirth of a united China; and third, the

[1] A. J. Toynbee, 'A dire view of the United States from abroad', *NYT*, 10 May 1970.

vast increase in political self-awareness and articulateness on the part of the masses of Asia. It would be difficult to argue that any of these aspects are as yet fully or satisfactorily covered in the scholarly literature of the West upon which most students rely. The shortfall between history and scholarship is, however, greatest in the case of the first dominant feature—the role of United States foreign policy in postwar Asia.

One only needs to look at the output of Chatham House in its books and periodicals over the past twenty years to see how the subject of American foreign policy has received a dispropor-tionately small amount of attention, whether with reference to Asia or to the rest of the world except, in a small degree, to Europe. From 1950 to 1965 the quarterly journal *International Affairs* only published two articles, at an interval of nine years, which were concerned in any detail with American policy in the Far East. The score-card for American foreign policy elsewhere was not much better—one article on policy towards Latin America, half a dozen on relations with Britain or Europe, and two on the effect of American public opinion upon foreign policy-making.[2] This is sparse coverage indeed, when the total number of articles on international affairs carried by the journal in this sixteen-year period was close on 400. The picture changed considerably after 1965, the year when the Vietnam war first burst the bounds of Anglo-American scholarly restraint, but meanwhile almost a generation of writing and discussion had been lost.

This academic oversight is even more noticeable if one scans the Chatham House booklist. The catalogue of the Oxford University Press only lists one Chatham House book in print in its North American section—Dr Coral Bell's essay on Anglo-American relations. In the early 1950s there were two Study Group reports on *The Atlantic Alliance* (1952) and *Britain and the United States* (1953). And that is, amazingly, all that was

[2] The two articles on US Asian policy were by Richard V. van Alstyne and Saville Davis in the issues for 3 July 1956 and 4 Oct. 1965 respectively. The record of Chatham House's monthly journal, *The World Today*, is only slightly better. Apart from a brief show of interest in US–China relations in 1955–6, the subject was barely touched until 1963 and onwards. Out of over 700 articles in the fifteen-year period 1950–64, only three dealt with any other aspect of US foreign policy in Asia. However, *The World Today* did provide a better coverage than *International Affairs* on US policy in Latin America.

published by the major institution outside the United States concerned with the academic study of international affairs, over a twenty-five year period dominated by an expanding American foreign policy in every part of the world.

To borrow the language of Mao Tse-tung's Cultural Revolution, it might be said that Chatham House was 'afraid to touch the buttocks of the tiger', or to challenge the authority of the Number One Nation in Power Taking the Capitalist Road. Academics are as human as anyone else, and some criticism of American foreign policy may have been somewhat muted, at least in print, out of consideration for those transatlantic colleagues who frequented the same conferences at Ditchley, Bellagio, or 58 East 68th Street. But Mao's metaphor does not sufficiently explain the self-effacing nature of British scholarship. It was not just for reasons of prudence that there was a general failure to question the principles and goals of American foreign policy, but because few people thought that there were any questions worth asking. Nor was it even necessary to define those principles and goals for the benefit of the general public, since they were after all an integral part of the intellectual luggage of the free world.

In 1950 a Chatham House Study Group published its report on *Defence in the Cold War* (subtitled 'The task for the free world'), described as an 'analysis and assessment' of the international situation 'by a non-political body'. The task for the free world was to devise more effective means of countering the communist attack which, it was now clear, 'was being switched to Asia'. It was not the Study Group's function to speculate about the nature of the communist threat or the origins of the cold war, far less to take a critical look at the official Western view (of, for instance, the monolithic nature of world communism). As the author of the Group's report explained (p. 8), '[We] were in no position to improve on, or indeed to question, the information and analysis on which Western estimates of the present situation had been based.' Two years later the same Study Group had no difficulty in concluding that it was essential to maintain 'for a considerable period the hegemony of the West', in order to keep in check the world-wide 'march of Communism'.[3]

This is not to say that there was no discussion of American

[3] RIIA, *Atlantic Alliance: NATO's role in the free world* (London, 1952), p. 134.

foreign policy at all. If its ends were taken for granted, its means were not, and certainly not when they affected British interests. From the Study Group report of 1953 (*Britain and the United States; problems in co-operation*) up to Dr Bell's essay of 1964, Chatham House displayed a constant concern with the 'relationship', as it is delicately called, and especially with those areas of friction which concerned policy in Asia. The list of these was impressively long: recognition of Peking, sales of Malayan rubber to China, conduct of the Korean war, the Japanese peace treaty, attitudes towards Indian neutrality, the Indo-China settlement, and onwards in an endless line of local difficulties.[4] But the analysis was strictly limited to its Anglo-American context, and the scholars took the shared goals of the transatlantic politicians for granted. Ask not what the United States is doing to the rest of the world, one might paraphrase John F. Kennedy. Ask rather what it can do for (or to) Britain. America's Pacific policy is of interest in so far as it reflects a different order of priorities from that of Great Britain, and disturbs the harmony of the 'relationship'. 'America, unlike Britain, lives in the Pacific, and has to think of the East Asian states as a set of neighbours, the group of powers who share with her the shores of that ocean, and who must affect her security interests in quite a direct and immediate manner.'[5] What many people, including some Americans, might consider to be a debatable proposition is stated here as a necessary fact.

The overall picture of American postwar policy in the Far East, as it emerged in the publications of Chatham House and in the bulk of those published, until the late 1960s, in the West, was homogeneous and bland. The picture was one of a reactive

[4] The 'contradiction', as the Chinese would describe it, between British and American interests concerning the sale of Malayan rubber to China is more than usually piquant. As described in RIIA, *Britain and the United States* (p. 197): 'Partly because of the presumed effect on rubber prices, which some Americans thought were being kept aloft by Chinese purchasers, partly because of the delivery to China of material considered to have strategic value, the rubber trade became for a time the object of sharp American attack. In this case the British were in a difficult position. On the one hand supplying the Chinese Communists meant strengthening the power upon which depended the hopes of the terrorists in Malaya, also Chinese in great part. On the other hand, the prosperity of the Malayan economy was felt to be an important factor in keeping the terrorist guerrilla from gaining more support.'

[5] Coral Bell, *The Debatable Alliance: an essay in Anglo-American relations* (London, 1964), p. 33.

and reluctant United States, dragged into the mire of Asia by
the inexorable force of events (and events which were mostly
communist-inspired). As Dr Peter Lyon writes in an essay, itself
the result of a recent Chatham House Study Group on Asia:

> Thus the United States, as the world's principal *status quo* power,
> has found herself increasingly in recent years in the invidious posi-
> tion of deeming it necessary to try and perform some of the regional
> stabilizing roles, by the show and use of military force and of
> economic strength, which were once performed by some of the
> former European imperial powers in this area. . . . There can in
> reality be small room for doubt that this role as an ordering power
> [the ambiguity in the word 'ordering' seems doubly appropriate
> here] is as distasteful to United States leaders in principle as it is
> irksome and uncertain—and yet almost inescapable—in practice.[6]

We are all familiar with the agonies of conscience experienced
by those who wield supreme power to the detriment of others.
And we are fortunate that the United States is an 'open' society,
whose political leaders are expert in baring their souls to the
public gaze, thus affording us some insight into the stops as
well as the starts of their foreign-policy adventures. If we were
privileged to share the doubts and distaste for foreign involvement of the Soviet or the Chinese leadership, one hopes that we
would be equally understanding. But as it is, this line of analysis,
when applied exclusively to one of the great powers, tends to
distort the whole picture. They—the other side—have goals
and objectives, while we—the Western side—have problems
and scruples. This partial view of the foreign-policy process
in the West, which emphasizes its accidental and reactive
elements while underplaying those of a more purposeful nature,[7]
is further encouraged by the intermingling in academic life of

---

[6] *War and Peace in South-east Asia* (London, 1969), p. 110.
[7] I do not intend to suggest that the formulation of US foreign policy is a wholly
conscious and articulate process, perceived as such by those who take part, or that
it does not react to external stimuli. But I would argue that it is based upon certain
assumptions about what is desirable in the international system, and that these
assumptions, which are shared (although not always explicitly) by those responsible
for US policy-making, have imparted a dynamic and expansionist quality to this
country's postwar foreign policy in Asia. The possession of this quality by the US
is usually underrated, while it is attributed in excess to the communist powers.
Although the making of foreign policy is as replete with contradictions and inconsistencies as any other political process, a general and consistent tendency can be
discerned.

so many distinguished people who have been 'on the inside' of government, or who perhaps still are. Naturally they too will emphasize, in off-the-record conversations with their scholarly colleagues, their liberal views and their opposition to the more unfortunate aspects of official policy. Just as it is difficult to find an ex-Nazi who did not either serve on the Eastern Front or take part in a plot against Hitler, so it is hard to find a former US administration official who would not have liked to recognize Peking in 1950 or to withdraw from Vietnam in 1965.

As far as Asia is concerned, the view that American foreign policy has been essentially reactive and involuntary is not confined to the postwar period. It is, rather, an extension of the same historical approach which regards the Open Door policy more as an expression of benevolence than of commercial self-interest, that sees American imperialism as different in quality from the more sordid British, French, and Tsarist versions with which it co-operated. If America came to be involved in Asia, it was by a combination of accident and of quixotic impulse, as Louis Halle has explained:

> Our unexpected acquisition of the Philippines embroiled us permanently in the Far East. It required us to maintain power overseas, in alien territory, or to ally ourselves with power overseas, in order to meet our new commitment. . . . Our commitment to defend the Philippines was dwarfed by our subsequent commitment to defend the administrative and territorial integrity of China itself, that vast and crumbling empire which reached into the remotest parts of Asia. It was this commitment that was the direct cause of our long quarrel with Japan. . . .
>
> [This commitment] can hardly be explained except as the impulsive commitment of a Don Quixote. We saw China as a lovely lady by the wayside beset by bullies, and we gallantly interfered. We didn't draw our sword, because we had none to draw, but we said we would defend her against the bullies who did have swords. The consequences of this gallantry, undertaken so casually and with so little thought of where it would lead, have been far-reaching. For half a century the lady looked to us for a protection which we were hardly prepared to give her.[8]

The note of whimsy struck by Professor Halle is not sufficiently ironical for us to acquit him of believing in what he has

---

[8] *American Foreign Policy, theory and reality* (London, 1960), pp. 217–18.

written. It is a serious argument, and one which is shared by, for example, Professor John Fairbank, who has described how:

We have a record there [China] of 50 years or so of real sacrifice on our part in some cases to preserve a Chinese nation, to prevent it being taken over by the various imperialist powers and finally, of course, by the Japanese, and this is something that we have to our credit in the annals of history which we don't try, perhaps, as we should, to capitalise on.[9]

It is these indulgent interpretations of the past century of United States policy in Asia which William Appleman Williams has described as 'the veils that Americans have woven to obscure the harsh reality of their imperial record', arguing instead that 'Empire is as American as apple pie', and that 'the history of the American empire is the history of the famous frontier thesis: that hallowed but false syllogism by which Americans have traditionally asserted that their prosperity, freedom and security —and that of other peoples—is the inexorable product of the expansion of the United States.'[10] Just as the 'reactive' view of United States postwar policy in Asia is rooted in this quixotic interpretation of America's imperial past, so the 'revisionist' school of contemporary cold-war critiques owes a large intellectual debt to Professor Williams and other historians of his school. While the historical approach is important, the 'reactive' view of postwar United States policy does not rely solely upon historical forces, generous impulses, or accidents of fate to explain the reasons for American involvement in Asia. The main argument is more narrowly based upon the interpretation of certain key developments in contemporary Asia as inspired by forces hostile to the United States which could not remain unchallenged. It is no longer a question of accidents, but of deliberate initiatives by the communist side to which the United States was obliged to respond. This view has reached such proportions that a whole range of American actions in Asia are commonly presented, in a manner inconsistent with the verifiable facts, as reactions to initiatives by the communist side when in fact the latter succeeded rather than preceded the former.

---

[9] 'Legacies of Past Associations', in U. G. Whitaker, ed., *The Foundations of US China Policy* (Berkeley, 1959), p. 84.

[10] 'Rise of an American World Power Complex', in N. D. Houghton, ed., *Struggle against History* (New York, 1968), pp. 1–3.

The linch-pin of this reactive argument is the (obviously communist-inspired) Korean war, which is supposed to have played a crucial role in galvanizing the United States into actions and policies that would not otherwise have been undertaken. The containment of China, the intervention in Indo-China, the rearmament of Japan, all these policies and the wider view of Asia as a battleground with communism which accompanied them, are frequently described in Western secondary literature on the subject as a sort of regrettable political 'spin-off' from the Korean war.

As Dr Lyon has written in his Chatham House essay, the Korean war prompted 'the beginning of an attempt to apply "containment" in Asia as well as in Europe',[11] while Professor Hans Morgenthau has described how 'China's intervention in the Korean War radically transformed the Asian policies of the United States. The United States responded to that intervention with two policies: the policy of isolating China and the policy of peripheral military containment.'[12]

Statements of this kind, although almost commonplace in the literature of international affairs, are misleading in that they fail to distinguish between the formulation of a new policy and the implementation or acceleration of an existing one. Not only had the doctrine of 'peripheral military containment' of China been adopted in principle before the Korean war, but steps had been taken to put it into effect. The war certainly resulted in an 'acceleration' of this policy (the term used by President Truman to describe the stepping-up of United States aid to the French in Indo-China). It also involved an expanded definition of the 'periphery' which it was deemed expedient for the United States to underwrite militarily. However, the underlying definition of United States interests in Asia had not changed—it was already there—and while a different set of circumstances might have led to different sorts of intervention, the trend towards greater involvement was inherent in the nature of the basic policy commitment.

The doctrine of containment had been expressly formulated by Secretary of State Acheson in a memorandum of 18 July 1949, to Ambassador Philip Jessup, requesting him to make a thorough

---

[11] Lyon, p. 107.
[12] 'The US and China', in Tang Tsou, ed., *China in Crisis* (Chicago, 1968), ii. 98

study of the ways and means of 'halting the spread of totalitarian communism in Asia'. In so doing, Jessup was to act on the assumption that 'It is a fundamental decision of American policy that the United States does not intend to permit further extension of Communist domination on the continent of Asia or in the Southeast Asia area.'[13] Jessup's conclusions are not known; and in his recent memoirs, Dean Acheson neither mentions the fact that he requested a report of this nature nor gives any indication that the containment policy had been adopted.[14] Reminiscences of the type of Acheson's memoirs lean heavily on the 'reactive' alibi, fostering the impression that the administration had no policy at all other than to appease its domestic critics by a series of piecemeal concessions. While the domestic political aspect is important, there is sufficient evidence to indicate that crucial decisions were taken on the grounds of general and well-defined policy at a high level in the direction of a greater involvement in Asia during the twelve months preceding the Korean war. Although many of the primary documents are still inaccessible or are known only in summary form, this is an area which should be rewarding for the more adventurous researcher.

In Japan the State Department had decided by the autumn of 1949 that it was necessary to maintain an American military presence there indefinitely. Plans had also been laid for a peace treaty with Japan which would exclude China and the Soviet Union, and for a national police force which was to be the forerunner of the future Japanese army. In Indo-China the State Department was waiting with some impatience for the ratification by the French Assembly of the Élysée Agreement, which would create a nominally independent state of Vietnam to which American recognition and aid could be accorded. As for policy towards China, the object of containment, the dust of domestic politics only served to obscure the fact that it was already set in a rigid and hostile mould. (The evidence for this

---

[13] Nomination of Philip C. Jessup: Hearings before a sub-committee of the Committee on Foreign Relations, US Senate, 82nd Congress, 1st sess. (Washington, 1951), p. 603.

[14] Dean Acheson, *Present at the Creation* (London, 1970). There is a reference to Jessup and his two fellow 'consultants on China', which makes no mention of their brief, on p. 344, although it does suggest that 'new policy conclusions' were hoped for.

description of US Asian policy in 1949–50 is provided in the following pages.)

These specific moves were made not in order to appease Congress (which was hardly aware of them) but in the light of a considered policy of no negotiations with the 'communist world' until the United States had achieved a bargaining position of massive military superiority. Acheson explains that 'four years of trial had convinced us that agreement with the Kremlin was not then possible. Certain obstacles stood in the way that had to be removed. Among them was the existence in the non-Communist world of large areas of weakness, which by its very nature the Soviet system had to exploit.'[15] Writing at the time (1950), the Chatham House Study Group on *Defence in the Cold War* does not suggest that the effort to negotiate seriously had been kept up for so long. 'The decision that no real co-operation by the Soviet Government with the free world could be hoped for', it states, 'seems to have been taken by American and British statesmen in the first half of 1947' (p. 4). In either case, this rigid and self-righteous policy led to the decision in January 1950 to proceed with research and development of the hydrogen bomb. It also led to the drafting early in 1950 of the national security plan known as NSC-68, which recommended a programme of massive rearmament in order to increase 'free-world capabilities', and which had reached a stage of advanced planning before the Korean war broke out.[16] Europe was still envisaged as the primary theatre of operations, and to that extent the Korean war did result in a significant shift of emphasis. What is of greater significance, however, is the existence of a well-defined policy in which Asia was included, towards the (supposedly unified) communist bloc, before the Korean war began. It is in this light that one should assess the benign view of a reactive American policy in Asia.

Let us examine by way of illustration Acheson's famous speech

[15] Acheson, p. 379.
[16] Most writers stress the point that it was the outbreak of the Korean war which speeded up the implementation of NSC-68, and raised defence spending to an even higher level than it had anticipated. This may be so. But the principles behind NSC-68 had already been accepted by the President and by the Secretaries of State and Defence. It was being planned and costed before the war began. The question which we should ask is this: Under what circumstances would NSC-68 *not* have led to a very significant increase in defence expenditure very soon?

of 12 January 1950 to the National Press Club. Every student
is taught that in this speech the American Secretary of State
defined the United States 'defensive perimeter' in the Pacific
in such a way as to exclude both Taiwan and South Korea, and
that in all probability this gave the green light to the 'communist
side' to proceed with plans for the crossing of the 38th Parallel
in Korea. Further, it is argued that his disavowal of the defence
of Taiwan, coupled with a previous statement to the same effect
on 5 January by President Truman, indicated a relatively com-
plaisant 'hands-off' policy towards the new People's China.

This interpretation is strengthened by the partisan attacks
which were launched against Acheson after the Korean war
broke out on the grounds that he had given encouragement to
communist aggression, thus making his own position appear all
the more moderate. But it ignores the main thrust of this speech
as seen at the time by those whom it most directly concerned.
For the issue was not so much South Korea or Taiwan as it was
Japan.

> . . . the defeat and the disarmament of Japan has placed upon the
> United States the necessity of assuming the military defense of Japan
> so long as that is required, both in the interest of our security and
> in the interests of the security of the entire Pacific area and, in all
> honor, in the interest of Japanese security. . . . I can assure you
> that there is no intention of any sort of abandoning or weakening the
> defenses of Japan and that whatever arrangements are to be made
> either through permanent settlement or otherwise, that defense must
> and shall be maintained.[17]

Thus Acheson, it has been argued in a 'revisionist' analysis of
US policy towards Japan, 'had come closer than any previous
government spokesman to acknowledging the American inten-
tion to retain an indefinite military presence in Japan' regardless of what 'settlement'—i.e. peace treaty—might be reached.
Yet at the time and afterwards the inclusion of Japan, a country
still theoretically under international occupation, as 'an integral
part of the US line of defence in Asia was not regarded as worthy
of particular comment in the United States'.[18]

The People's Republic of China was not inhibited from com-

[17] *DSB*, 23 Jan. 1950, pp. 115–16.
[18] John W. Dower, 'The eye of the beholder: Background notes on the US–Japan
military relationship', *Bull. of Concerned Asian Scholars*, Oct. 1969, p. 20.

ment. What impressed Peking in its published analyses was not
what was excluded from the 'defensive perimeter' but the far
greater expanse of territories which it did include. 'It is clear',
stated an editorial[19] in *People's Daily* on 1 February 1950, 'that
the American imperialists have assigned a major and permanent
position to Japan in their defensive perimeter' and that the US
intended to annex the Ryukyus. (In October 1949 Congress had
authorized the expenditure of $58 million for military construc-
tion on Okinawa, and in April 1950 it was confirmed that the
United States would occupy the Ryukyus indefinitely.)[20]

Were China's fears of a Japan with permanent American
military backing unjustified, or merely voiced for reasons of
propaganda? This interpretation rests largely upon another
chronological myth to the effect that the form of the Peace Treaty
of September 1951 and the accompanying bilateral security
pact was dictated by the outbreak of the Korean war, and hence
that it too was essentially a reactive response to communist
aggression. Yet Acheson's own memoirs confirm that while the
outbreak of the Korean war produced a sense of 'new urgency'
in the State Department, work on the treaty had already been
actively begun under the direction of J. F. Dulles.[21] George
Kennan has also confirmed that already in the winter of 1949 a
consensus had been reached in Washington that such a treaty
would be accompanied by 'a separate agreement with the
Japanese' providing for the retention of American bases in
Japan.[22]

On Korea itself, a Washington-watcher in Moscow or Peking
would not have concluded so readily as his domestic critics that
Acheson had washed his hands of the southern half of the peninsula. Acheson distinguished between American responsibilities in
the northern part of the Pacific area, including Korea as well as
Japan, and the southern part (Indo-China and South-east Asia)
where 'the direct responsibility lies with the people concerned'.

---

[19] 'US imperialists never learn.'   [20] Dower, p. 20.   [21] Acheson, ch. 46.
[22] *Memoirs* (New York, 1969), pp. 416–18. Kennan argues that there may have
been some connection between the decision to conclude a peace treaty with Japan
and 'the Soviet decision to unleash a civil war in Korea'. Acheson (pp. 429–30)
retorts that the Soviet Union could hardly have acted 'in anticipation of United
States decisions taken almost three months later'. Yet the true chronology is evident
from his own narrative, although he ignores it when provoked into polemics with
Kennan. It is a good illustration of how the reactive myth affects even those who
were involved in the actual events.

Korea belonged to the upper half of the league table, together with Japan although 'in a lesser degree' than the latter. The exclusion of Korea from the 'defensive perimeter' which Acheson traced around the Pacific stemmed from an essentially military definition of those interests in the area whose defence could reasonably be guaranteed by a direct United States military presence. It was not a political definition of the extent of those interests.[23]

After all, in a portion of the southern part of Asia (Indo-China) the United States had taken the critical first steps towards underwriting the French colonial war, even if this was an area where the responsibility lay 'with the people concerned'. The decision to do so had been made in the previous year, although its implementation had to await ratification of the Élysée Agreement. It may be objected that the size of the first US aid mission in Saigon and its initial grant was minuscule by future standards. Again it is proper to ask in reply under what conditions such a commitment, reflecting the sombre view of communist 'expansionism' expressed in NSC-68, would *not* have continued to escalate as the French position continued to deteriorate.[24]

Acheson's abandonment of Taiwan may also have seemed rather less unequivocal to the Chinese than it did to his Republican critics at home. President Truman's statement of 5 January is, like Acheson's speech of the following week, an oft-quoted document, but the wording is not wholly unambiguous.[25] The Defense Department, backed by General MacArthur in

[23] It is interesting to note that the same Chinese reaction to Acheson's speech, already quoted (n. 19 above) failed to omit Korea from its description of Acheson's 'defensive perimeter'. From China's point of view, the distinction between the northern and southern parts of Asia, with Japan and Korea in the former area of 'direct responsibility', would be more significant. But no doubt the Chinese understood that Korea was not in the permanent or 'back-up' line of American defence requiring US occupation.

[24] On the timing of US aid to Indo-China, see further Gittings, 'The Great Asian Conspiracy' in E. Friedman & M. Selden, eds., *America's Asia* (New York, 1971), pp. 132–6. The 'reactive' view that the US commitment came in response to the recognition, early in 1950, by Moscow and Peking of the Democratic Republic of Vietnam is chronologically incorrect.

[25] Truman stated that the US had no desire for special rights or military bases on Formosa 'at the present time', that it did not intend to make any military intervention, and that it 'will not pursue a course which will lead to involvement in the civil conflict in China', or provide military aid or advice to the forces of Formosa. This sounds categorical enough today, but it is slightly weakened by the final two

Japan, disputed the State Department view that military aid to Taiwan could no longer be effective, and this disagreement was publicly known. It was still common ground between the State and Defense Departments that Taiwan *was* of 'strategic importance' to the United States and Truman's decision not to become involved militarily 'at the present time' was taken on grounds of expediency rather than out of respect for the territorial integrity of China.[26] Meanwhile the United States continued to recognize the fugitive Nationalist regime on Taiwan, and to seek to deter its allies from extending recognition to Peking. Taiwan was authorized to continue to purchase military supplies from American sources, to use the small unexpired portion of military aid extended in the China Aid Act of 1948 and the much larger sum of unexpired economic aid. A partial trade embargo was imposed upon China, and steps were taken to deny China certain vital resources, including the major part of its civil aviation fleet.[27] The general climate of Western opinion over the Taiwan question may be illustrated by the remarkable proposal of Secretary-General Trygve Lie that Taiwan should be put under UN trusteeship. This suggestion, made to Truman and Acheson in April 1950—before the outbreak of the Korean war—and repeated to Attlee and Kenneth Younger (as Minister of State) in London, was based on the grounds that if China occupied Taiwan, the island would 'remain a military threat on the flank of the United States and other countries with interests

sentences, at least from the viewpoint of a sceptical reader in Peking. These sentences are omitted in the otherwise lengthy quotations provided by Tang Tsou (*America's Failure in China 1941–50*, Chicago, 1963, ii. 531) and Robert Blum (*The US and China in World Affairs*, New York, 1966, p. 108). They read as follows: 'In the view of the United States Government, the resources on Formosa are adequate to enable them to obtain the items which they might consider necessary for the defense of the Island. The United States Government proposes to continue under existing legislative authority the present ECA program of economic assistance' (*DSB*, 16 Jan. 1950, p. 79). In other words, intervention and fresh aid were out; the sale of arms and the continuance of existing aid was not. This formula, whatever political purpose it served in Washington, still entailed a degree of 'involvement in the civil conflict in China'.

[26] On the strategic importance of Taiwan, and the Defense Dept proposal in December 1949 to send a military assistance mission to the island, see Acheson's testimony in June 1951, *MacArthur Hearings*, p. 167, quoted in Derek Bryan, *China's Taiwan* (London, 1959), pp. 4–5.

[27] For further discussion of these US policies see my 'The Origins of China's Foreign Policy', in D. Horowitz, ed., *Containment and Revolution* (London, 1967), pp. 197–200.

in the South Pacific' for years to come.[28] It is narrated by Lie
in his autobiography with apparent pride, as if unaware that
it is not the function of the UN Secretary-General to align himself with any particular set of great-power interests.

The Korean war

Any serious attempt to touch the buttocks of the American
tiger in Asia must lead to a hard look at the established version
of the origins and circumstances of the Korean war. It may
be an academically perilous exercise, since for many people of
that generation the war is still the touchstone which distinguishes the social democrat from the fellow-traveller. Yet it is
a safe bet that if the Korean war occurred today under similar
conditions, it would be far less enthusiastically championed in
the West. To the contemporary student, with the Tonkin Gulf
incident and other examples of official American mendacity
fresh in his mind, cries of communist aggression will not be
echoed without a very thorough investigation.[29]

Such an investigation has never been accorded to the Korean
war. I. F. Stone's iconoclastic study of *The Hidden History of the
Korean War* (1952) still stands alone. Exposing the same kind
of contradictions and evasions in American policy statements
which are now familiar to any student of the Vietnam 'credibility gap', but writing without the benefit of this comparative
hindsight, Stone succeeded in raising a number of awkward
questions. Some form of South Korean military provocation,
backed by a degree of encouragement from the diehard camp
of General MacArthur at Supreme Commander Allied Powers'
headquarters in Tokyo, does not seem wholly implausible.
Certainly those who argued for a more aggressive policy of
containing China, for the defence of Taiwan against liberation,
and for a general extension of the 'perimeter' of United States
'security' in Asia, found the Korean war of great assistance to
their arguments.

Relations between the communist actors in the war also
require much closer investigation. Here too one book stands

[28] Trygve Lie, *In the Cause of Peace*, pp. 264–6.
[29] J. C. Goulden, *Truth is the First Casualty: the Gulf of Tonkin affair—illusion and
reality* (New York, 1970). See also the review by P. Dale Scott in *New York R. of
Books*, 29 Jan. 1970.

alone—Allen Whiting's analytical study of China's decision to enter the war, which is a vital but small part of the whole picture.[30] If it is a case of North Korean aggression, was Pyongyang fully or partially backed by the Soviet Union? Did it jump the gun or did it act alone? Or is there any evidence for Harold Hinton's sketchily argued view that 'Mao probably urged Stalin to give the North Koreans the permission and logistical support necessary for a formal invasion of South Korea?[31] These questions are difficult but not unanswerable; Whiting's own analysis shows that much of value can be deduced by spelling out the 'esoteric content' of communist documents of this period.

A further tiger-tweaking note on the Korean war should be added. The communist campaign accusing the United States of germ warfare in Korea may appear to be ludicrous in some details, but the case against this charge is unproven as well as the case for it. Contrary to general supposition, there is no *a priori* reason why the United States should not have contemplated or actually used such weapons in Korea. There are practical reasons of a technical nature why their use might be militarily counterproductive, though these are not conclusive.[32] It should not be thought that this kind of warfare would have been ruled out of consideration by the United States on humanitarian grounds, especially since it is now known that America was stockpiling nerve gas for possible use in Korea. Chemical weapons are only slightly more easy to control than bacteriological weapons; both are anti-personnel devices which do not discriminate between military and civilian targets, and this is why they are regarded with equal horror in the civilized world.[33]

[30] *China Crosses the Yalu; the decision to enter the Korean war* (New York, 1960).

[31] *Communist China in World Politics* (London, 1966), p. 207.

[32] Robert Leckie has a two-page discussion on why the germ warfare accusation was a 'hoax'. He argues that such warfare has no use at the front, where it will also infect friendly troops, and that its only purpose is to weaken support for the enemy in his rear areas. He seems unaware that it was principally in these areas (including the Manchurian rear) that the Chinese alleged germ bombs were being dropped. Leckie also argues that germ warfare is of little value 'in a poor country such as Korea, where disease is constant and various, where there is frequent contact with animals, where there is no sanitation, and where, as a consequence, fear of disease is low and immunity is high'. In sanitary countries such as America, however, it would be 'a new and fearful thing, whereas in Korea it would not' (*The Korean War*, London, 1962, pp. 349–50).

[33] '. . . the gas GB [Sarin] was derived from Nazi German research and manufactured by the American "defence" establishment during the Korean war as a

Taiwan

Let us now conclude this examination of the reactive myth in United States policy towards postwar Asia by looking at a typical example of the kind of question of fact which becomes distorted in responsible secondary sources. It is a small detail in itself, but taken in conjunction with other errors of the same kind, it helps to build up a historical mosaic of events in which the United States is always more sinned against than sinning.

Item: Mutual Defence Treaty, signed between 'Nationalist China' and the United States on 2 December 1954.

Question: Why was the treaty signed?

Answers: (1) According to Harold Hinton, in his textbook on Chinese foreign policy, China shifted its primary attention to Taiwan in August 1954, after the Geneva agreements, as 'the only area' where it 'could put pressure on the United States'. This led to the bombing of Quemoy in September and the Offshore Islands crisis which then developed. The outcome was that in December the United States signed a mutual defence agreement with Taiwan.[34]

(2) According to the Chatham House *Survey of International Affairs, 1955–6*, the outcome of the Geneva Conference had strengthened America's resolution 'to resist from the outset any further signs of communist infiltration'. It was this attitude which underlay the Manila Pact. And so when, in the autumn of 1954, tension increased in the Formosa straits, 'the United States was quick to see a new danger-spot developing, which required new measures. What these new measures were was seen when, on 1 December 1954, it was announced that the United States had concluded a mutual security alliance with the authorities in Formosa' (p. 7).

weapon against mass Chinese infantry attacks. Yet, there is no evidence that the Chinese were using gas. These circumstances alone make a mockery of all those solemn assurances given by every President and innumerable generals that this country would never be first to use gas warfare' (Tom Wicker, 'Nerve gas and national security', *Internat. Herald Tribune*, 12 Aug. 1970). See also the *NYT*, 10 Aug. 1970 story, in the *IHT* of the same date, which reported that 'by the mid-nineteen-fifties, the Army was manufacturing thousands of gallons of Sarin . . .'. These reports were occasioned by the publicity given to US Defense Dept plans in 1970 to dump unwanted stocks of nerve gas off the coast of Florida. The Korean episode was a historical footnote to the story which attracted little attention.

[34] Hinton, p. 261.

Fact: On 21 July 1954, at a press conference timed to coincide with the final day of the Geneva Conference on Indo-China, President Eisenhower stated that the conclusion of a mutual defence pact with the government on Formosa had been under study for some time, but that this did not necessarily exclude Formosan participation in a South-east Asia pact. There were numerous press reports in June and July 1954, quoting named American officials, that discussions on the proposed bilateral pact were in active progress. These reports all antedate the beginning of the Chinese propaganda campaign against Taiwan which started in August, and the shelling of Quemoy which started in September. In fact Chinese propaganda included several denunciations of the American plans to conclude this treaty. The treaty was neither a 'new measure' nor the 'outcome' of Chinese initiatives in the Taiwan area. One might more fairly conclude that these initiatives were taken partly in response to the news that the treaty was being discussed.[35]

Soviet Asian policy

There are several good studies of a politico-economic nature on the Soviet Far East, but very few of Soviet policy *in* the Far East. Here the reactive myth has operated in reverse; until recently the view of a hyper-active Soviet diplomacy in postwar Asia was still widely held. According to the classic mythology, it was by means of Soviet directives, transmitted at the South-east Asia Youth Conference in February 1948 (the 'Calcutta Conference'), that the first wave of Asian revolution was stirred up.[36] As Soviet expansionist aims were progressively thwarted in the West, by the Truman Doctrine, the Marshall Plan, the Berlin airlift, and the establishment of NATO, 'Moscow turned

---

[35] *NYT*, 22 July 1954; *Manchester Guardian*, 5 July 1954; *NYHT*, 21 July 1954 (statement by Karl Rankin, US Ambassador to Taiwan); *NYT*, 7 Nov. 1954 (State Dept disclosure that discussions had been in progress 'for almost a year'). Eisenhower makes no mention of the treaty in his memoirs except to record that it was signed in December.

[36] Even if there were no 'directives', there was a general 'line', which was communicated at Calcutta. See e.g. Joseph Frankel, 'Soviet Policy in South East Asia', in Max Beloff, *Soviet Policy in the Far East 1944–51* (London, 1953), pp. 208–10. For the contrary view that if a Soviet 'line' existed, which is unproven, it was unintelligible to any Asian who actually had to make revolution, see Gittings, 'The Great Asian Conspiracy', cited above, n. 24.

East'. While the victory of Chinese communism was always hard to accommodate to this Machiavellian myth of the great Soviet conspiracy in Asia, the Korean war certainly fitted very nicely. As Malcolm Mackintosh has written in his textbook study of Soviet foreign policy:

> The year 1949 brought a strategic stalemate in Europe: no further Soviet territorial advance could be made. . . . However, in the Far East an entirely new set of circumstances . . . opened up great possibilities for Soviet strategy. From 1949 to 1953 it was the Far East that claimed priority among the planners of Soviet strategy in Moscow.[37]

Lately a rather more sceptical view has been taken of the Soviet commitment to revolution in Asia, which the current war in Indo-China has revealed to be less than wholehearted. By backward projection, a similar picture seems to obtain for the whole postwar period. Charles McLane's excellent study of Soviet strategies in South-east Asia under Lenin and Stalin demonstrates the low priority given to this area by the Russians after the war, and their poor level of knowledge and understanding of the area.[38] The myth of the Calcutta Conference dies hard, but McLane has cut it severely down to size, as did Dr Ruth McVey previously in an important but neglected monograph.[39] It is also doubtful whether David Dallin's unequivocal assertion that the Korean war was 'planned, prepared and initiated by Stalin' would be so widely accepted today, although this phase of Soviet policy still awaits closer study.[40] The assumption that the Soviet Union continued to call the shots during the war, to the extent of being able to influence decisively the course of the negotiations conducted by China and North Korea with the United States and its allies at Panmunjom, is also questionable. It is argued that Stalin artificially

[37] *Strategy and Tactics of Soviet Foreign Policy* (London, 1962), p. 33.

[38] *Soviet Strategies in Southeast Asia, an exploration of Eastern policy under Lenin and Stalin* (Princeton, 1966).

[39] *The Calcutta Conference and Southeast Asian Uprisings* (New York, 1958). That the myth dies exceedingly hard is illustrated in a recent Chatham House publication, Wilfrid Knapp's *History of War and Peace 1939–65* (London, 1967), where we learn (p. 217) that in February 1948 the Malayan Communist Party 'received instructions from Moscow, through the communist-led youth conference in Calcutta, to resort to open revolt'. No evidence has ever been produced to support this or any similar claim.

[40] *Soviet Foreign Policy After Stalin*, p. 60.

prolonged the course of these talks for reasons of Soviet policy, obliging Peking and Pyongyang to adopt intransigent postures at the negotiating table. It was only after his death that the Chinese were able to make the necessary concessions on the prisoner-of-war issue which led to the signing of the armistice. As Professor Adam Ulam remarks, 'the fact that the negotiations which began in July 1951 were to last two years can also be taken as an indication that it was Russia which decided that a complete cessation of hostilities in Korea, and the release of a portion of the American forces for service in Europe, was not in her interest'.[41]

This problem is worth analysing further in order to demonstrate how tangled is the path which the revisionist historian has to retread. On the face of it, Professor Ulam's interpretation stems from a particular view of the nature of Soviet dominance over the communist world in the early 1950s. One may question the validity of this view, both on general grounds and on the specific evidence that Peking pursued independent policies from Moscow even in the first years of the Sino-Soviet alliance, including those policies which concerned the Korean war. Having done so, one may then come to the conclusion that if it was not the Russians, then it must have been the Chinese who delayed the signing of the armistice agreement for so long.[42]

Yet it is not enough only to question the explicit assumption of Soviet dominance upon which Professor Ulam's interpretation of the Panmunjom negotiations is based. One must then go on to question his implicit assumption that it was the communist side in these negotiations which behaved in an intransigent manner. Once again there is a contemporary analogy with the present war in Indo-China, where the American position on negotiations has suffered progressively from loss of credibility. Armed with this hindsight (and a measure of scepticism not possessed at the time by many writers except Wilfred Burchett

[41] *Expansion and Coexistence* (London, 1968), p. 534.
[42] According to this interpretation, the death of Stalin was still important. His successors were prepared to grant China the kind of aid in return for which Peking consented to end the Panmunjom deadlock—a deadlock which the Russians feared might otherwise lead to a renewal and intensification of the war. Stalin had been more sympathetic to China's reluctance to lose face on the POW issue, but less willing to give additional aid.

and others who openly espoused the communist cause) one may find the standard account of Panmunjom less than convincing. The communist negotiators rant and rage, and then rat on their promises. The American side tables its reasonable demands and if provoked beyond endurance suspends the negotiations in a dignified manner. This interpretation, presented in the works of Leckie and Rees, remains unchallenged by any serious academic study, although the subject is now receiving some attention (as yet unpublished) by the present generation of American graduate students.[43]

Much work also remains to be done on the nature of Sino-Soviet relations from the time of the 1950 alliance until the 'dispute' began officially (in the Chinese version, which is followed by many Western analysts) in 1956. This artificial dividing line between amity and discord cannot be seriously maintained, although it would be equally wrong to treat the whole post-1949 relationship as if the same degree of tension existed all along. Once, however, one has discarded the myth of China's subservience to Moscow, one can without too much difficulty use the technique of 'esoteric analysis' to detect evident divergencies of policy between Moscow and Peking throughout the early period, by a closer comparison of their formal and overt statements and commentaries on the various crucial issues which arose. Some important analyses of Sino-Soviet ideological differences were made at the time by a few American scholars, although these made no impact upon the 'monolithic' mythology preached by Acheson and Rusk which formed the starting-point for official policy throughout the 1950s.[44] Sino-Soviet

---

[43] As Professor Ulam himself points out, 'some of the substantive demands on the American side were extremely hard for the Communists to acquiesce in'. Apart from the POW issue, injected into the negotiations by the US at a point when they were close to being concluded, which led to a delay of one and a half years, there were other issues, such as the earlier US refusal to accept a truce line along the 39th Parallel, although the talks had been agreed to on this basis. There is a useful study of the parallel negotiations and debates taking place at the UN in Shiv Dayal, *India's Role in the Korean Question* (Delhi, 1959). Otherwise one is left with Leckie's *Korean War* and David Rees, *Korea: the limited war* (London, 1964).

[44] B. I. Schwartz, 'China and the Soviet Theory of "People's Democracy"', in *Communism and China: ideology in flux* (Harvard, 1968), first published as a pamphlet under the same title by the MIT Center for International Studies in 1954; P. L. Bridgham & others, *Chinese and Soviet Views on Mao as a Marxist Theorist and on the Significance of the Chinese Revolution for the Asian Revolutionary Movement*, mimeo. paper dated 8 Sept. 1953.

differences on issues of practical policy have received even less attention, although there is also some contemporary evidence.[45]

It seems unlikely that the fundamental disagreements between the Chinese and Russians which emerged after 1956, over the correct road to socialism, policy towards the imperialist camp, and questions of peace and war, were ever far beneath the surface. Already in 1953–5, a close reading of the Chinese press reveals much the same sort of concern with Soviet 'summitry', and a dislike of being left out of the East–West dialogue, which was openly displayed in 1959–60. Likewise the Soviet response to the first Offshore Islands crisis in the winter of 1954 contained the same element of hesitation for which the Chinese later reproached Moscow after the second crisis of 1958. Further research in this very interesting and underdeveloped field should lead in the long run to a more rounded picture of post-1949 Sino-Soviet relations, in which the peaks of honeymoon friendship and the depths of polemical dispute assume less prominence in the light of the permanently operating causes of disagreement.[46]

Chinese foreign policy

The study of Chinese foreign policy in itself is still very much an under-researched field, and one should welcome the greater interest shown in it in recent years. During the 1950s serious study of the subject was partly inhibited by the feeling that the Chinese had very little foreign policy of their own worth talking about. Fortunately the Sino-Soviet dispute has laid that misconception at rest. However, a residue of doubt still exists as to whether Peking had many serious thoughts about foreign policy until after the Korean war and the inauguration of its 'people's diplomacy' in 1954–5. The belief that the Chinese communists were uninterested and unversed in the analysis of international affairs before 1949, and that they were generally content to follow the Soviet line, is often asserted. So is the view that in the

[45] See Harold Macmillan's account of how Soviet leaders expressed doubts about Chinese policy at the Geneva summit of July 1955 (*Tides of Fortune, 1945–55* (London, 1969), pp. 619, 622).

[46] See further my *Survey of the Sino-Soviet Dispute* (London, 1968), pp. 17–20. I shall discuss China's concern in 1953–5 about Soviet 'summitry' in a forthcoming study of Chinese foreign policy.

immediate post-1949 period the Chinese Foreign Ministry was guided more by preconceived dogma than by the 'realities' of the world situation.[47]

Yet although the Chinese communists were faced with many new problems in the conduct of foreign policy when they assumed power, and perhaps also suffered from a shortage of skilled and reliable diplomatic staff, the whole history of their relations with the Kuomintang (and at various times with the Americans and Russians) during the anti-Japanese and civil wars had manifested a semi-diplomatic character. A close reading of the pre-1949 communist press reveals that their analysis of external affairs was usually well-informed, and that their conclusions were by no means always in line with those of the Soviet Union. Much more work needs to be done upon the Chinese 'world outlook' in this vitally formative period, when the future of China along with the whole Pacific area was in the melting-pot of the war and its aftermath, before we can fully understand the conceptual background with which the Chinese communists tackled the formulation of a national foreign policy after 1949.

It is not only a question of doing more research, but of making a determined effort to jettison the preconceived categories with which Western scholarship has tended to approach the subject of Chinese foreign policy. There is, for example, the view that the Chinese communist government actively 'needs' a foreign enemy in order to encourage its population to greater efforts, and to persuade it to accept with docility a coercive system. As a recent writer explains: 'Maoist theory, and the practice of the last decades, demands enmity. The Chinese people must be led to see themselves threatened; invasion must always appear to be a realistic possibility. While Mao rules the peasant-based giant there cannot be meaningful détente between China and the Soviet Union or the United States.'[48] There is nothing in Maoist theory to justify this assertion, nor can it be easily inferred from the practice of Chinese foreign policy. It derives from an

---

[47] 'Whatever might be said about the uniqueness of the domestic program of the Chinese Communists, there could scarcely be any doubt that in international affairs their attitudes were precisely the same as those of other Communist parties' (Tsou, *America's Failure*, p. 213).

[48] J. D. Simmonds, *China's World; the foreign policy of a developing state* (Canberra, 1970), p. 7.

interpretation of the Chinese political system as dependent upon coercion rather than consensus and upon the related view that the communist model of modernization is basically unacceptable to the bulk of the population. This kind of argument tells us more about the value-loaded judgements of those who advance it than about the Chinese system which it views so unsympathetically.

Another view of China's foreign policy starts from a very different premise but arrives at much the same conclusion. This interpretation places great stress upon the 'traditional' or 'Middle Kingdom' element in the Chinese world outlook. Peking's alleged failure to perceive the realities of the current situation is attributed to a historical deformation in her vision of the outside world. A rather crude version of this thesis has been offered by Professor Morgenthau:

> As the present relations between China, on the one hand, and Cambodia and Burma, on the other, can be regarded as a modern version of the tributary relations of old, so the present ignorance of the Chinese leaders of the outside world, their verbal assaults on it, and their ineffective policies with regard to it can be understood as a modern version of China's traditional ethnocentrism.[49]

References of this type to the sinocentric features of the Chinese empire and its tributary system are commonplace, although there is little attempt to show why the underlying attitudes should still survive in China under very different circumstances. Nor is it entirely clear whether we have an accurate picture of what these traditional attitudes were; recent research tends to underline the ambiguities in the tribute system, which was sometimes more a matter of diplomatic style than of sinocentric content. The degree of Chinese receptivity to outside influences also fluctuated very widely from one dynastic era to the next.[50]

There is a more sophisticated view of the way in which China's historical legacy has supposedly deformed her present world outlook. Here the Chinese are seen as acting out on the contemporary world stage the kind of defiant anti-imperialistic role which they were unable to perform successfully in the bad old

[49] In Tsou, ed., *China in Crisis*, ii. 94.
[50] Much new and penetrating light has been thrown upon these problems of interpreting the imperial world order in J. K. Fairbank, ed., *The Chinese World Order* (Harvard, 1968).

days of real nineteenth-century imperialism. Their sense of nationalist outrage against the rape of China in the past is projected against the unfortunate and unimperialistic Americans of today. As Dr Ishwer Ojha explains in a recent study of Chinese foreign policy (which he subtitles 'The diplomacy of cultural despair'): 'In the final analysis, it is not a Marxist-Leninist evaluation of international relations which shapes the attitudes of Chinese leaders and molds their perceptions of the United States and the world. It is rather their reconstruction of Chinese history and their sense of continuity with the age of imperialism.'[51]

All of these approaches to the analysis of Chinese foreign policy have one characteristic in common—the tendency to minimize, if not to deny, those elements in the contemporary American world performance which might entitle the Chinese to regard the United States as hostile and imperialistic to boot. The 'reality' which China fails to understand is the world as it is perceived from Washington; there is some reluctance to concede that it looks rather different from Peking, and if it is conceded to be different, the Chinese are still likely to be accused of over-reacting to the threat which they erroneously perceive.

The kind of specific questions conventionally asked about Chinese foreign policy are often burdened by Western value judgements to a degree which make them of doubtful utility. Is China aggressive? Has she or will she renounce the use of force? Here it is assumed that while Western foreign policy strives towards the avoidance of international conflict, that of the communist powers, and of Mao's China in particular, does exactly the opposite. As A. M. Halpern has described it: 'The world-view in which conflict is not a temporary malfunction, but an inherent structural feature, requires recognition [by China] of a permanent enemy and does not permit mental reservations in one's basic attitude towards him';[52] while another scholar writes that for Mao and his followers 'violence [is] the highroad for reaping the fruits of . . . instability'.[53] There is here

---

[51] *Chinese Foreign Policy in an Age of Transition* (Boston, 1969), p. 89.

[52] 'China in the postwar world', *China Quarterly*, Jan.–Mar. 1965, p. 22.

[53] Richard Lowenthal, 'Communist China's Foreign Policy', in Tsou, ed., *China in Crisis*, ii. 2.

a serious confusion between Chinese analysis and practice, between the view that conflict is an integral element in international relations and the practical steps that China may take either to advance or to allay such conflict. Conversely, the denial in theory that conflict is an inevitable feature of the world scene need not inhibit the United States from actually promoting it on a large scale.

Yet it is in terms of the 'worst possible case' that Chinese foreign policy is so frequently discussed, while American policy towards China habitually enjoys the benefit of the doubt. It is thought natural to inquire of China's nuclear programme whether she may use her capability to hit targets in X, or practise nuclear blackmail against Y. To ask whether the United States might under certain circumstances threaten or use nuclear weapons against China is not usually considered a very 'realistic' question (although Peking may recall that nuclear threats were issued from Washington more than once in the days of Dulles). The obvious explanation for the Chinese nuclear programme—that it is pursued for the purpose of acquiring some form of minimum deterrent—is made to sound a trifle apologetic, even naïve.

There is a lot more we would like to know about Chinese foreign policy, even if the material at our disposal is limited. (The actual progress of policy-making, for instance, is a closed book and is likely to remain so, and our knowledge of the organizational structure is almost non-existent. For more than two years after the Cultural Revolution we were unaware of the identity of the acting Foreign Minister.) It may, however, be possible to establish some links between shifts in foreign policy and changes in the internal politics of the party leadership, although the evidence to this effect provided in the polemics of the Cultural Revolution must be treated very cautiously. Other areas remain wide open for research, including the operation and effects of Chinese aid overseas, a subject which affords a rare opportunity for fieldwork on the spot. Yet unless the myths and categories which inform so much of Western academic opinion are brought out into the open and rigorously reassessed, little of value will be learnt.

The Vietnam war

The reactive view of United States foreign policy in Asia is not confined to the first postwar decade which has been discussed in some detail earlier in this paper. It is, however, the events of that decade that established the terms of reference within which the bulk of Western research in this field has since been conducted.

Just as the United States was seen to be 'entangled' in China before 1949, so it is now regarded as having become regrettably 'involved' in Indo-China. Its liberal critics may deplore a certain lack of judgement on Washington's part in allowing itself to become ensnared; they rarely question the honourable intentions of those who are responsible (except for a few wild men in the Pentagon whose influence is, fortunately, held within bounds). If it is a question of blame, it is to be attached to the other side. Just as the Chinese communists in 1950 were deemed to have 'provoked' the United States into non-recognition, while the Soviet communists in the same year lured the Americans back into Asia by instigating the Korean war, so today the communist side in Indo-China is held culpable, first for provoking United States intervention, and second for refusing to lie low and allow the Americans a decent 'way out'.

The academic literature on the Vietnam war is disfigured by the same kind of chronological myths which are a characteristic of the earlier history.[54] It drinks deeply and uncritically from the same tainted sources in the twilight world where the universities and the various government agencies hold hands and intermingle. 'Captured enemy documents' are quoted without reserve; it is not surprising that the only full-length study of the National Liberation Front of South Vietnam should be written by a USIA foreign service officer.[55]

But in sharp distinction to its performance during the Korean war, Western scholarship is no longer unanimously lulled by the myth-making or cowed by its political overtones. The Vietnam war has served to radicalize the views of many liberal academics

[54] e.g. that the insurgency in the South was initiated in 1959–60 as a result of organizational steps taken by Hanoi—the creation of the Fatherland Front and the National Liberation Front. This ignores the part played by President Diem's repressive policies in provoking rural resistance as early as 1956.

[55] Douglas Pike, *Viet Cong* (Cambridge, Mass., 1966).

in the United States (although much less so in Britain). It is no criticism of such distinguished scholars as George McTurnan Kahin and John Wilson Lewis to suggest of their *The United States in Vietnam* (rev. ed. 1969)—by far the best survey of the subject—that it is based upon assumptions about the nature of United States foreign policy whose focus was greatly sharpened by President Johnson's escalation of the Vietnam war. The same war has also served to impart a much more effective cutting edge to the anti-imperialist analyses of the new 'revisionist' historians. Gabriel Kolko's massive study of United States diplomacy in the closing years of the second world war, when its global perspectives of the postwar era were first fully developed, ends significantly with the definition of American objectives in China and Vietnam.[56] At the base of the scholarly pyramid which supports the closely argued research of historians like Kolko stands a new generation of Western scholars of Asia for whom academic maturity has closely coincided with the trauma of Vietnam.

Those political leaders who have sought to 'fill our ears with silver and tell us lies about Vietnam' (the words are those of the British poet Adrian Mitchell) have not had such an easy time of it as their predecessors in the 1950s. A growing body of critical writing has kept pace with the step-by-step escalation of the war in Indo-China, most of it of at least a semi-academic character. The extent of this enterprise may be gauged by the fact that when, in May 1971, a copy of the secret Pentagon study on the origins of the Vietnam war was leaked to the American press, the great majority of its damning 'revelations' had already been anticipated in the scholarly anti-war literature.[57]

[56] *The Politics of War* (London, 1969).

[57] Apart from Kahin & Lewis, one should mention two earlier surveys: *The Politics of Escalation in Vietnam* (ed. Franz Schurmann & others) and *Vietnam* (ed. Marvin Gettleman), both published in New York in 1966. There is a mass of periodical literature in such journals as *I. F. Stone's Weekly*, *Viet Report*, *New York R. of Books*, and the Committee of Concerned Asian Scholars' *Bulletin*.

There was something slightly disingenuous about the howl of liberal outrage on the lines of 'we were deceived' which greeted publication of the Pentagon documents, as if the essential facts which were now illustrated in a new wealth of documentary detail had in themselves been previously unknown. If the Johnson administration succeeded in deceiving the public for a time, those liberal politicians and academics who were much better equipped to assess the evidence but who hesitated to 'take sides' were equally guilty of self-deception.

What, we may legitimately ask, would American foreign policy in Asia look like if it had been consistently submitted to the same processes of critical scholarship and documentary exposure which have accompanied the post-1964 escalation of the Vietnam war? It is a strange sort of historical irony which leaves us much better informed about the details of target bombing against North Vietnam in 1965 than about the origins of the containment policy in Asia in 1949–50. What is now required is a rigorous and lengthy process of historical re-examination of the course of the 'cold war' (more frequently hot in character) in postwar Asia, and particularly of the American part in it.

Such an investigation should not be confined to the American side, but it should start with it. For this is the most neglected aspect of the postwar Asian scene in our understanding, and the balance badly needs to be adjusted. Any distortion in our view of American aims in this area cannot fail to produce a corresponding, or much greater, distortion when we move on to consider the policies of the other participants. Indeed, much of the talent and financial resources at present being expended upon Asian 'area studies' might more usefully be directed into the area of American studies until this much-neglected aspect has received sufficient attention. This enterprise may come rather late in the day, but it is never too late to start revising myths and taming tigers.

12   South Asia: the Colonial Backlash

HUGH TINKER

I

SINCE the second world war, international attention has often shifted from the familiar European scenes to focus upon events and places in the third world, hitherto remote from our own world: Congo, Biafra, Sinai, Cuba, Vietnam. During the last quarter of a century this international concentration of attention was principally directed to South Asia only during the long labour which preceded the birth of India and Pakistan and the violent events which followed immediately after. It is true that certain international arguments occur in South Asia—notably the long controversy over Kashmir, and the quarrel between India and Pakistan which erupted into a two-week war, and the Sino-Indian dispute which also briefly flared into open hostilities. Yet even these events have seemed to take on the character of non-events.[1] The international community correctly estimated that the chance escalation into global conflict which could be precipitated over Cuba, or Suez, or perhaps on the Mekong, has never emerged on the South Asian horizon. In South Asia, problems do not cry out for solutions: they just need to be kept simmering, well below boiling point.

Yet our minds have continued to hover around South Asia

---

[1] The most striking example of how far the outside world chooses to ignore South Asia has been provided during the first half of 1971 with the repression of the Bengali nationalist movement in East Pakistan. For three months, March–May, Pakistan military forces, comprised exclusively of western personnel, systematically destroyed the urban middle-class leadership (together with the physical destruction of large areas of the major towns) and then turned upon the resistance movement, the Mukhti Fauz, in the countryside. This operation precipitated the panic flight of rural people across the borders into India. The world almost entirely ignored these events (in marked contrast to the massive response to the Biafra campaign in Nigeria), and it was only when four or five million people had become refugees, and a cholera epidemic had flared up, that attention was aroused. Even now (June 1971) not one foreign government has responded to Mrs Gandhi's call for an approach to President Yahya Khan of Pakistan.

simply because of the vast size of its largest component, India.
China and India are the two world giants, two or three times
larger than the superpowers, the United States and the Soviet
Union, in terms of population. And in a strange way, India
stands at the centre of the world (quite literally, of course, if we
look at a world map on Mercator's projection). India was the
birthplace of universal religions. India was the magnet of
Europe—the Land of Gold—from Roman to Renaissance times.
India was the brightest jewel in the British Empire. India was
the first new nation (in any real sense). And India has been open
to the world, so that any television network can send a camera
crew there any time to put before us the slow misery of famine,
the fevered madness of religious or community conflict—whereas in China, as in much of Africa, we are excluded from this
form of vividly vicarious experience.[2] So India is important in
international affairs just 'because it's there' (like its greatest
mountain). India's vast scale (*c.* 530 million population, 1971)
dominates even Pakistan (population *c.* 140 million, 1971).
Bigger than Japan or West Germany, Pakistan has acquired a
small-state psychology in relation to India. The other neighbours—Burma, Ceylon, Nepal, Afghanistan, and tiny Bhutan
and Sikkim, dwindle into insignificance beside India though
—with the exception of the latter two—they are middling
states, ranking ahead of most of the African countries in
population.

As we in the west have focused upon India we have concep-
tualized our ideas in terms of India to the neglect of her neighbours. A striking example of this kind of treatment is found in
Gunnar Myrdal's *Asian Drama* (1968), which purports to be an
analysis of Third World development with special reference to
Southern Asia, but which is in essence a study of India. The
crux of South Asia's problems has been discerned as the success
or failure of parliamentary democracy. Among many observers,
this question became a moral imperative. I do not find that European or American observers of contemporary Africa are under
the same constraint: as Ghana, Nigeria, and other African states
abandoned parliamentary forms of government and adopted
ad hoc solutions to their political situations, the process was

---

[2] It is too early to discern whether the 'ping pong revolution' early in 1971 will
lead to more of an Open Door policy by China.

analysed in a cool, relatively value-free manner.[3] But, perhaps because we were all more naïve in the first 'outbreak of independence', the future of democracy in India became a kind of test of a set of universal ideas and values. Because India in the 1950s appeared to be deriving strength and confidence from the parliamentary process, this vindicated democracy and reassured those liberals who felt that the cold-war struggle was really a test of two sets of ideologies in practical terms.[4] When Pakistan, Burma, and Nepal departed from the parliamentary mode, this was seen as a moral lapse (particularly in the case of Pakistan) and much inquiry was directed to answering the question: why did democracy fail? So, in Western eyes, South Asia is most important as a laboratory of democracy. And the writers and thinkers native to South Asia have, by and large, mirrored this concern in their own attitudes. The need to discover and define 'real' democracy has exercised all the leaders of South Asia, even though they may, in seeking democracy 'of the type that people can understand and work', stray outside the corridors of Westminster.

It was very largely due to Nehru that the leadership of South Asia went on to ask what democracy meant, beyond the formal political structure. Nehru argued that democracy only became meaningful when it gave a better, fuller life to the mass of the people. And so emerged the conception of democratic planning and development; the attainment of a socialist society through a combination of control and voluntarism. A very high proportion of Indian brainpower—of politicians, officials, academics—was applied to realizing the goal of 'the take-off into self-sustained growth'.

The West also endorsed the importance of this goal, and during the 1950s fostered the contrast between 'democratic' development (the Indian model) and communist, authoritarian development (the Chinese model).

[3] Though Nyerere's Tanzania is different, and many observers, African and Western, feel they have a stake in Tanzania, just as ten years ago we had a stake in Nehru's India.

[4] The present writer does not wish to pretend that he was different, and, unconsciously, perhaps, *The Union of Burma; a study of the first years of independence* (1957) was an assertion that in maintaining the framework of parliamentary democracy through the first decade of independence the peoples of Burma had demonstrated qualities of individualism and rejection of authoritarianism. Even today, though he is compelled to reshape his conclusion (see 4th ed., 1967), he does not discard the main thesis.

There were always significant groups in India to challenge the concept of total planning within the framework of a centralized state. Gandhi's teaching had always stressed that 'that state is best which is governed the least'. During millennia of history, Indian society has resisted the 'big' state, and even under foreign conquest—under the Mughals and the British—there were powerful forces working for decentralization and adjustment towards a *social* order rather than a *political* order. These forces became increasingly assertive after the death of Nehru. Thus, after the first thrust into freedom, and the discovery of a new India, liberated from the trammels of the past, people found themselves returning to an older India in which religion, custom, and language are determinants of local and sectional loyalties. This rediscovery of an older India has not meant a reversion to the past. There are certain new factors bearing upon the old elements which transform the whole situation. In particular, whereas in the past society was hierarchic, with a whole complex of master–servant, patron–client relations, and only a limited number of escape routes from the hierarchy (notably, those of the man on horseback, and the man with the sacred word), today social relations are in a flux, and although mobility is still far less than in the West there is growing mobility which in some areas (such as Gujarat or Punjab) is inducing active social change. As a concomitant of this interaction of social and religious pressures, there is also the *politicization* of the pressures, whenever they are transformed from the latent to the active. In the past, the creative individual or the group mobilized a network of individual loyalties only: today, there is organization—professional, supplied with funds, exploiting the media of communications. The link-figure in this process of change was Gandhi. He functioned as a traditional leader, personally sending out hundreds of messages to his followers, counselling them on their diet, their health, their marital mode. But he also exploited the capacities of the Congress for organization and mass communication and persuasion, to mobilize all-India campaigns of political pressure.

The search for democracy and development, and the readjustment and restructuring of tradition, have also been at the centre of the problems of India's neighbours. Though some states (Afghanistan, Nepal, Bhutan, Sikkim) have not ventured far down this road, which we have now become used to calling 'modernization', Pakistan, Ceylon, and Burma have all wrestled seriously with these problems. India's neighbours have also participated in the technique and philosophy of international relations which is termed non-alignment. This was evaluated in the 1950s as a contribution to the growth of a moral order in world affairs, and Nehru's bridge-building operations in the early and middle 1950s were watched with the same concern and commitment as was evident in the attention paid to parliamentary democracy and planned development. In the 1960s Western attention has relaxed, as non-alignment has been unable to solve conflicts in inter-state relations with any more visible success than other techniques. Nevertheless, non-alignment has remained the *modus vivendi* of South Asia. Elsewhere, in reply to the concept of political development (which seems to me to have no precise or definable meaning) I coined the term 'broken-backed states' to explain the situation of so many third-world countries.[5] Non-alignment is a form of broken-backed international politics, and as I observed in my analysis: 'Broken-backed government may seem a poor thing to those fortunate enough to live under more dynamic systems of government. But it has a quality which hard-bitten politicians rate highly: survival.' The world may be thankful that there is one major area where international problems simmer and do not boil over: and much needs to be learnt about the nature of politics and society in the area to discover just why this should be an area of international lassitude between the two areas of extreme phreneticism: the Middle East and South-east Asia.

Before attempting to examine how far research has explored the themes postulated above, we are to notice the books published under Chatham House auspices. In my view, the one study sponsored by Chatham House with a claim to be considered a permanent and fundamental contribution to our understanding remains *Modern India and the West* (1941), edited

---

[5] H. Tinker, *Reorientations* (London, 1965). This phrase has been my one original contribution to the terminology of politics and political science. It has been picked up by the leaders of Singapore as a cautionary comment on the fate of new states: see Lee Kuan Yew, *The Times*, 21 July 1969 and Goh Keng Swee, *The Straits Sunday Times*, 23 Nov. 1969. It has also been accepted by the doyen of British professors of government, W. J. M. Mackenzie, *Politics and Social Science* (London, 1967), p. 345.

by L. S. S. O'Malley.[6] The entire South Asian scene has been altered, and in many respects revolutionized, since O'Malley's massive work appeared. Yet there is much that is still relevant within its twenty-six chapters. I would place O'Malley along with the Chatham House 'giants': Toynbee, Hailey, Hancock, Purcell, though this assessment would be challenged by some. The only work with anything like the same panoptic view to appear since is B. B. Misra's *The Indian Middle Classes; their growth in modern times* (1961), which is a social history. In terms of size and significance, A. H. Hanson's *The Process of Planning; a study of India's five-year plans, 1950–1964* (1966) is apart; a shrewd analysis of how top level government planning affects (or does not affect) sectors and segments of the economy and polity.[7] A small book with a big influence was *The China–India Border; the origins of the disputed boundaries*, by Alastair Lamb (1964). Lamb showed how, in taking over Britain's imperial pretensions in the Himalaya, independent India got involved in what was essentially an imperial or post-imperial quarrel.

Chatham House policy on studies of India's neighbours must appear puzzling to the outsider. There have been no studies at all of Pakistan.[8] *Foreign Aid and Politics in Nepal* (1965), by Eugene B. Mihaly was a controversial study of a controversial programme in what is still an Asian Ruritania. B. H. Farmer's *Pioneer Peasant Colonization in Ceylon* (1957) opened up a genre of economic-political geography which has an unrealized potential. Finally, the present writer's *The Union of Burma* was a panoramic view of a small country tossed, unprepared, into the stormy seas of independence. Just by luck, the fieldwork was undertaken after the first civil war had abated (1954–5) and before the total blackout of the present military dictatorship had been imposed. For this study, and for about two or three years only, it was possible to travel to the farthest corners of Burma; leaders in the Cabinet Office and in the village were willing to be interviewed, and records and registers were opened. Then dark clouds obliterated the scene.

[6] For a fuller discussion of the place of *Modern India and the West* in South Asian studies, see the present writer's 'The Rediscovery of India', *International Affairs*, Jan. 1969.
[7] There is also a symposium, *The Crisis of Indian Planning* (1968), ed. Paul Streeten & Michael Lipton.
[8] Though Chatham House's publisher, Oxford University Press, has a most comprehensive list of political, geopolitical, and economic studies of Pakistan.

This slim list does not comprise all the work on South Asia attempted by Chatham House. There have been study groups and meetings which have gone further. But the list does indicate the shortcomings manifest in modern or contemporary South Asian studies. Aspects of economic development have been reasonably covered but politics—especially the field of inter-state relations—has remained largely unworked. Compared with other areas, there has been a lack of serious proposals for Chatham House to consider: and the 'under-development' of South Asian studies by Chatham House truthfully reflects the state of the subject in contemporary Britain. When this point was made in *International Affairs* ('The Rediscovery of India', January 1969) some of those working on the subject seemed to feel that this was a reflection on their work. It was not intended to be so: and it is worth stressing again that unless there is a deliberate investment in young British research workers, who can look forward to appointments in British universities, then modern South Asian studies will fade into unimportance in Britain. This would be regrettable from several points of view, but most of all because today there are more than half a million people originating from South Asia resident in Britain, and it is essential that this intermeshing of peoples should be invigorated by mutual understanding and knowledge.

However, the plight of modern South Asian studies in Britain is of less consequence than the impoverished intellectual situation of these studies in the countries of South Asia. Thanks to the leadership and example of M. N. Srinivas, there is an encouraging beginning in sociology and anthropology. Economic studies make a good showing, quantitatively, especially those connected with the Delhi School of Economics; though Indian economics remains hypnotized by the mirages of the planning era of the 1950s, and has barely adjusted to the harsh realities of the 1960s. Contemporary history, political science, and international relations (which resemble a somewhat ill-organized chain store under optimum conditions) are in poor shape in India, and barely exist as recognizable disciplines in the other countries. Of course, we can identify creative scholarship: but only by reference to a few individual names—a Rajni Kothari in India, a Jeyaratnam Wilson in Ceylon. In India, advanced academic work in politics and international relations has been hived off from the universities into specialized centres and institutes existing in isolation. The rationale of this is, presumably, that the atmosphere of the universities discourages creative work: but the effect has been to set up congeries of little intellectual 'empires' which are often more concerned to demarcate their place in the sun than to foster original scholarship. Pakistan and Burma have not catered for critical, evaluative scholarship during the last army-supervised decade, while the ups and downs of Ceylon's politics seem to have had an enervating rather than a stimulating effect on Ceylonese writers. Perhaps because of lack of opportunity at home there has been a steady drain from South Asia of political scientists and historians to Europe and North America. Some return, in time, but many have permanently settled into a South Asian diaspora which the area can ill afford.

More than two decades after independence, South Asia still continues in a post-colonial situation, with regard to modern political studies. The trail-blazing work has largely taken place outside the area; much of it in North America. The style of scholarship, and the models and methodology are largely borrowed from the West. One Indian historian (himself an expatriate), Damodar Singhal, has commented:

> History does not offer a parallel to this phenomenon where efforts for learning produced such a pathetic class of self-complaisant and servile scholars. The nearest example, perhaps, may be that of the English themselves during the Norman period when it was fashionable to be French in speech, appearance, and behaviour.[9]

The 'colonial' state of South Asian studies is dramatically illustrated by the approaches adopted towards the basic event —the partition of the sub-continent—from which so much of the subsequent history of South Asia has flowed. The partition of India may have been partly caused by the twists and turns of British policy, both in the Government of India and at Westminster: but it was also the result of a thousand years of indigenous history in which Muslims had resisted assimilation by Hinduism and asserted their separateness. Our view of partition is focused almost exclusively upon British policy, about which we are now fully informed. The first authoritative account was

---

[9] *India and World Civilization* (Michigan, 1969), ii. 301.

given by V. P. Menon,[10] constitutional adviser to the Viceroy, and it has now been supplemented (and in respects replaced) by an account of the Mountbatten period written by a previous constitutional adviser, H. V. Hodson.[11] Though one writer is Indian, and the other British, both have essentially the same viewpoint: that of British New Delhi and Simla. There are numerous other studies, including accounts by participants,[12] unofficial versions based upon access to some or all of the records,[13] and at least one attempt at a synthesis of views by the techniques of confronting former participants and observers in a re-enactment of 'battles long ago'.[14] All these contributions will in time be evaluated against the monumental series of official British documents on the period, 1942–7, edited by Nicholas Mansergh and E. W. R. Lumby, which are to appear in about twelve volumes between 1970 and 1977.[15] This series will give us access to all the layers of British decision-making from the Cabinet Room down to the Provincial Governors. Although Burma's fate was intimately linked with that of India (and the Pakistan to be) during the last phase before independence, an unfortunate choice has been made: to exclude all material relating to Burma, even if this means slicing a letter in half!

All this tells us only half the story, at best. There are two big questions to be answered about the claimants for power in the 'Freedom Struggle' in the last phase. Why did the Congress choose the path of negotiation, rather than that of resistance, and then demonstrate such chronic inflexibility in negotiation? And how did the Muslim League transform itself from near-impotence in 1937 to mass action in 1947 (only to fall back into impotence after independence)? Thus far, only a handful of autobiographies by persons close to the leading actors have appeared, giving highly personalized accounts of causes and

[10] *The Transfer of Power in India* (London, 1957).

[11] *The Great Divide; Britain–India–Pakistan* (London, 1969).

[12] e.g. A. Campbell-Johnson, *Mission with Mountbatten* (London, 1951); Penderel Moon, *Divide and Quit* (London, 1961).

[13] E. W. R. Lumby, *The Transfer of Power in India, 1945–7* (London, 1954); Hugh Tinker, *Experiment with Freedom; India and Pakistan 1947* (London, 1967).

[14] C. H. Philips & M. D. Wainwright, eds., *The Partition of India; policies and perspectives, 1935–47* (London, 1970).

[15] *The Transfer of Power 1942–7*, i: *The Cripps Mission, January–April 1942* (1970); ii: '*Quit India*', *30 April–21 September 1942* (1971).

consequences.[16] We may hope to penetrate further into the collective mind of Congress when the projects at present under way for full-length biographies of Nehru bear fruit: one study is being undertaken by B. N. Pandey, and one by S. Gopal (both scholars of the diaspora).[17]

But what we need above all is an adequate study of Jinnah. Soon after his first meeting with Jinnah, Mountbatten wrote: 'This was the man who held the key to the whole situation', and, he added, 'I did not succeed . . . in diverting him by one degree from his set purpose of establishing a separate Muslim majority state in India.'[18] It is a matter of deep regret that the initiative of Z. H. Zaidi in setting up a Jinnah archive, and in tracing documents in forgotten corners of Pakistan, has ended in checkmate. The collection survives: but it has become a pawn in the game of Pakistani politics. And so we are left with legend: or rather legends: for the dead *Qaid-i-Azam*, the Great Leader of his people, is a political symbol, to be manipulated by each successive ruler, to fulfil his particular need for legitimacy.[19]

The greatest leader of all in the search for freedom, Gandhi, has received the fullest treatment; South Asian scholarship has responded nobly to the challenge of his enigmatic and polymathic personality and message. *The Collected Works of Mahatma Gandhi* are being collated and published.[20] A massive, eight-volume biography has been completed and revised,[21] and other individual studies (notably those of Gandhi's assistant, Pyarelal) have amplified our knowledge.[22] Indians and foreigners seem to have found a rare meeting ground of mutual discovery when joining in exploring Gandhi's meaning for the world.[23] If we

[16] Cf. Abul Kalam Azad, *India Wins Freedom* (London, 1959): an embittered but enlightening interpretation of the motives of Congress leaders.

[17] At present Michael Brecher's *Nehru; a political biography* (London, 1959) continues to hold the field.

[18] His unpublished *Report on the Last Viceroyalty*, esp. pp. 17–18.

[19] Chaudhri Muhammad Ali, *The Emergence of Pakistan* (New York, 1967), has vignettes of Jinnah as leader, though the Chaudhri fails to grasp his political role.

[20] By the Indian Ministry of Information, 1958– .

[21] D. G. Tendulkar, *Mahatma: life of Mohandas Karamchand Gandhi*, rev. ed. (Delhi, 1960–3, 8 vols.).

[22] A. Carter & others, compilers, *Non-Violent Action, theory and practice; a selected bibliography* (London, 1966) covers the Gandhi literature thoroughly to date of publication.

[23] C. F. G. Ramchandran & T. K. Mahadevan, eds., *Gandhi: his relevance for our times* (Delhi, 1964), and Sibnarayan Ray, ed., *Gandhi, India and the World* (Melbourne, 1970).

can penetrate the meaning of Gandhi we are some way towards grasping what India is all about. And this will not only involve philosophical profundities but also pettiness and peculiarities: which are Gandhi's and India's. At this level, the obscure publication, *Letter-Box of an Unknown Man,* by Kazi Ashraf Mahmud, deserves to be known.[24] This gives a glimpse of a Gandhi who was fussy, interfering, wrongheaded: it is only the great who can be petty and yet still be great.

II

The first quarter of a century of Indian independence falls into three main stages: there was the emergence of 'Nehru's India'—a unified, secular state, a parliamentary democracy, a socialistic, planned economy. Then came the intrusion of regional and communal politics into the all-India nexus. Finally, we have seen the phase of the challenge to parliamentary democracy, through the internal crisis of the Congress party, and the broader crisis of democratic politics by threat of overthrow from the Far Left—and perhaps the Far Right.

The first phase is commemorated by a classic work, W. H. Morris-Jones's *Parliament in India* (1957). Before this appeared, we had to make do with a series of legal and constitutional studies which told us a great deal about the formal structure, but omitted any evaluation of its working.[25] Morris-Jones ended by citing this estimate of the Indian parliament: 'Pericles said that Athens was the school of Hellas. Mr Nehru without boasting may say that Delhi is the school of Asia', and he himself endorsed this assessment. This was written at the springtime of Indian unity: quite soon the summer's heat was scorching that unity. The change was heralded by a remarkable study, *India: the most dangerous decades* (1960), by an American foreign correspondent, Selig Harrison, who then departed for other fields. His analysis of the forces of regionalism, casteism, and 'linguism' has had to be refined by subsequent research; but his main thesis has held. Some have reduced the Harrison thesis to the

---

[24] Dacca, 1969 (not for sale).
[25] In this rather arid area, two studies are rewarding, Sir B. N. Rau's *India's Constitution in the Making* (ed. B. Shiva Rao, Bombay, 1960) and Granville Austin, *The Indian Constitution; cornerstone of a nation* (Oxford, 1966).

conclusion that the fissiparous tendencies, based on language and religion, will sever the precarious control of New Delhi, and will eventually lead to the break-up of India. However, it can plausibly be argued that if powerful forces emerge at the regional level, they will need to establish a working relationship with the power-holders at the centre; if only because the centre retains control over the major financial resources, including access to foreign aid. The connection is demonstrated in a sophisticated study of Sikh political techniques (which function in terms of keeping national and regional alternatives open), made by Baldev Raj Nayar, a Punjabi whose home is in North America.[26]

Another dimension was given to our awareness of India as 'a land of minorities' (as the Simon Report had once called it) by Donald Eugene Smith's *India as a Secular State* (1963). This employed a multidisciplinary analysis and took us into politics, law, sociology, and comparative religion. Smith demonstrated that in the debate between the secular and the religious, India was constantly impelled towards the latter. All this was placed in a somewhat different perspective by Lloyd and Susanne Rudolph in *The Modernity of Tradition* (1967). Rebelling against 'the imperialism of categories', they protest against Western-centred concepts which accept North American or Nordic models of government and society as 'developed' and the Afro-Asian models as 'under-developed'. They attempt to portray Indian political evolution in Indian terms. Paradoxically, the first serious Indian attempt to make a comparable evaluation, A. D. Moddie's *The Brahmanical Culture and Modernity* (1968), largely rejected the past as a curb on development.

The latest phase of political fragmentation and realignment was heralded in the literature by *Factional Politics in an Indian State* by Paul Brass (1965). In Nehru's last years, the Congress was already satiated with power, and politics was all about Who Gets What. For twenty years the break-up of Congress had been predicted; but when it came it was on much more complex lines than a mere split into Left, Right, and Centre. Brass worked out the dynamics of factionalism and defection at the vital state level: and he set a trend which is still being developed. Myron Weiner took the analysis further in his studies of state politics,

---

[26] *Minority Politics in the Punjab* (Princeton, 1966).

and others chronicled the evolution and devolution of parties.[27] However, such is the time-lag between fieldwork and publication that we still have to base our assessments on studies completed before, or at best in, the 1967 general election. We lack accounts of the subsequent polarization of politics towards Far Right and Far Left, and in particular we have only superficial reports upon the emergence at the head of the Indian communist movement of the Naxalites, operating both as rural Maoist guerrillas, and also as urban guerrillas. The principal work upon communism—that of Overstreet and Windmiller—is now twelve years out of date; while even a substantial recent study—by Victor Fic—was completed before the significance of the latest wave was apparent.[28]

The victory of Mrs Gandhi in the general election of 1971, with the overwhelming defeat of the Old Guard Congress and the right-wing parties, may appear to represent the reappearance of the Nehru style of government, with a charismatic leader able to create a personal political pattern which has to be accepted by lesser politicians, both at the centre and in the states. Before there is a rush to rewrite the record, political scientists will need to examine the underlying meaning of this unexpected *bouleversement*. How far does the factional explanation of Indian politics still apply, none the less? Or has there been a return to the direct dialogue between the national leader and the people which Nehru in his prime was able to articulate? The problem demands techniques of analysis which can interrelate all the levels of political promise and performance: local, state-level, and national.

We do not find the same range of studies for Pakistan as for India. The attempt to establish parliamentary democracy has been analysed in two first-class works: *Pakistan; the formative phase* (1960), by Khalid Bin Sayeed, and *Pakistan; a political*

---

[27] *Party Building in a New Nation; the Indian National Congress* (Chicago, 1967), and Myron Weiner, ed., *State Politics in India* (Princeton, 1968). Also Marcus F. Franda, *West Bengal and the Federalizing Process in India* (Princeton, 1968), Stanley A. Kochanek, *The Congress Party of India; the dynamics of one-party democracy* (Princeton, 1968), H. L. Erdman, *The Swatantra Party and Indian Conservatism* (Cambridge, 1967).

[28] G. D. Overstreet & M. Windmiller, *Communism in India* (Berkeley, 1959); Victor M. Fic, *Peaceful Transition to Communism in India; strategy of the Communist Party* (Bombay, 1969).

study (1957), by Keith Callard.[29] These writers concentrate upon the inadequacies of politicians and political institutions. The influence of religion can hardly be described as an intrusion in a country which was deliberately created as a homeland for Muslims: and Leonard Binder's *Religion and Politics in Pakistan* (1963) considers Islam as a fundamental feature of national life. The subject is explored further in a symposium edited by Donald Smith, *South Asian Politics and Religion* (1966), in which Part III: 'Pakistan: the Politics of Islamic Identity' is generally excellent.

When democracy was superseded in 1958 by martial law, political scientists were nonplussed. They did not then recognize military rule as a legitimate subject of study, and still have not really found their bearings. A cool assessment of the first phase was made by Herbert Feldman in *Revolution in Pakistan* (1967). An attempt to relate the regime of Field-Marshal Ayub Khan to political development was supplied by G. W. Choudhury.[30] In Pakistan, as in India, regional and linguistic tensions have jostled within the lower echelons of politics, and although some of these tensions are chronicled in Choudhury's work, the subject demands much fuller study.

Throughout the changes of political direction in Pakistan, the army and the civil service have remained to referee and supervise the life of the nation. We still await a study of the political impact of the Pakistan Army, but several works on the bureaucracy have appeared, among which the giant *Asian Bureaucratic Systems Emergent from the British Imperial Tradition* (1966), edited by R. Braibanti, includes a thorough account of Pakistan and the other countries of South Asia. The latest phase, beginning with the rebirth of mass politics, is quite beyond the scholars: but a very personal work by a leading actor in the present drama—Zulfikar Ali Bhutto—reproduces some of the rhetoric with considerable style and verve.[31]

One of the main lessons of the tragedy of 1971 is that the populist politicians—whether Bhutto in the west, or Sheikh

[29] The early death of Keith Callard sadly impoverished the slender ranks of scholars of Pakistan.

[30] *Constitutional Development in Pakistan*, 2nd ed. (London, 1969). The author was singularly unlucky in that both his 1st and 2nd editions coincided with the overthrow of the regime he was describing.

[31] *The Myth of Independence* (London, 1969).

Mujibur Rahman in the east—did not have the capacity to tackle the big issues. When the talking ended, they were unable to direct the action. This tragedy of 1971 provides a theme of historical magnitude equalled only by the events of 1945–7. Once again, the theme is of unity and disunity, of ideologies in conflict, and of leaders who could not understand the nature of the challenge which confronted them. Whereas one aspect of the 1945–7 story is exhaustively documented (the dialogue among the British authorities, and with the Indian leaders), the disintegration of the Pakistan ideal cannot be related to documentary guidelines. The myth-making has already begun; and accepted versions are likely to be steeped in conspiratorial explanations, compounded of broken promises and treachery. To unravel this story will be a major problem for the future historian of South Asia.

The smaller countries have attracted proportionately less attention from foreign scholars. Some kind of Gresham's Law has been at work, and less interesting or exciting political situations have produced studies which are theoretically less interesting. Burma has always exercised a fascination over outsiders (both European and Asian) and work of a greater quantity and quality has appeared on Burma than on the other small South Asian states. Although Burma since independence has returned to its own roots to a greater extent even than India or Pakistan, there are few interpretations by Burmese to explain this process to the outside world. Dr Maung Maung wrote a number of accounts of the emergence of democracy in Burma, of which *Burma's Constitution* (1959) is probably best known. He has since become (it seems) the official interpreter of General Ne Win's regime. Dr Htin Aung illuminates our understanding of the Golden Land through his researches in folklore and customary law: his *History of Burma* (1967) has an epilogue which discusses Burma since independence. Otherwise, we have to see Burma through the eyes of foreigners—mainly Americans— viewing this tradition-bound land through their own, alien traditions. *Economic Development in Burma, 1951–60* (1962), by Louis J. Walinsky, is as much an account of American projections of development techniques as it is of Burma's plight under these ministrations. Two studies of Buddhism and politics, *Buddhist Backgrounds of the Burmese Revolution* (1965), by

E. Sarkisyanz, and *Religion and Politics in Burma* (1965), by Donald Smith, also tell us almost as much about the authors' presumptions as about their subject. A recent monograph by John Badgley, *Politics Among Burmans; a study of intermediary leaders* (1970) takes us into rural Burma ('the real Burma', as many would say), but its illuminating conclusions relate to the period before the present black-out on communications. It is likely to be some time before Burma returns into the sphere of international communication.

The reasons why Ceylon's lively and acutely politically conscious intelligentsia have not written accounts of their country's unique political system (in which two core-forces have competed in politics during the last decade) would no doubt provide an insight into the Ceylonese political culture. Perhaps it is because most of them are so personally committed; so that the tract becomes the only possible form of statement. Even a detached scholar like Jeyaratnam Wilson has produced only article-length contributions.[32] However, Sinnappah Arasaratnam's *Ceylon* (1964)—essentially a historical study—strikingly illuminates the present by way of the past. Among Western studies, Howard Wriggins's *Ceylon: dilemmas of a new nation* (1960) retains its value as an 'over-view'. B. H. Farmer's *Ceylon, a Divided Nation* (1963) examines communal politics, while *Communalism and Language in the Politics of Ceylon* (1967), by Robert Kearney, has greater analytical content.

Although Nepal has a larger population than Ceylon, it is usually perceived as a tiny, mountain principality. There are many works on Nepal in the field of social anthropology, but few in the field of politics. *Democratic Innovations in Nepal; a case study of political acculturation* (1966), by B. L. Joshi and L. E. Rose, is the most sizeable account of Nepal's journey into its own version of 'modernization'. We have noted Mihaly's study of foreign aid, and attempts to gain influence in this strategic Himalayan frontier zone. Similar works include Girilal Jain's *India meets China in Nepal* (1959): and this sector is likely to be more closely observed in future.

Moving on to review what are more properly international studies, rather than national or intra-national studies, we find

---

[32] See 'Oppositional politics in Ceylon (1947–1968)', in *Government and Opposition*, Winter, 1969, special no. on 'Political Forces in Asia'.

that in South Asia we are concerned with inter-state relations and hardly at all with international relations more broadly defined. During the 1950s there was the attempt to create a new climate of international relations called non-alignment. But the 1960s have been mainly occupied with an older kind of inter-state problem: that of territorial disputes, mainly arising out of the imperial past.

Non-alignment has its own rather slender literature.[33] A much wider range of studies covers the various territorial disputes. A good introduction is provided in Alastair Lamb's *Asian Frontiers; studies in a continuing problem* (1968), in which most of the disputes are under the heading 'Legacies of the Imperial Age'. The major dispute—to which no solution can be seen—is the controversy between India and Pakistan over Kashmir. There is a considerable body of works published both in India and Pakistan, but most belong to what a recent reviewer (Neville Maxwell) designated as the 'flat-earth' school of scholarship.[34] Probably the most percipient works on both sides of the quarrel are Sisir Gupta's *Kashmir; a study in India–Pakistan relations* (1966), and G. W. Choudhury's *Pakistan's Relations with India, 1947–66* (1968). Once again, Alastair Lamb gives us a pungent study which, because he is not afraid to make judgements on highly contentious issues, will not be universally acceptable.[35] One issue has been argued from the start: were the Pakistan authorities in collusion with the Pathan tribesmen who invaded the Vale of Kashmir? It is curious that unimpeachable information is now available on this question; and nobody seems to have noticed![36]

The conflict over Kashmir degenerated into war in 1965. Thus far, no really significant account has appeared, though *The Indo-Pakistani Conflict* (1968), by Russell Brines is adequate. The Himalayan encounter between India and China in 1962 has yielded a study with much more depth: Neville Maxwell's

[33] Cf. Peter Lyon, *Neutralism* (Leicester, 1963); Willard Range, *Jawaharlal Nehru's World View; a theory of international relations* (Athens, Georgia, 1961); Michael Brecher, *India and World Politics; Krishna Menon's view of the world* (London, 1968).

[34] *International Affairs*, Jan. 1971, p. 215.

[35] *Crisis in Kashmir, 1947–66* (London, 1966).

[36] The source is *Sir George Cunningham*, by Norval Mitchell (Edinburgh, 1968). Cunningham was Governor of the North-West Frontier Province at the time, and his diary indicates that Pakistan cabinet ministers were supporting the tribal adventure.

India's China War (1970): which is, however, unlikely to gain complete acceptance from all concerned.

Burma's attempts to live at peace with an unsettled frontier and powerful neighbours have been described in William H. Johnstone's *Burma's Foreign Policy; a study in neutralism* (1963), and Dorothy Woodman's *The Making of Burma* (1962). Although both appeared during the last decade, they are already dated.

There are very few international studies above this 'local' level of inter-state relations. One of the few is *India, Pakistan and the Rise of China* (1964), by Wayne Wilcox, but this is an essay, not a full-length study. One major difficulty is that most of those who work on South Asia are linguistically equipped only to handle English-language sources: perhaps with a competence in one or more South Asian languages. Very few are fluent in Russian or Chinese, the languages now most relevant to the power politics of the area. Thus attention has been given to themes like the Commonwealth, or American involvement, which are little more than peripheral to the situation today. This observation applies as much to South Asian scholars as to outsiders. Until yesterday the Indian Ocean was a low-pressure area in global politics. From about 1800 to about 1960 the British Navy effectively neutralized the Indian Ocean by the deployment of relatively small-scale forces. The attempt by Japan to explode this low-pressure system between 1942 and 1945 ended in total disaster. Today the Soviet navy has become a bogey, for political purposes, but there is still no hard reason for assuming that Soviet surface vessels operating at extended distances have transformed the situation. Though Soviet nuclear submarines, armed with nuclear warheads, may use the Indian Ocean in order to 'get lost', this is a factor in super-power politics rather than regional politics. Nevertheless, the Indian Ocean—and South Asia—will now become increasingly involved in international politics, instead of the imperial and post-imperial power which has thus far provided the environment.

It follows that the major innovation in South Asian studies which we ought to look for is the development of transcontinental studies. Till now there has been no satisfactory investigation of the impact of the Soviet Union on India and Pakistan. Russia as now the main supplier of military materials to India, is ineluctably involved in the growth of heavy industry, and has the second biggest aid and debt relationship with India. What has all this meant, internally and internationally? Similarly, during the last ten years, Pakistan has been transformed, in the Soviet view, from a running dog of American imperialism into a client and agent in the Soviet diplomatic and economic advance down through Central Asia to the Indian Ocean, to outflank Turkey and Iran. At the same time Pakistan has become China's principal non-communist associate, the recipient of major Chinese arms supplies, and a partner in many enterprises. India's relationship with China, which veered from a friendship based on false premises to animosity also based on questionable premises, is now being revised in Delhi as well as in Peking; though China's involvement in the revolutionary movements in eastern India may provide a counter-force. The relevance of all this to Sino-Soviet relations, and also to the emergence of Central Asia out of the twilight into the contemporary Asian context, has to be evaluated. Till now, South Asian and Central Asian studies have pulled along on parallel courses, but in the future they must converge.

Another aspect of transcontinental relations which needs to be investigated is the absence of regional associations between the maritime nations of the continental rimland which reaches from South Asia up to Japan. In the 1950s there was a putative move towards association among the 'Bandung Powers' (India, Ceylon, Pakistan, Burma, and Indonesia), but this soon faded away. The 'Colombo Powers', called into partnership by Mrs Bandaranaike to ameliorate the Sino-Indian conflict (Ceylon, Burma, Cambodia, Indonesia, Ghana, the UAR) also could not stay the course. Other groupings, such as SEATO and CENTO, have never looked like anything but what they are: groups of clients of the United States. Economic grouping has not really advanced beyond the consortium arrangement whereby the poor are given some say in the aid dispensed to them by the rich (the Colombo Plan was one bright hope that has faded). Studies of these various aspects of regional co-operation—or non-co-operation—have seldom penetrated far into the dynamics of the situation. One notable effort in this direction was *The Indus Rivers; a study of the effects of partition* (1967), by Aloys Michel. Taking a technical subject—irrigation—as the baseline, Michel explored the atmosphere of Indo-Pakistani inter-state bargaining, and the stratosphere of World Bank politicking. This angle of study is one that could be usefully extended.

III

In addition to these levels, which are properly those of international studies, we shall be required to observe the working out of the democratic process in South Asia as a measure of how far these countries can maintain the present unstable stability: which, imperfect though it may be, gives considerable support to national and international life.

It has been argued above that the 1960s were a period of transition in South Asia, the early 1970s are likely to prolong this period (of course, all periods of time are transitional from one kind of polity and society to another: but some periods are more transitional than others). Despite the apparently final break between West Pakistan and the eastern wing, and Mrs Gandhi's apparently overwhelming victory over the Old Guard, 1971 is unlikely to see the crystallization of politics in Pakistan or India into a fixed and permanent mould. The contradictions in society and politics run in so many cross-cutting directions that clear trends cannot be perceived, either by participant or observer.

In Burma the strange domination of General Ne Win over a nation of rebels and individualists is likely to continue, despite implacable underground resistance by communist and communalist forces. Ceylon, while giving the appearance of making a radical move to the Left under Mrs Bandaranaike, has still been unable to make the transfer from urban, élitist government towards a system admitting new political forces into the power structure. It may be that political scientists will just have to wait patiently for the kaleidoscope to sort itself into a recognizable pattern (other than those political scientists whose ideology enables them to predetermine the approaching pattern). It seems quite possible that the pathfinding studies which emerged during the early and mid-1960s will have no counterparts in the early 1970s. Yet in a few years time we may be set as exciting a challenge as ten years ago.

It seems certain that the new pattern will only take shape when a reasonably stable balance has been attained between the forces of regionalism and those of nationalism. Thus far, there is a tendency to consider the state or province and the centre as two different political arenas. Perhaps because a fairly sizeable intellectual investment has to be made in, say, Maharashtra or Bangladesh, the specialist tends to see 'his' region as the meaningful arena, and to discount the processes of interaction between region and nation. There could be a danger of ending up with a bagful of regional studies, with no particular attempt to create a synthesis between them. *India and Ceylon; unity and diversity* (1967), edited by Philip Mason, was a symposium on the problem of synthesis. Baldev Raj Nayar's *National Communication and Language Policy in India* (1970) explores the subject of communication as a key factor of national unity and diversity. Although Ceylon and Burma do not contain such a range of regional and communal differences as in India or Pakistan, they also have to work out a concept of nationhood which provides an equal place for minorities. It would seem that this field of study—the nexus of nation and community—should be the special concern of the people of South Asia. They are likely to possess superior cultural capacity for thorough research: and it is, peculiarly, their problem. However, it must be said that so far Asians have (with exceptions such as Nayar and Wilson) appeared somewhat reluctant to attempt academic studies in what is a field of controversy.

It was observed earlier that South Asian studies still remain a 'colonial' subject. A very probable trend in the immediate future may be that decolonization will occur without independence being established. Interest in South Asia in British universities appears to be dormant: perhaps awaiting the stimulus of discovery by our own United Kingdom Asians, who, in their present approach to university education, think more in terms of science and technology. In North America, there was almost a boom in South Asian studies during the 1960s; but the boom may be followed by an equally dramatic slump. Federal support has dried up under the Nixon administration, and business support has shrunk during the present economic 'pause' (a shrinkage accentuated by disapproval of student radicalism), while the foundations are rethinking their strategies and concentrating upon fields of utmost urgency. South Asian centres are hard put to maintain present commitments, and there is talk of 'rationalization', i.e. pooling the programmes of different universities, so that efforts are not duplicated anywhere. American post-graduate students are quick to smell success or failure in different fields of study: and the present generation is not venturing into the field of South Asia. Yet if Asian Studies fade away in North America and Western Europe, will India and its neighbours be ready to respond?

Postscript

This chapter was set up in type before December 1971, when the glare of world attention was again focused upon South Asia as, once more, a new country was born in bloodshed: Bangladesh. In a longer perspective, 1971 may, like 1947, appear as a watershed in world events, for the spectator of international affairs will do well not lightly to dismiss this as a unique event. Whereas there have been many attempts by submerged groups in the Third World to claim their right to nationhood—Kurds, Ambonese, Nagas, Anya Nya in South Sudan—only once has such a movement come near to winning through: Biafra. Now, at last, a submerged nation has broken away from an established Third World state; and it might, therefore, happen again.

This has introduced a new and uneasy element into the unstable stability of South Asia. Yet the superpowers are still excluded from the overt forms of intervention practised in the Middle East or South-east Asia. Another notable event of December 1971 was the approach of the US Seventh Fleet into the Bay of Bengal; and its silent disappearance. Similarly, China observed a marked caution while its main Asian ally, Pakistan, suffered grievous defeat. But we cannot say for sure that the Great Game delineated by Kipling will no longer be played in the high Himalaya. The observation recorded earlier in this chapter on the importance of systematic studies of Soviet and Sino-Soviet relations with South Asia takes on ever greater urgency.

The sun has set on the British Empire; the J. F. Dulles hegemony has dissolved in the presidency of Richard Nixon; but the colonial backlash still remains a factor, in the political reality as well as the academic study of South Asia.

13   The Study of International Politics

ROGER MORGAN

Introduction

DAVID RIESMAN tells the story of an American anthropologist, wearied by endless conclaves in which his colleagues debated the new methodologies of their discipline, who finally cried in despair, 'Why can't we just go out and *do* ethnography the way we used to?'[1] A similar reaction on the part of the busy diplomat, politician or commentator on world affairs is quite understandable, when he is invited to take heed of some of the activities of academic specialists in international relations. He may, of course, be very willing to turn for advice to scholars he knows to be expert in the politics of the Middle East, South-east Asia, Germany, or the Balkans. But what possible benefit, he may ask, can he draw from the work of those academics—particularly the Americans, but also a substantial minority of their British colleagues—who seem to spend their time arguing about how far the study of international relations can be 'scientific', about the various alternative meanings of the term 'international theory', or about whether the student of international politics can learn more from mathematics or from Machiavelli?[2]

The flow of books and articles (again, largely but not entirely American) on the methodology, prospects, and problems of the study of international politics has now reached such proportions

---

[1] *Constraint and Variety in American Education* (New York, 1958), p. 87
[2] Michael Banks, 'Two Meanings of Theory in the Study of International Relations', in *Year Book of World Affairs, 1966*, pp. 220–40; E. Raymond Platig, *International Relations Research: problems of evaluation and advancement* (New York, 1966); Klaus Knorr & James Rosenau, eds., *Contending Approaches to International Politics* (Princeton, 1969); and Nigel Forward, *The Field of Nations* (London, 1971) provide useful introductions to these debates. This essay follows the conventional—though ambiguous—academic terminology in treating 'international politics' and 'international relations' as synonymous.

that even those engaged in the subject full-time find it hard to keep up. The interested non-specialist, perplexed about which of the rival academic prophets can offer him practical guidance (if any), may well be tempted to feel that all of them should be segregated in some other place until they have resolved their differences and can return with something positive to offer him. His situation may be likened to that of a politician —or even a simple voter—who attempts to understand the disputes of the economists about the causes and cures for inflation or stagnation, and finishes by declining to take seriously all the pretensions of what Michael Postan has pleasantly suggested calling the 'plague of economists'[3] until they have agreed among themselves at least about some of the answers.

What, for a start, is the academic study of international politics about? Its practitioners, like those of any other branch of the social sciences, aim at the deepest possible understanding of a particular aspect of human activity. A recent survey of the branch in question, after defining its concern as 'political activity at the level of diplomatic or international society, the relations between the members of that society, and the forces and factors, both internal and external, which affect these relations', summarizes the three main subdivisions of the field as follows:

The first, the *international political system*, covers the emergence and growth of the system of sovereign states (from the sixteenth century to the present), and the political processes at work within it. The second, *foreign policy analysis*, is concerned with how foreign policy is made and executed. The third, *international institutions*, involves the identification and examination of the well-established rules and usages of international society, and the assessment of their contribution, whether they are world-wide or regional, to the maintenance and strengthening of world order.[4]

The whole idea of attempting a systematic classification, analysis, and explanation of these phenomena certainly appears ambitious enough to explain the often pejorative connotations of the word 'academic' in the mouths of practical men of affairs. In view of this, it is ironical to recall that the present

---

[3] *Encounter*, Jan. 1968, pp. 42–7.
[4] SSRC, *Research in Political Science* (London, 1968), pp. 32, 34: the formulation is by Professor Geoffrey Goodwin.

quest of those involved in the study of international relations (the quest for understanding or diagnosis) has its historical roots deeply embedded in a concern to solve the problems of the real world (a concern with prognosis and even with prescription).

The Carnegie Endowment for International Peace, which has played a leading part in promoting the study of international affairs ever since its establishment in 1910, was set up under a trust ordaining that the Endowment's first objective should be 'to hasten the abolition of international war' and continuing with the optimistic proviso that as soon as this end was achieved, the funds of the Endowment should be diverted to other reforms. A few years later, when the first university chair of International Relations in the world was established—the Woodrow Wilson Chair of International Politics at the University College of Wales, Aberystwyth—its benefactor, David Davies, made it a condition of the endowment that the incumbent should undertake studies that would help to further the work of the newly-founded League of Nations; the Montague Burton Professor of International Relations at Oxford, again, is enjoined by statute to promote the study of world government.

The notion that the study of international relations should make a direct contribution to peace and security—like the view that university specialists in economics or social administration should produce some results of practical utility—has continued to exercise a considerable influence, though this may take very different forms. A wide gap separates the sort of 'policy-orientated' work on strategic problems undertaken in many American universities (often financed by direct contracts from the Department of Defense) on the one hand, and on the other the various branches of 'peace research' or 'conflict research' practised and taught in Scandinavia or at University College, London.[5]

The development of international relations, in the fifty years that separate the reforming naïveté of the pioneers from the sophisticated tones of the SSRC report just cited, has been considerable. It has been marked by a steady growth in rigour,

---

[5] A survey of peace and conflict research in Germany and elsewhere is given by Karl Kaiser, *Friedensforschung in der Bundesrepublik* (Hanover, 1970). See also John Burton, *Conflict and Communication* (London, 1969).

coherence, and readiness to take account of all the relevant factors—from economic motives to moral values—in formulating hypotheses about the nature of international political processes. This development has reflected, in part, the natural growth of any academic discipline from infancy to something approaching maturity. 'Natural growth', however—in the sense of a disinterested search for truth—has only been the side marked 'theory' of a coin whose other side reads 'practice'. One strand in the intellectual history of the discipline of international relations has been precisely the successive accusations of each generation of innovators that their predecessors, by arguing from false premises about the real world, were offering false remedies for its problems. When the 'realist' school, headed by E. H. Carr and Hans Morgenthau, between the late 1930s and about 1950 attacked the dominant 'idealist' school of the inter-war years (notably Arnold Toynbee and Sir Alfred Zimmern), the burden of their criticism was not simply that the latter were intellectually inaccurate in arguing that the foreign policies of states were determined by political ideologies or 'immorality', or that there existed a 'real' harmony of interests between states, which would form the basis of a new international order if all states were rational and perceptive enough to realize it:[6] a graver part of the accusation was that by presenting a false picture of the way individual states and the international system functioned, the idealist school was hindering rather than promoting the development of a more peaceful international order.[7]

The triumph of the realists was resounding (no doubt they were helped by the activities of Hitler and Stalin out in the real world): by the 1950s, the majority of academics were analysing the foreign policies of states essentially in terms of 'power politics' or 'national interest'—even when international encounters occurred within the 'paddock' of the UN, let alone amidst the 'jungle' of traditional diplomacy.[8] This victory was,

[6] E. H. Carr, *The Twenty Years' Crisis* (London, 1939); Hans Morgenthau & Kenneth W. Thompson, eds., *Principles and Problems of International Politics* (New York, 1950).

[7] Criticizing 'visions of a world federation' and 'blue-prints of a more perfect League of Nations', Carr concluded his book (p. 307): 'Those elegant superstructures must wait until some progress has been made in digging the foundations.'

[8] The terminology is that of Herbert Nicholas, *The UN as a Political Institution* (London, 1959). The title *Power Politics* was used both for a successful textbook by

however, short-lived. Having become the established orthodoxy, the 'realists' were in their turn assailed by a fresh wave of Young Turks—or rather, in this case, by several simultaneous and often very tumultuous ones. The waves broke first in America, though their ripples have since been felt in Europe. This time the newcomers ranged all the way from mathematicians and economists, men with a *penchant* for quantification or the application of games theory or economic bargaining theory to inter-state relations, to neo-'harmony-of-interests' men with the quasi-Benthamite conviction that international conflict was largely due to misperception.[9] Again, part of their case against those they challenged was concerned with policy: the charge was that the 'realists', by constructing their theory from the building-blocks of 'national interest' and 'power', were not only presenting a false picture of reality but were also, in consequence, guilty of preaching meretricious and counter-productive solutions to the problems of war and peace. (It is true that the chief American 'realist', Hans Morgenthau, was also criticized—notably by Inis Claude in *Power in International Relations* (1962)—on the strictly intellectual grounds that his use of the terms 'power' and 'national interest' contained internal inconsistencies.)

Every stage in the development of theorizing about international relations—'idealist', 'realist' (now sometimes called 'classical'), 'behavioural', 'scientific' and 'anti-scientific' (or 'traditional')—has thus been marked at least to some extent by the wish to shed light on the causes of international conflicts, and this has been reflected in the research undertaken and the courses offered at universities. At the same time, in a quite natural reaction against this view of international relations as a 'policy science' (and quite irrespective of what particular policy recommendations resulted from, or lay behind, the respective theories), there has of course been the equally clear-cut view that the business of academic specialists in international relations was precisely *not* to offer practical solutions, or even to pretend that their professional expertise was of an order

Georg Schwarzenberger (1st ed. 1941) and for a notable short study by Martin Wight published for Chatham House in 1946.

[9] Cf. the works of Bruce Russett, Morton Kaplan, Thomas Schelling, Karl Deutsch, and John Burton.

that qualified them to do so. In some cases this doctrine led to the view that the academic approach to international relations should be limited to the study of recent *history*: this view until quite lately dominated both research and the teaching of the subject at Oxford—where the international relations papers for the PPE course covered mainly the history of the League of Nations and the UN, and the diplomatic history of the period from 1870 onwards—and even today it powerfully influences international studies at Cambridge. The emphasis on history is in many ways a tenable doctrine: it is, at first sight, hard to refute the argument that international relations, like political science or any other social science, *can* only draw on the past for its evidence (if thinking about the future is discounted as mere speculation), and that a deliberately historical approach is therefore not merely the most suitable form of training for undergraduate minds but also the true way of understanding the subject.

Most professional scholars in the field would in fact agree that history provides the data for their inquiries. They would, however, argue that their *use* of this evidence differs from the use to which the historian puts it. Whereas he is concerned to establish the truth about a specific episode or sequence of events, they—like other social scientists—approach historical evidence in the hope of establishing valid general propositions, in their case, about international political behaviour. To quote the SSRC's report again:

international history, either as part of or closely allied to international relations, provides the raw material for the formulation and testing of these propositions; it gives depth and perspective to the study of the present; and above all it can impart the sense of the concrete, of the particular and the contingent in human affairs, which is an enriching experience in itself and a check upon over-ready generalization (p. 33).

Another form of reaction against 'policy-orientated' studies has been the attempt to analyse, write about, and teach international affairs 'objectively'—i.e. *without* trying to offer solutions to problems—but concentrating on contemporary events rather than following the historians into the past. A large number of area specialists—experts on the 'government and politics' of, say, the Middle East, or South-east Asia, rather than on international relations properly speaking—would argue that their job is to analyse and teach their subject in an objective or factual manner, following closely on the heels of contemporary problems without pretending to solve them.

Studies of this kind—dealing with the affairs of a foreign area, or even of a single foreign country—have, of course, formed a sizeable and distinguished part of the research output of Chatham House, as of the Council on Foreign Relations and other comparable institutions. This is clear from the other essays in this book—many of which deal with a branch of international studies defined in terms of a geographical area—and from Wilfrid Knapp's recent survey of 'Fifty years of Chatham House books'.[10]

In this very fact of the close attention paid by Chatham House research to the domestic affairs of foreign countries lies a fairly distinct difference between the study of international affairs as interpreted by the RIIA and the academic study of international relations strictly defined. In the Chatham House research programme as a whole, studies of the internal affairs of foreign countries have been very prominent—this is true of the Institute's political and economic research, if not of its legal work—as well as studies of genuinely international topics. (Many of the 'domestic foreign' studies—for instance Andrew Shonfield's *Modern Capitalism* [1965, paperback 1969]—have, of course, been international in the sense of being comparative in approach and dealing with transnational phenomena.) In other words, the Institute has covered what the political science profession calls the sub-discipline of 'comparative government' as well as that of 'international relations'.

Theory: pure and applied

Meanwhile, back in the latter field, certain eminent scholars have been apparently confusing the issue—and perhaps confirming practical-minded research institutes in their distrust of theoretical studies—by producing essays with such negative titles as 'Why is there no international theory?' Martin Wight has written a brilliant and paradoxical piece bearing this title;

[10] *International Affairs* (special issue to mark the 50th Anniversary of Chatham House, Nov. 1970), pp. 138–49.

his thesis, very crudely, can be boiled down to the proposition that 'international society' can produce no political theory comparable with that produced by the existence of the state, since citizens within a state can pursue and philosophize about 'the good life', whereas states in the international system must needs be concerned merely with survival. He has then threatened to bemuse the lay public still more by writing at least one further essay which triumphantly demonstrates that international theory *is* possible after all. This last essay, 'The Balance of Power', published in the same book as the one just mentioned, is a perfect illustration of what a theoretical approach to an international phenomenon can achieve: it systematically elucidates the various meanings given to the term 'balance of power', and explores their differing implications for the policy of states.[11]

In one sense, then, 'theory' starts from the definition and elucidation of terms, and this leads, as in any branch of inquiry, to a clearer view of the subject-matter to which these terms relate. The next question is whether 'theory', having accomplished this important first step, can take us any further, and whether such a thing as a general theory of international politics is possible.

A recent writer, P. A. Reynolds, contrasting the precision and predictive value of theory in the natural sciences with the indeterminate results so far obtained in respect of the more intractable data available to the social sciences, reaches the following conclusion: 'Theory in international relations . . . has first a simple taxonomic purpose—to classify data in such a way that similar sets of data may be similarly arranged, and so in a superficial way compared.' Reynolds offers as an example the analysis of the main elements in the foreign policy decision-making process to be identified in any state at any time:

Differences in the ways in which decisions are arrived at in different states may be observed by classifying data about the respective processes into the analytical categories of information, communication, constitution of decision-making groups, and so on. Moreover,

---

[11] These summaries of Martin Wight's two essays are like the Prussian officer's outline of the plot of Schiller's *Wilhelm Tell*: 'Some fool of a civilian shooting at fruit.' The reader should turn to the originals in Herbert Butterfield & Wight, eds. *Diplomatic Investigations* (London, 1965), pp. 17–34 & 149–75.

a set of categories of this kind will, if well designed, ensure that the relevant questions about the decision-making process in any state will be asked.[12]

Although, as Reynolds here suggests, the drawing-up of such a check-list of the factors requiring assessment, if any specific case is to be understood, is merely a first step towards a general theory, it may be for the moment the most valuable contribution the academic approach to the study of international relations has to offer. Attempts to construct general theories which will predict with any certainty either the behaviour of individual states in the international system—according to their economic, ideological, demographic, or any other characteristics—or the future evolution of the international system as a whole, appear unrealistic in view of the limited number of cases (judged by the normal standards of the natural sciences) on which such theories have perforce to be based. If theoreticians are modest enough to limit themselves to offering a classification of the factors that an assessment of any phenomenon requires— whether the phenomenon be 'foreign policy' or 'balance of power', or 'international integration'—a valuable purpose will be served. The key to the understanding of any phenomenon in international politics is in fact its comparison with others that appear at first sight to be comparable, i.e. the process of understanding requires the elimination of false analogies and a deepened awareness of true ones.

A useful example of the way in which theoretical approaches can illuminate a specific topic is offered by the developments of the last few years in the study of American foreign policy. The published literature on this subject has been enormous, ranging from polemical tracts on current issues to solid historical narratives. Much understanding can be gained from a critical reading of the memoirs and biographies of successive Presidents and Secretaries of State, and the published reflections of their advisers—notably the articulate White House staff of the Kennedy presidency. Various issues in American foreign policy have also been the subject of topical tracts, more or less polemical, some of which—e.g. the essays of Walter Lippmann and James P. Warburg—retain more than an ephemeral value.

[12] *An Introduction to International Relations* (London, 1971), pp. 258–9.

The more academic literature on American foreign policy has until recently been dominated by the writings of historians, notably the standard works by Samuel Flagg Bemis and Thomas A. Bailey.[13] On the postwar period, one of the most enlightening books is still the historical account by John A. Spanier, *American Foreign Policy since World War II* (2nd ed. 1962). For an understanding of specific aspects of American foreign policy, the relevant historical literature also provides an indispensable starting-point, e.g. the work of Trevor A. Reese on United States relations with Australia and New Zealand or, on American policy towards Western Europe, the short narrative by Max Beloff or the more detailed account by Ernst van der Beugel.[14] If, however, after learning what the historians can tell us about what happened in any specific episode in American foreign relations, we want to go on to ask *why* it happened, or whether its happening illustrates or results from any underlying theme of American policy, we must turn to studies which approach the subject-matter in more theoretical terms than those of the historian. Two interesting attempts to interpret postwar American foreign policy in terms of the underlying conceptions influencing the minds of policy-makers are the work by Michael Donelan, *The Ideas of American Foreign Policy* (1963), and the larger study by Seyom Brown, *The Faces of Power: constancy and change in United States foreign policy from Truman to Johnson* (1968), whose central theme (p. vii) is 'the basic policy premises that underlie and are expressed by the international behavior of the United States'. The works of Donelan and Brown are 'theoretical', in the sense that they look beyond the study of diplomatic behaviour to try to assess its underlying assumptions, but their approach is still 'historical', in the sense that they are writing, so to speak, the intellectual as well as the behavioural history of policy. A more advanced type of theoretical approach—which has illuminated hitherto obscure aspects of America's foreign relations—is represented in the writings of Dr Coral Bell, who offers not only her assessment of the premises on which American policy has been based,

[13] Flagg Bemis, *A Diplomatic History of the United States* (5th ed., New York, 1965); Bailey, *A Diplomatic History of the American People* (6th ed., New York, 1958).

[14] Reese, *Australia, New Zealand and the United States: a survey of international relations, 1941–68* (London, 1969); Beloff, *The United States and the Unity of Europe* (London, 1963); van der Beugel, *From Marshall Aid to Atlantic Partnership* (Amsterdam, 1966).

but also her own analysis of the contemporary international system, and the efficacity and relevance of various American policies, judged in relation to the realities of that system as she interprets them. Her first major study of a theoretical kind, *Negotiation from Strength: a study in the politics of power* (1962), assesses the aims and the achievements of America's policy towards the Soviet Union during the 1950s in terms of an explicit series of alternative propositions about the causes of war and the conditions of peace.

Broadly speaking [she writes] one may see the causation of war as lying in the nature of the state, or in the nature of the relation between states, or in the nature of man. From the first assumption of war as inherent in the nature of the state—whether of despotic states in general, or of Communist despotisms in particular, or (from the other camp) of capitalist states as such—it would logically follow that domestic change in the enemy is the only substantial hope of peace. From the second theory, of war as inherent in the nature not of individual states but of the relation between them, it would logically follow that diplomatic adjustment was a possible hope of peace, or at least of the avoidance of any particular war. On the third theory, seeing war as inherent in the nature of man, one would presumably have to pin one's hopes for long-range peace on psycho-analysis, or Christianity, or the transforming effects of Socialism on humanity (p. 30).

Taking as a point of departure this triptych—which echoes the formulation offered by Kenneth Waltz in his classic study *Man, the State and War* (1959) Dr Bell considers how far American foreign policy-makers acted according to the 'diplomatic-adjustment' thesis—as Acheson largely did—or—like Dulles—to the 'domestic-change' thesis. This classification of policy-makers according to their operating premises—and according to the appropriateness of these premises to the real world as perceived by an acute observer—illustrates the value of an explicit conceptual framework in offering a more satisfactory explanation of events than could be provided by a 'straight' historical narrative.

Dr Bell's subsequent books, both sponsored by Chatham House and concerned in large part with American foreign policy, are *The Debatable Alliance: an essay in Anglo-American relations* (1964) and *The Conventions of Crisis: a study in diplomatic management* (1971). In both, the facts of recent history are again interpreted in terms of a series of explicit hypotheses: in the first case, about the relevance for Anglo-American relations of the changing East–West power balance as a whole, and in the second case, about the nature and implications of international crises, which the author categorizes in a precise and rigorous manner.

Other approaches of a theoretical kind have also shed light on how American foreign policy is made: these have included the approach through the theory of decision-making, exemplified in the work of Bruck, Snyder, and Sapin,[15] and the thesis advanced in Richard E. Neustadt's study of Anglo-American relations, *Alliance Politics* (1970), that the main source of conflict in alliance relationships is to be sought within the domestic political purlieus of the respective allies. Neustadt's systematic analysis of crisis behaviour in terms of personalities, policies, priorities, and 'the rationality of individual decisions' (pp. 57–9), and his application of these categories to the two case-studies of the Suez and Skybolt incidents, do much to explain the nature of alliance relationships in American foreign policy. Not all students of alliances would agree with Neustadt's emphasis on domestic political factors: both George Liska in *Nations in Alliance* (1962) and Stanley Hoffmann in his analysis of the Atlantic alliance, *Gulliver's Troubles* (1968), ascribe more significance to broader international factors. In this, in my view, they are correct: the study of alliances needs to take account of 'systemic' or 'macro' factors as well as the 'micro' factors emphasized by Neustadt.[16] The latter's application of analytical categories to the historical data, however, considerably enhances our understanding of how American foreign policy works.

Turning from the study of American foreign policy to other examples, it is worth noting that a more or less explicitly theoretical approach underlies several pieces of research on international politics recently sponsored by Chatham House: Professor Karl Kaiser's short study *German Foreign Policy in*

[15] Richard C. Snyder & others, eds., *Foreign Policy Decision-Making: an approach to the study of international politics* (New York, 1962).

[16] The author has explained this view more fully in a review of Neustadt's book and in an article 'Washington and Bonn: a case study in alliance politics', in *International Affairs*, Apr. & July 1971 respectively.

Transition (1968) is based on a systematic analysis of the inter-action between foreign and domestic politics in West Germany; Dr Karl Birnbaum's study of *Peace in Europe* (1970) relies on elaborate methodological considerations about the value of statements of 'declaratory policy' as a guide to the understanding of 'action policy' in various national political systems; and a symposium on some of the main factors influencing British and West German foreign policy includes an assessment of which branches of 'international theory' are of value in the analysis of these factors, and of the implications of the study itself for the development of theory in future.[17]

The way ahead

It is hard to predict which of the various elements in the current spectrum of theorizing about international relations will prove to be the most significant in the long run. There are at least four aspects of the situation which seem particularly important (one is speaking here of the relations between theory and practice) and likely to remain so:

1. The increasing interdependence between studies of international politics and *strategic studies*, which at times goes so far as to resemble a merger.
2. The relative modesty with which the protagonists of *quantification* now press their claims, compared with their confidence a few years ago.
3. The development of attempts to construct *futurological models* of various aspects of the international system, or of the system as a whole.
4. The growing sense on the part of the theoreticians that they must descend—directly or indirectly—from the abstract level recently characteristic of some of their work and make it more relevant to the real world.

The first of these factors—and the one to be most fully discussed here—is the interaction between international politics and strategic studies.

[17] Karl Kaiser & Roger Morgan, eds., *Britain and West Germany: changing societies and the future of foreign policy* (London, 1971).

Strategic studies

Some people find it surprising that strategic studies should have broadened out from the analysis of strictly military affairs—what Clausewitz called 'the art of employment of battles as a means to gain the object in war'[18]—to inquiries which have become almost coterminous with that of the field of inter-national relations as a whole. Those who argue that strategic studies ought to be limited to the study of (military) strategy, and are surprised to find an Institute for Strategic Studies publishing works on such broad political questions as *The Asian Balance of Power: a comparison with European precedents*, or *Europe's Futures, Europe's Choices*,[19] fail to see that there are per-fectly valid reasons why such a development should have occurred. It can indeed be argued that studies of the strategic factor in international relations—touching, as they do, on the central question of the meaning of 'security' in the modern international system—are at least as central to studies of inter-national relations, and illuminate at least as many aspects of the subject, as the analysis of any other factor in international life, even the economic one which Susan Strange rightly em-phasizes.

The reasoning behind this argument is briefly as follows. Before the first use of nuclear weapons in 1945, despite the increasing horrors of each successive war, the development of military technology was so limited that states could still reckon actually to employ their most powerful weapons against each other, or plausibly to threaten to do so. As long as this was the case, students of strategy could regard their task as being the analysis of the means of concentrating enough military resources to win battles in wars which major states could expect actually to fight, using the most modern and effective weapons they possessed. It is true that strategy impinged directly upon dip-lomacy: for instance, Germany in 1914 was impelled into diplomatic ultimatums by the Schlieffen Plan, and the defensive strategy symbolized by the Maginot Line prevented France in the 1930s from pursuing the active interventionist policy in

---

[18] Quoted in Hedley Bull's important article, 'Strategic studies and its critics', *World Politics*, July 1968, p. 593.
[19] Adelphi Paper No. 44 (1968), by Coral Bell; *Europe's Futures, Europe's Choices*, ed. Alastair Buchan (London, 1969).

Eastern Europe demanded by her alliances with Czecho-slovakia and the Soviet Union. In many ways, however, strategy and diplomacy could still be separated. The advent of nuclear weapons, creating a situation in which major powers have unprecedented reasons for *not* employing their most modern weapons, has meant that *all-out* force, and hence the threat of it, has become less credible and therefore less effective as a means of international pressure. The challenge posed by nuclear technology is how states can manage their relations—including getting their way with potential adversaries—*without* using their principal weapons, or even coming near to threatening to do so. In this situation it has been quite natural for strategic studies to expand from their original subject-matter, the mobilization and use of military force, in two directions. The first has com-prised the development of theories about the ways in which nuclear power still might be used in international relations—essentially the threat of its use constituting a deterrent to unwelcome action by other powers.[20] The other new direction concerns a range of questions about the implications of the new strategic situation for the relations between states, i.e. the forms of interaction—ranging from 'conventional' armed conflict to close alliances—which still *are* open to them. As we have seen, the advent of nuclear weapons has forced states to think out the nature of security—for themselves and for the international system as a whole—in fundamentally new terms.

Each of these two branches of study—the theory of deter-rence, and the implications of the nuclear deadlock for con-ventional strategy, foreign policy, and international security—has produced a remarkable crop of writings.

What is striking is that while most observers of strategic studies would recognize the former branch of literature—the works of Kissinger, Kahn, Buchan, and others—as a legitimate development from the earlier and restricted acceptance of what 'strategic studies' were about, the same critics fail to see the second new branch—the studies of international security in the broader sense—as an equally logical step in the intellectual development of the subject. Yet inquiries into such questions

[20] The heyday of deterrence literature can be said to date from the publication of Henry Kissinger's *Nuclear Weapons and Foreign Policy* in 1957 to that of Herman Kahn's *On Escalation* in 1965.

as the nature of international security, the implications of nuclear weapons for the cohesion of alliances or the management of crises, or the causes of stability or instability in the balance of power, are in fact a quite logical development from the study of the new military technology itself.

These questions, moreover, indicate the central importance of strategic factors—defined in these broad terms—in the international politics of our time. All major governments, since the onset of the nuclear age, have been constantly preoccupied with precisely such matters as these.

Thus the strategic situation of today leads the analyst into broader questions of international politics, both at the level of decision-making within each state and also at the level of the international system itself. The first level embraces such questions as: what proportion of the gross national product can be devoted to the defence budget? is conscription politically possible? should the Ministry of Defence or the Ministry of Foreign Affairs have the last word in national security decisions and, if not, who should arbitrate between them? And the second level comprises such questions as: would a world of many nuclear powers be more stable than a world with only two? how can a superpower delegate decisions about nuclear matters to some of its allies without alarming the others, or the adversary?, and so on.

The central importance of these questions, and the interconnections between military strategy and the national interests of major powers, have been illustrated not only in the published works of specialists in strategic analysis, but also in the sociology of the profession. It is no accident that the Institute of War and Peace Studies at Columbia University has been founded and guided by Professor William T. R. Fox, most of whose writing has been on broad questions of international theory rather than on strategy strictly defined; that Professor Hedley Bull's work on arms control and international order should place strategic factors in their political context; that the founding Director and developer of the Institute for Strategic Studies, Alastair Buchan, has been elected to the Chair of International Relations at Oxford; that Laurence Martin should move from the Woodrow Wilson Chair of International Politics at Aberystwyth to the Chair of War Studies at King's College, London; or that the previous Professor of War Studies, now a Fellow in Defence Studies at All Souls, should be Vice-Chairman of the Council of Chatham House. Such links merely illustrate the central and inescapable bearing of strategic considerations on the whole field of the international behaviour of states. Just as institutes of strategic studies can appropriately bring out works dealing with the balance of power and other aspects of the international political system, so it continues to be appropriate for a more broadly-based institute of international affairs to promote studies with a fairly strong strategic emphasis: a recent example is the Chatham House symposium *International Security: reflections on survival and stability* (1971), edited by Kenneth Twitchett, which combines a theoretical analysis of the nature of security with more concrete case-studies of regional and functional aspects of the topic.

Quantification and the scientific approach

An example of the confidence exhibited a few years ago by the proponents of a 'scientific' approach to international affairs may be found in the widely-used book of Charles A. McClelland, *Theory and the International System* (1966), as follows:

> Tomorrow . . . the study of international relations may become a scientific discipline specializing in data-processing and analysis of international system phenomena, and providing routine reports and advice on foreign policy alternatives available to national governments. It is no longer an entirely fanciful projection to suggest that in two decades there may be a President's Council of Foreign Policy Advisers appointed from the circle of R and D and academic specialists in international relations theory and research. The route to future international system stability in a multi-nation world may lie in the direction of cross-national coordination of international communications and hence the rationalization of foreign policy decision process . . . (p. 136).

Similar views about the possibility of a scientific analysis of international relations are to be found in the writings of John Burton, notably in *International Relations: a general theory* (1965). Another study, published in the same year, undertakes to show 'how several kinds of simple quantitative data can be used to describe the world's international politics and to test hypotheses'.[21]

[21] Bruce M. Russett, *Trends in World Politics* (New York, 1965), Preface.

It is no exaggeration to say that, while some proponents of the scientific approach remain convinced of the value of quantification,[22] other pioneers of this approach have substantially modified their earlier expectations. This is clearly the case with Professor Karl W. Deutsch, whose stimulating textbook, *The Analysis of International Relations* (1968), is much more modest in the weight it places on quantifiable data than his earlier work, *The Nerves of Government* (1963).

These judgements do not amount to saying that the quantifiers and scientists have abandoned their quest: the truth is simply that at least some of them now make less ambitious claims for quantification as a method. They are more aware that the quantifiable aspects of an international situuation, while they give important clues to its nature, by no means tell the whole story. It is one thing to forecast, for instance, that the French gross national product in 1980 will be 50 per cent higher than the British, if the trends of 1969–71 continue; or that if Japan continues to spend only 1 per cent or 2 per cent of her GNP on defence, while China and the Soviet Union spend roughly 15 per cent, her defence capacity, even allowing for a faster growth-rate, will fall far behind theirs. It is something quite different—and completely non-quantifiable—to say how, if these trends in fact persist, the British, French, or Japanese governments are likely to respond to them.

Futurology

The attempt to apply futurological methods to the study of international society obviously suffers in an acute degree from the relative unpredictability of political behaviour in general, which makes even domestic politics less susceptible to these methods than, for instance, demographic or even economic processes. *The Year 2000* (1967), by Herman Kahn and Anthony J. Wiener, probably the most ambitious work of futurology so far published, offers some interesting speculations about possible future evolutions of the international system, but these—based on a mixture of the projection of economic and demographic

---

[22] e.g. David J. Singer's articles 'Patterns in international warfare, 1816–1965', in *Annals of the American Academy of Political & Social Science*, Sept. 1970, pp. 145–55, and 'Intergovernmental organization and the preservation of peace 1816–1964', *International Organization*, Summer 1970, pp. 520–47.

trends and ingenious speculation about political and strategic stability or instability—have not yet done much to inspire the more detailed analyses which might indicate the respective degrees of plausibility of the authors' various alternative models. Although the Commission on the Year 2000, established by the American Academy of Arts and Sciences, has in turn set up a working group on the future of the international system, this group has not yet been able to advance much beyond the sweeping projections of *The Year 2000*, and some rather disconnected shorter pieces published in *Toward the Year 2000: work in progress* (1969), edited by Daniel Bell. A more promising application of futurology is represented by the Institute for Strategic Studies' publication, *Europe's Futures, Europe's Choices: models of western Europe in the 1970s* (1969), edited by Alastair Buchan, which relies less on the projection of economic trends than on deductive reasoning about a range of alternative political structures for Western Europe's future. All Foreign Offices that employ planning staffs are to some extent engaged in futurology, but the timespan with which these staffs are able to concern themselves is naturally very limited: indeed, the experience of the Policy Planning Staff of the US State Department, established under George Kennan in 1947, that its members were often drawn deeply into current policy issues, is in no way untypical.

The challenge for the proponents of futurology as a potentially useful contribution to the making of foreign policy is to bridge the gap between such short-term expedients and the much longer-term speculation about the year 2000.

One such enterprise is *Europe Tomorrow: sixteen Europeans look ahead* (1972), edited by Richard Mayne (part of the joint research programme on European affairs of Chatham House and PEP), in which a team of authors attempts to predict (and perhaps to influence) various aspects of Europe's affairs over the next twenty years.

There have already been some successful attempts to predict the likely course of international events—one of them being the ISS Adelphi Paper No. 26, *Sources of Conflict in the Middle East* (1966), which succeeded in foreshadowing the course of the Middle East crisis of 1967—but the business of thinking systematically about the medium-term future of the international system is one which academic specialists, and still more policy-orientated research institutes, are likely to take increasingly seriously.

Relevance to the real world

This problem is summarized in the title of a recent interesting symposium, *Theory of International Relations: the crisis of relevance* (1968), edited by Abdul A. Said. Even the most abstruse theoreticians in international relations will argue that the long-term object of their exercises is to evolve models of international political behaviour—along the lines of models of economic behaviour—which will ultimately have some explanatory relevance to the real world.[23] Raymond Aron, one of the outstanding representatives of the 'classical' school of theoreticians, in an attempt to summarize what might be called 'the theory of practice' (a phrase reminiscent of the American dictum 'there's nothing so practical as a good theory'), has used the term 'praxeology'.[24] This has been described as a 'revolting neologism',[25] but it usefully expresses the notion that theory and practice should go together. Their relationship is aptly described by Stanley Hoffmann in the introduction to *Gulliver's Troubles*, where he disclaims any wish, as a theorist, to make practical policy recommendations:

. . . My discussion of the alternatives available to the United States and of their effectiveness will be less detailed than that of other writers in this series; their primary concern is to make policy recommendations, whereas mine is to demarcate the area of effective choice. . . . One should not expect an apple tree to produce cherries—one should judge it by the quality of its apples. A man without practical experience as a policy-maker or as an adviser to policy-makers is unlikely to contribute much by usurping a role for which he is unqualified; his best chance of being useful lies precisely in the realm of academic analysis. Indeed, the value of prescriptions is not unrelated to the strength of the basic analysis (pp. xviii–xix).

[23] e.g. Michael B. Nicholson, 'A Model of Crisis Decision-Making', a paper presented to the Annual Conference of the Political Studies Association of the UK at Birmingham in Mar. 1971.

[24] *Paix et guerre entre les nations* (Paris, 1962). English trans. *Peace and War, a theory of international relations* (London, 1966).

[25] By Michael Howard, 'Power politics: Raymond Aron's theory of peace and war', *Encounter*, Feb. 1968, pp. 55–9.

This attempt—to explain the nature of the real world in such a way that the practitioners of foreign policy are more likely to make the right decisions—represents a restatement, in more modest terms, of the intentions of those who first promoted the academic study of international relations in the early years of this century. There is no denying that in some ways the academic analyst can be a positive nuisance to the policy-maker. For instance, although it may suit supporters of NATO to describe it, for public relations purposes, as a 'collective security agreement'[26]—a phrase which conveys reassuring hints of Woodrow Wilson and the ideals of the League—the scholar will have to point out that the alliance is *not* a collective-security organization but a collective-defence pact.[27] A deliberate blurring of terms, as in this case, may be a great help to the politician in his public statements. When he is actually formulating policy, however, such a confusion of terminology may entail a dangerous confusion of thought. Putting the practical value of theory at its very lowest, it could be said that the academic can prevent the practitioner from making false analogies, of the kind that made Anthony Eden in 1956 regard Nasser as he had regarded Hitler and Mussolini in 1938. In fact this is only a small part of the contribution that theory can make to practice, as the growing interest of Foreign Offices in the world of academic research fully demonstrates.

[26] e.g. the reference to NATO in Dean Acheson's memoirs, *Present at the Creation* (New York, 1969), p. 369.
[27] See the discussion of this point by Kenneth Twitchett, in *International Security*, pp. 31–9.

Contributors

DENNIS AUSTIN is Professor of Government, University of Manchester. He was Fellow of the Institute of Commonwealth Studies from 1959 till 1968 and of Chatham House from 1964 till 1965. He is author of *Politics in Ghana* (1964, paperback 1970), *Britain and South Africa* (1966), and *Malta and the End of Empire* (1971).

J. E. S. FAWCETT has been Director of Studies and Stevenson Research Fellow at Chatham House since 1969. He is a former Fellow of All Souls College, Oxford. From 1945–50 he was Assistant Legal Adviser, Foreign Office, from 1950–60 was General Counsel to the International Monetary Fund in Washington, and has been since 1962 a member and since 1969 Vice-President of the European Commission of Human Rights. His principal publications include *The British Commonwealth in International Law* (1963), *International Law and the Uses of Outer Space* (1968), *The Law of Nations* (1968), and *The Application of the European Convention on Human Rights* (1969).

JOHN GITTINGS is the author of *The Role of the Chinese Army* (1967) and *Survey of the Sino-Soviet Dispute* (1970), and was the China specialist at Chatham House in 1963–6. He has since worked for the *Far Eastern Economic Review*, at the LSE Centre for International Studies, and as acting editor of the *China Quarterly*. He is now working on a study of Chinese foreign policy and the cold war in Asia.

DR ROSALYN HIGGINS is research specialist in international law and organization and UN affairs at Chatham House and is a Vice-President of the American Society of International Law. Her principal publications include *The Development of International Law Through the Political Organs of the United Nations* (1963), *Conflict of Interests: international law in a divided world* (1965), *The Administration of United Kingdom Foreign Policy through the United Nations* (1966), and two volumes (on the Middle East and Asia) of *United Nations Peacekeeping 1946–67: documents and commentary*, for which she received the award of the American Society of International Law.

MICHAEL KASER is Lecturer in Soviet Economics at the University of Oxford and Fellow of St Antony's College. He has worked on Soviet and East European economic affairs since 1947, initially in the Foreign Service and from 1951 to 1963 in the UN Economic Commission for Europe. His principal publications are *Comecon: integration problems of the planned economies* (2nd ed., 1967) and *Soviet Economics* (1970).

CAROLINE MILES has been a British and an international civil servant. From 1966 till 1970 she was a research specialist at Chatham House, when she contributed to both the Institute's journals. She is now associated with a merchant bank, looks after various business interests, and continues to write.

BRUCE MILLER is Professor of International Relations, Research School of Pacific Studies, Australian National University. From 1957 till 1962 he was Professor of Politics, University of Leicester. His publications include *The Commonwealth in the World* (1958), *The Nature of Politics* (1962), *Britain and the Old Dominions* (1966), and *The Politics of the Third World* (1966). Since 1963 he has edited *The Australian Outlook*. His *A Changed but Continuing Commonwealth 1952–69*, in a new Chatham House *Survey of Commonwealth Affairs* series, is in preparation.

ROGER MORGAN, Deputy Director of Studies at Chatham House, has been a Lecturer at various British universities and Visiting Professor at Columbia and Johns Hopkins Universities. He is author of *The German Social Democrats and the First International* (1965), *Modern Germany* (1966), and co-author of *European Political Parties* (1970). He edited (with Karl Kaiser) *Britain and West Germany* (1971).

DR ROY PRYCE is Director of the Centre for Contemporary European Studies at the University of Sussex. He is also Visiting Professor and a member of the Academic Board of the College of Europe in Bruges and is Trustee of the Federal Trust for Education and Research. His publications include *The Italian Local Elections of 1956* (1957), *The Political Future of the European Community* (1962), and (with John Pinder), *Europe after de Gaulle* (1969).

ANDREW SHONFIELD, who was Director of Studies at Chatham House from 1961 till 1968, when he became Chairman of the Social Science Research Council, returned to the Institute as its Director at the beginning of 1972. In 1965 he was a member of the Royal Commission on Trade Unions and in 1968–9 of the Review Committee on Overseas Representation (the Duncan Committee). His principal publications include *British Economic Policy since the War* (2nd ed., 1959), *Modern Capitalism* (1965, paperback 1969), *The Attack on World Poverty* (1960), and he is editor (with Charles P. Kindleberger) of *North American and Western European Economic Policies* (1971).

SUSAN STRANGE taught international relations and organization at University College, London, until 1964 and from 1951–7 was at the same time Economic Correspondent for the *Observer*. Since 1965 she has been a research specialist at Chatham House and also teaches at the London School of Economics. She is author of *The Sterling Problem and the Six* (1967) and *Sterling and British Policy* (1971).

DR HUGH TINKER is Director of the Institute of Race Relations, London. He is author of *The Foundations of Local Self-Government in India, Pakistan and Burma* (1954), *The Union of Burma* (1957, 4th ed. 1967), *India and Pakistan, a political analysis* (1962), *Ballot Box and Bayonet; people and government in emergent Asian countries* (1964, 3rd ed. 1966), *South Asia, a short history* (1966), *Experiment with Freedom, India and Pakistan 1947* (1967), and *The Mission to the Court of Ava in 1855* (1969).

D. C. WATT is Reader in International History in the University of London; editor, *Survey* and *Documents on International Affairs* since 1962; author of *Britain and the Suez Canal* (1956), *Britain looks to Germany* (1965), *Personalities and Policies* (1965), *A History of the World in the Twentieth Century* (1967); editor of *Contemporary History in Europe* (1968), and *Hitler's Mein Kampf* (1969).

Subject Index

(*Note*: SU = Soviet Union)

Saudi Arabia, 116
Scandinavia, 177, 187; creation of
  Nordic Council, 178; Soviet and E.
  European studies in, 200; and peace
  research, 273; *see also* EFTA
Scarborough Commission, 198
School of International Studies (New
  Delhi), 137
Scientific and technological co-opera-
  tion, 187n.
SEATO, 35, 267
self-determination, 23–4; *see also* human
  rights
Senegal, 52, 168n., 173n.
Sikkim, 250, 252
Singapore, 70, 253n.
Sino-Soviet relations, 75, 131f., 199,
  238–9, 240–1, 267
Soblen case, 59
social science, sociology: role of, in
  international studies, 3–4, 7–12, 62,
  76; in economic relations, 65–6; in
  Soviet & E. European studies, 202–11
Social Science Research Council (UK),
  10–12, 272f., 276
Somalia, 162, 166, 168n., 169, 171
South Africa, 60, 134, 154, 156, 162,
  165n., 172; UN attitude to apartheid
  33, 47, 159f.; ICJ and, 54f.; Rhodes-
  ian sanctions and, 57; Afrikaner
  Nationalists, 140, 142; Commonwealth
  studies and, 138, 143–4, 148f., 154;
  need for political studies on, 163;
  expansionist role of, 164–5
South Asian studies, 249–70
South-East Asia, 118, 121, 131, 161,
  165, 253; US policy, 133, 231, 237;
  Soviet policy, 238; *see also* individual
  countries
South Korea, *see* Korean war
South-West Africa, 54, 60, 165
South West Africa Cases (1966), 49,51–2, 54
South West Africa (Voting) Case, 49
Soviet & E. European studies, 117–18,
  197–202; postwar research in UK/
  US, 198–9, 200f.; – in Europe, 200;
  – by international organizations,
  201–2, 206; linguistic problems,
  198–9
  Socio-political studies, 202–4; con-
  temp. Russian novels, 204–5; non-
  Russian republics, 205–6; Jews,
  206–7; Christianity, 207; hist. of

CP, 207–8, 209; post-revolutionary
  hist., 208–9; education, 209–10;
  topics for further study, 210–11
Economic studies, 211ff.; planning
  system, 214–17; economic reform,
  217–18; agriculture, 218
Soviet News, 122, 126
Soviet Union, 43, 52f., 106, 171, 285;
  and UN, 41, 132; and Cuban
  missile crisis, 123; relations with US,
  132–3, 176, 228f., 231n., 281;
  interests in Africa, 162, 165–7; and
  Asia, 237–41; *see also* Czechoslovakia;
  German Federal Republic; India;
  Korean war; Sino-Soviet relations;
  Soviet & E. European studies
Spain, 20, 52, 127–31, 153; and UN
  membership, 27–8; Council of Europe
  and, 28; territories in Africa, 28–9,
  171n.; Civil War, 104f.; *see also*
  Gibraltar
Spanish Sahara, UN and, 28–9
Statute of Westminster, 140f., 143ff.;
  see also Commonwealth studies
sterling area, studies on, 153–4
strategic studies, 64, 273, 283–7
Sudan, 161, 166
Suez canal, 46, 166
Suez crisis, 43, 60, 249, 282
Survey of Commonwealth Affairs (RIIA), *see*
  Commonwealth
Survey of International Affairs (RIIA), 13f.,
  103–35; origins and evolution, 103–7;
  complexity of problems of producing,
  107–8, 114–31; comparable inter-
  national publications, 108–9; as work
  of contemporary history, 110–14,
  134–5; new proposed plan for,
  131–5; *see also* contemporary history
Sweden, 20, 31, 52; *see also* EFTA
Syria, 116f.

Taiwan: US and, 230, 232–4, 236–7;
  PRC and, 236–7
Tanzania, 161f., 165ff., 173, 251n.
third world, 160, 170–1, 194, 250; *see
  also* Afro-Asian bloc; non-alignment
totalitarianism, 24–5, 31, 117
trade, *see* international business and
  trade
trade unions, and multinational corporations, 95–6
Turkey, 20, 88, 117, 119f., 267

Index of Persons and Authors